Journalism and the Russo-Japanese War

Journalism and the Russo-Japanese War

The End of the Golden Age of Combat Correspondence

Michael S. Sweeney and
Natascha Toft Roelsgaard

LEXINGTON BOOKS
Lanham • Boulder • New York • London

Published by Lexington Books
An imprint of The Rowman & Littlefield Publishing Group, Inc.
4501 Forbes Boulevard, Suite 200, Lanham, Maryland 20706
www.rowman.com

6 Tinworth Street, London SE11 5AL, United Kingdom

Copyright © 2020 The Rowman & Littlefield Publishing Group, Inc.

All rights reserved. No part of this book may be reproduced in any form or by any electronic or mechanical means, including information storage and retrieval systems, without written permission from the publisher, except by a reviewer who may quote passages in a review.

British Library Cataloguing in Publication Information Available

The hardback edition of this book was previously catalogued by the Library of Congress as follows:

Library of Congress Cataloging-in-Publication Data

ISBN: 978-1-7936-1790-3 (cloth : alk. paper)
ISBN: 978-1-7936-1792-7 (pbk. : alk. paper)
ISBN: 978-1-7936-1791-0 (electronic)

Names: Sweeney, Michael, 1958- author. | Roelsgaard, Natascha Toft, author.
Title: Journalism and the Russo-Japanese War : the end of the golden age of combat correspondence / By Michael S. Sweeney and Natascha Toft Roelsgaard.
Other titles: End of the golden age of combat correspondence
Description: Lanham, Maryland : Lexington Books, [2019] | Includes bibliographical references and index. | Summary: "This book examines Japan's victory over Russia in 1904-05 and how it overhauled press-military relations, ending sixty years of battlefield freedom for correspondents. The authors argue that Japan controlled access and allowed only a narrowly constrained view of the war to circulate, thus creating the template for all modern wars."— Provided by publisher.
Identifiers: LCCN 2019040541 (print) | LCCN 2019040542 (ebook) |
  ISBN 9781793617903 (cloth) | ISBN 9781793617910 (epub)
Subjects: LCSH: Russo-Japanese War, 1904-1905—Press coverage. | Russo-Japanese War, 1904-1905—Journalists. | Russo-Japanese War, 1904-1905—Censorship. | Freedom of the press—Japan—History—20th century. | Government and the press—Japan—History—20th century. | War correspondents.
Classification: LCC DS517 .S94 2019 (print) | LCC DS517 (ebook) |
  DDC 070.4/4952031—dc23
LC record available at https://lccn.loc.gov/2019040541
LC ebook record available at https://lccn.loc.gov/2019040542

To Carolyn, now and forever,
and
to Kathinka, for your endless support.

Contents

Acknowledgments		ix
A Note about Names		xi
Introduction		xiii
1	Japan Meets the Press	1
2	Lionel James and Stanley Washburn	45
3	Jack London	69
4	John Fox Jr.	91
5	Richard Harding Davis	113
6	Luigi Barzini Sr.	131
7	Photographers and Illustrators	147
8	Hector Fuller	171
9	With the Russians	183
10	Conclusion	199
Bibliography		215
Index		229
About the Authors		239

Acknowledgments

This book is the work of two authors, but it would not exist without the talents of many people who have given their time and wisdom. The authors particularly wish to thank the following for their assistance: Atsuko Shigesawa for her invaluable service in obtaining primary documents from Tokyo; Francesca Colloredo for her help with translations from Italian; Beth Llewellyn McGlaughlin for her help with the translations from French; and Giovanna Dell'Orto, Steven Miner, and Aimee Edmondson for their comments on drafts of the manuscript. In addition, Michael S. Sweeney would like to thank Ohio University for its financial assistance on his many travels to libraries and archives around the United States and in Italy, and Dr. Robert K. Stewart and the faculty of the E.W. Scripps School of Journalism for supporting his period of leave to allow him to research and write. He also thanks the graduate students in his sections of Journalism 8110, Historical Research in the Mass Media, for in-class discussions that helped sharpen the analytical rigor of the two authors.

A Note about Names

The Russian city of Port Arthur was originally known as Lushun and is known today as Lüshunkou District in the city of Dalian, China. This book refers to Port Arthur by the English version of its Russian name to be true to contemporary sources and the modern scholarship that relies on them. Likewise, the city of Dalny, meaning "Distant" in Russian, retains that name in this work rather than the modern name of Dalian. Battles known by the former names of cities and villages, such as Mukden, retain their original nomenclature. Otherwise, most obsolete geographical names have been updated to their modern versions, followed by the contemporary name on first reference in parentheses. For example, the text refers to the Japanese First Army landing at Incheon (Chemulpo). An exception occurs in direct quotations, such as Jack London's references to "Ping-yang" instead of Pyongyang.

There are several options to translate Russian names from their original Cyrillic letters into the English alphabet. This book follows the usage in Rotem Kowner, *Historical Dictionary of the Russo–Japanese War* (Lanham, MD: Scarecrow Press, 2006).

The surname appears first in Japan. Thus, for example, Oku Yasukata becomes Oku on second reference.

Introduction

It is tempting to begin a book such as this by saying, "Once upon a time . . . ." The phrase calls to mind fairy tales and myths, stories so disconnected from our reality that they make us smile and scoff.

And yet there was a time, long ago, when journalists enjoyed what Phillip Knightley, the pre-eminent historian of wartime journalism, called the "golden age" of war correspondence.[1]

It was an era when Western journalists could see, hear, and write virtually without hindrance from their vantage point at the center of combat's noisy and chaotic arena. In the first war covered by professional journalists, the invasion of the Second Federal Republic of Mexico from 1846 to 1848 by the United States, reporters were free to ride and camp with American armies in a system later generations would call "embedding." They talked to generals and ordinary soldiers, and sometimes, long before journalists paid much attention to ethics, they joined the fight with gun and bayonet. When he wasn't writing one of his two hundred stories, George Kendall of the New Orleans *Picayune* served as a courier of military messages and as a judge who passed sentence on American soldiers accused of crimes. A woman, Jane McManus Storms, writing under the byline Cora Montgomery for the *New York Sun*, gathered information for her stories from inside Mexican territory.

There was no censorship, no need for passes to provide access, and little or no military suspicion of the embedded civilian press. War reports gathered in the Mexican interior traveled by pony and steamship to the nearest American city, New Orleans, to be set in print or forwarded to the closest terminal of that brand-new invention snaking its way across the country—Samuel F. B. Morse's telegraph. Any dispatch printed in the United States would take weeks to find its way back into Mexico, making any news of tactical value—troop strength, deployment, or expected movements—too stale to contain secrets. Storms and Kendall felt free. So free, in fact, that they did not hesitate to print criticism of U.S. officers and their decisions when they felt it was merited. Kendall, for example, documented a serious lack of supplies and blamed a poor plan of assault on Mexico City for what he considered an unacceptable number of American casualties.[2]

This golden age continued into the next major war for those covering the British armed forces. It was on the Crimean Peninsula in the 1850s that William Howard Russell, sometimes deemed the "father" of war correspondence, filed stories to the *Times* of London. Russell's accounts, and those of other war correspondents, revealed horrors that contributed to the downfall of the British government, sparked Alfred Lord Tennyson to write "The Charge of the Light Brigade," and helped prompt Florence Nightingale to travel to the war zone and create the field of modern nursing. Despite stirring up antipathy in some elevated political circles, Russell eventually earned a knighthood as a Commander of the Royal Victorian Order. War correspondents were heroes.[3]

In Crimea and in the American Civil War a decade later and the Spanish-American War and Boer War at century's end, not much changed. Reporters saw battles. Their newspaper and magazine accounts moved only as fast as horse and steam train could carry them, limiting the speed with which printed news spread and therefore the potential to alter the course of ongoing conflicts. Occasionally officers detained or banned journalists who wrote something they disliked, but only after the correspondents had enjoyed the opportunity to witness and to report.

Through the end of the nineteenth century, reporters from friendly or neutral countries still could tag along with Western troops and warships, going and coming mostly as they pleased. Nearly as free as children at play. *Once upon a time* . . . .

Jack London expected just such freedom when he traveled to Japan for his first opportunity to cover the clash of armies, the Russo-Japanese War of 1904–1905. William Randolph Hearst had paid him well, expecting a good return on his investment when one of the world's brightest young literary stars turned his pen to describe death and destruction on a monumental scale. London wrote, "I had heard . . . of all sorts and conditions of correspondents in all sorts of battles and skirmishes, right in the thick of it, where life was keen and immortal moments were being lived. In brief, I came to war expecting to get thrills."[4]

Instead, he got nothing. Virtually overnight, it seemed, the rules had changed, and they had changed dramatically. Japan walled off war correspondents from the news, keeping them figuratively blind, deaf, and mute. True, the Russo-Japanese War brought together two adversaries that had no history of British- or American-style press-military relations, no constitutional guarantees of press freedom. The Japanese played by their own rules, and in so doing they, and to a lesser extent the Russians, created a virulent bacillus of censorship and propaganda. The outside world kept watch and noted Japan's eventual victory. It wasn't long before the armed forces of the West caught and spread the infection.

Chances are, most readers are unfamiliar with the Russo-Japanese War. That is a shame. World War I copied so many of its elements of strategy and tactics, as well as its deployment of huge civilian armies in the field, that the conflict of 1904–1905 is sometimes called World War Zero.[5] The Russo-Japanese War gave to total war the demonic elements of machine guns, barbed wire, torpedoes, land mines, and hundreds of thousands of conscripted and volunteer soldiers facing each other on a scale never before seen. Battles dwarfed the conflicts at Waterloo, Gettysburg, and Sedan. The climactic conflict on land, the Battle of Mukden in February and March 1905, threw 276,000 Russians against 270,000 Japanese.

The war marked the first time an Asian power defeated a European one. Japan emerged as a player on the world stage, while Russia's stunning defeat added to domestic unrest that led a decade later to the toppling of the tsar, the establishment of the Soviet Union, and, eventually, the Cold War.

Few expected Japan to win. Nevertheless, the tiny island nation marshaled all its resources in a bid for victory. Beyond soldiers, horses, ships, guns, and other materiel of war, Japan forged nearly total control of information at home and in the war zone. It established restraints on war correspondents we recognize today, which include:

- An elaborate set of regulations reporters pledge to follow in order to gain accreditation to cover forces in the field, coupled with penalties for disobedience.
- Press pools, in which a military spokesperson shares information with one reporter, who then is expected to share it with all other journalists on hand.
- Military liaisons, also known as "guards" or "minders" (and derisively as "nurses" in the Russo-Japanese War) who are ordered to accompany journalists everywhere—and, in this particular war, were accused of spying on them as if they were the enemy.
- Strict censorship, coupled with total control of the means to share information with the world in a timely way.

In short, the victors forged the news into a weapon. The Japanese shaped it to contribute to the war effort on the home front by censoring anything that might hurt morale. And they shaped it to ensure it would propagandize at home and abroad. Reporters saw nothing of true combat in the war's early stages, and even then, censorship reduced their hearsay accounts to mush.

It was only after months of complaints by reporters in the field—including some to the president of the United States—that Japan somewhat reluctantly reached the conclusion it had to factor Western popular opinion into its equations if it were to maximize the use of mass communication as a weapon of war. In late summer and autumn 1904, after Jack London, Richard Harding Davis, John Fox Jr., and other literary stars of the day had left the Far East to return to the United States and the United Kingdom of Great Britain and Ireland, Japan finally lifted its restrictions a bit. But by then, military attachés and other Western observers had come to a shared realization: Control the press and you control the story. People on the home front would then react to a carefully shaped and censored version of war instead of the bloody, barbarous real thing.

Captain Peyton C. March of the U.S. General Staff was one of a handful of American military attachés (including Captain John J. "Black Jack" Pershing and Major General Arthur MacArthur, the father of Douglas MacArthur) who observed Japan's control of the press. March correctly predicted in a 1905 report to his country's War Department that all of the world's armies would copy the Japanese template:

> One of the most striking things in connection with this war has been the way in which Japan has handled the question of the censorship. There can be no doubt that the standard set in this war has furnished an object lesson which will be presented to all the great powers by their attachés in the field in such a way as to make some similar method a necessity in all future wars.[6]

Writing in 2002, historian Greg McLaughlin agreed. The Japanese system became "the real blueprint for modern military censorship," he wrote.[7]

And thus ended the golden age. That blueprint was not only accepted but also expanded in World War I. France and Britain clamped down on journalists' access to the Western Front almost before the echoes of the opening shots faded there in August 1914. The British government agreed to accredit *one* American correspondent to cover the entire Western Front that autumn. That assignment fell to Frederick Palmer, who had reported about the Japanese army from Manchuria in the Russo-Japanese War. He filed from France for the Associated Press, United Press, and the International News Service. Any information Americans received beyond his independent observations most likely was British and French propaganda. Only after the intervention of former president Theodore Roosevelt, in January 1915, did more reporters gain accreditation.[8]

This book aims to restore the Russo-Japanese War to the understanding of modern audiences and, in particular, to explain the Japanese system of information control. It examines the evolution of Japan's carefully orchestrated public relations and press correspondence campaigns and their impact on how news of the war filtered through an official lens and arrived in the West.

Chapter 1 provides an overview of significant developments in Japanese political and military history, beginning with the start of the Meiji era, and focuses on the interplay of Japan's press and government. This chapter culminates with the war itself and the plans set in motion by Japan and Russia to deal with an unexpected throng of war correspondents. A parallel narrative describes the evolution of war correspondence from the 1840s through the beginning of the Russo-Japanese War in February 1904, detailing how Japan's methods differed from what had come before. Chapter 2 examines attempts in spring 1904 to report the war by Lionel James and Stanley Washburn, who chartered boats to avoid censorship and observe events from the open sea. But in James's case, there was a twist; in a devil's bargain, he agreed to the placement of a Japanese spy on board his boat. This chapter includes radio's debut as a tool of war correspondence, made possible by one of the founders of radio broadcasting, the inventor Lee de Forest, who provided his expertise and the necessary equipment at cost. Chapter 3 looks at novelist Jack London's tireless but utterly frustrated efforts to report on the Japanese First Army during the early stages of the war without authorization from Japan. He returned to California thinking of himself as a failure, when in fact he had helped contribute to a vigorous, emerging template of war correspondence that did more than regurgitate dry details of objectives won or lost, or armies broken or victorious. Chapters 4 and 5 focus on two of the most popular novelists and war correspondents of the era, John Fox Jr. and Richard Harding Davis, who submitted themselves to Japanese regulations but gave up and went home after many months. They, too, understood a new era had been born but did not fully appreciate its changes. Chapter 6 examines one of history's best war correspondents, Luigi Barzini of *Corriere della Sera* in Milan, Italy, and how he managed to make friends with Japanese officers and soldiers in the Second Army and eventually witness the largest battles fought until that time. Chapter 7 looks at the unique challenges faced by the artists and photographers of the war, including Robert L. Dunn and James "Jimmy" Hare of *Collier's Weekly* magazine. Chapter 8 restores to history the lost saga of Hector Fuller, who risked his life to sail through Japanese waters and became the only Western reporter to observe from within besieged Port Arthur and get out again. He got his scoop, making the English-speaking world pay attention to his hometown newspaper in Indianapolis, at a cost of being discharged from the war zone for his troubles. Chapter 9 visits the Russians and their treatment of war correspondents, including Frances McCullagh, Frederick McCormick, and Douglas Story. Chapter 10 provides a conclusion applying the lessons of the Russo-Japanese War to World War I and subsequent conflicts, even into the twenty-first century.

Primary sources consulted for the book include the archives of Jack London at Utah State University; Richard Harding Davis at the University of Virginia; John Fox Jr. at the University of Kentucky; Willard Straight at Cornell University; Stanley Washburn and William H. Brill at the Minnesota Historical Society; Hector Fuller at the Indiana Historical Society; Luigi Barzini at Italy's l'Archivio Centrale dello Stato, Rome; the Oral History Archive at Columbia University in Manhattan; the digital images archive at the Library of Congress; and Japan's national archive, Dokuritsu Gyosei Hojin Kokuritsu Kōbunshokan, Tokyo. More than thirty war correspondents' memoirs and autobiographies, as well as hundreds of contemporary newspaper and magazine accounts, were examined.

Japan showed the world that it could defeat two foes it found exceedingly frightening: an army of well-equipped enemy soldiers and a phalanx of correspondents devoted to freedom of the press. It won two victories, yes, but this book tells not only how and what happened, but at what cost.

Here's a hint: The world did not live happily ever after.

NOTES

1. Phillip Knightley, *The First Casualty: From Crimea to Vietnam; the War Correspondent as Hero, Propagandist, and Myth Maker* (New York: Harcourt Brace Jovanovich, 1975), 46, 62.

2. George Wilkins Kendall, *Dispatches from the Mexican War* (Norman: University of Oklahoma Press, 1999), 8–19; and Tom Reilly, "Jane McManus Storms: Letters from the Mexican War, 1846–1848," *The Southwestern Historical Quarterly* 85, no. 1 (July 1981): 27–34. The only book-length account of the American correspondents in the Mexican-American War is Tom Reilly, *War with Mexico! America's Reporters Cover the Battlefront*, ed. Manley Witten (Lawrence: University Press of Kansas, 2010).

3. Michael S. Sweeney, *From the Front: The Story of War, Featuring Correspondents' Chronicles* (Washington, DC: National Geographic Press, 2002), 32–39.

4. Jack London, "Japanese Officers Consider Everything a Military Secret," *San Francisco Examiner*, June 26, 1904.

5. The phrase "World War Zero" appears to have been coined in 2005. Those making the case for the appropriateness of this label note that the war was fought on foreign territory (neither Russia nor Japan), financed in large measure by loans from other nations, and used ships and weapons built by other nations. Even the peace was forged on foreign territory—Portsmouth, New Hampshire, in 1905. See John W. Steinberg, Bruce W. Menning, David Schimmelpenninck van der Oye, David Wolff, and Shinji Yokote, eds., *The Russo-Japanese War in Global Perspective: World War Zero* (Leiden, Netherlands: Brill, 2005), xix–xxi. Other historians dispute the application of this "zero" label, asserting that the war, while on a grand scale of death and

destruction, was merely a regional conflict. See John W. Steinberg, "Was the Russo-Japanese War World War Zero?" *The Russian Review* 67, no. 1 (January 2008): 2.

6. Peyton C. March, "Report No. 6, War Department, Office of the Chief of Staff, Washington, January 3, 1905," Reports of Military Observers Attached to the Armies in Manchuria During the Russo-Japanese War, Part I (Washington: Government Printing Office, 1906), 55.

7. Greg McLaughlin, *The War Correspondent* (London: Pluto Press, 2002), 55.

8. Nathan A. Haverstock, *Fifty Years at the Front: The Life of War Correspondent Frederick Palmer* (Washington, DC: Brassey's, 1996), 164, 174.

Chapter 1

Japan Meets the Press

> *All he really sees at the front are shells bursting at a distance of three or four miles, and, close at hand, a friendly battery which is firing these shells. He makes friends with the battery commandant, who is profane, preoccupied, and quite ignorant of what is going on in other parts of the field. Besides, he does not speak any language with which the journalist is acquainted.*
>
> —Thomas F. Millard, Russo-Japanese War correspondent[1]

When the commander of the first wave of air attacks on Pearl Harbor looked down upon an unsuspecting American fleet on December 7, 1941, he scarcely could believe his eyes. "Had these Americans never heard of Port Arthur?" Mitsuo Fuchida asked.[2] A student of naval history would have known that twice before in times of escalating international tensions, Japanese forces had sprung a surprise attack before declaring war. The first instance transformed Japan's faceoff with China on the Korean Peninsula into a shooting war, setting off the Sino-Japanese conflict of 1894 to determine hegemony over the Hermit Kingdom. The second occurred just before midnight on Monday, February 8, 1904, when a fleet under the command of Admiral Tōgō Heihachirō startled the crews of Russian warships outside the fortified city of Port Arthur on China's Liaodong Peninsula. Boats equipped with the latest Whitehead torpedoes worked their way close to the Russian fleet in the dead of night, disabled two battleships and a cruiser, and disappeared. The next day, the Japanese fleet returned, firing eight- and twelve-inch shells at Russian warships and exchanging fire with big artillery anchored in the city of Port Arthur itself.

By chance, one journalist at sea witnessed the start of the Japanese-Russian hostilities. Francis McCullagh, representing the *New York Herald*, sailed aboard a civilian ship, the *Columbia*, which had been returning to Port Arthur across the Bohai Strait separating Korea Bay and the Bohai Sea. "At exactly 11:30 I was undressing in my cabin when I heard three muffled explosions, which made the ship rock, and which were followed almost immediately by the discharge of small guns," he recalled. "The transition was so abrupt, the silence of the night was torn so rudely, that for a second I was startled, and the wild thought, 'The Japanese are on us!' rushed through my brain."[3]

McCullagh wasn't the only one surprised that night. Japan had gagged the press in its home islands to prevent any leak from reaching the Russians. Japan's army and navy opened hostilities without notifying their enemy or their own people. Although a Russian officer in Korea received notice of a state of war three hours after the attack on Port Arthur, a formal declaration did not reach Saint Petersburg, the Russian capital, until February 10. "The Japanese Government must be heartily congratulated upon the measures it has taken to prevent the publication of a single item of news disclosing its plans or the position of any part of its armed forces," Charles à Court Repington, military correspondent of the *Times* of London and a citizen of Great Britain, a Japanese ally, wrote approvingly of the surprise attack.[4]

After the attack on Port Arthur, the Japanese navy blockaded the remaining Russian fleet in the city's fortified harbor and occupied the Korean capital of Seoul, a strategic stop on the road to expected battlegrounds in Manchuria, the massive northeastern region of China. In an action coordinated with the Port Arthur engagement, Japanese ships disabled a Russian cruiser and a gunboat at Incheon (Chemulpo), on the coast near Seoul, and began landing nearly three thousand soldiers.[5]

Russia should have known peace could not last. Japan's ambitions to extend its influence in Asia—as well as the political and military muscle it needed to realize that goal—had been growing almost since a U.S. Navy squadron commanded by Commodore Matthew C. Perry threatened Japan in summer 1853, and then forcibly opened the xenophobic shogunate the following spring. Westerners perceived Japan's easy capitulation to Perry's gunboats as evidence of weakness. Japan felt shamed for being powerless to stop foreigners from dictating policy. Aggressive political parties, fuming at the insult, subsequently arose in Japan. Internal unrest culminated with the creation of the imperial Meiji government in 1868. Japan's new leaders decided that the only way to deal with superior Western technology was to emulate it. In the following decades, Japan embarked on a crash course of modernization, sending students abroad and inviting the aid of foreign experts to reconfigure the country's political, military, and scientific institutions. Changes swept through the civil administration, army, and navy, as Japan decided it had to colonize or be colonized.[6]

Japan flexed its muscle in the Sino-Japanese War, winning control of Taiwan, the Pescadores Islands, and the Liaodong Peninsula, which juts southwest from Manchuria into the Yellow Sea. Acquisition of the peninsula provided a clear route for expansion into East Asia. Japan aimed to extend complete control over Korea and Manchuria, as it would finally succeed in doing four decades later at the beginning of World War II. This nascent desire of the late nineteenth century attracted the attention of European powers. France, Germany, and Russia intervened to keep Japanese ambitions in check in 1895, forcing Japan to cede the Liaodong Peninsula to China. Within two years, Russia stepped in to lease the peninsula to fit its own expansionist designs and to counter the landing of German troops on the Shandong Peninsula. Russia chose a naturally defensible harbor at Port Arthur on the Liaodong Peninsula for its center of operations and began construction of a fortress and naval base.[7]

Russia had its own expansionist ambitions in the nineteenth and early twentieth centuries. In particular, it had long desired an ocean port that would always be free of ice. But where to go? To the west, Britain, Germany, Austria-Hungary, and Turkey dominated, with Turkey posing an immediate barrier to Russia's ice-free bases along the Black Sea. To the south loomed the natural barriers of mountains and deserts. To the north, Siberia slumbered in frost. That left the east. In 1860, China, weakened by its loss to Britain in the Opium War, agreed to give Tsar Aleksandr II the island of Sakhalin—which Japan had always considered part of its territory—as well as the coast of Manchuria from Korea to the Amur River. Russia established a coastal colony that year near the Korean border and called it Vladivostok, "Lord of the East." It would become a base for naval operations in the Pacific, but it was less than ideal because ice closed it at least three months each year. By contrast, Port Arthur and nearby Dalny, a Russian settlement on the Liaodong shoreline, were a particular prize because they remained ice-free throughout the year.[8] To supply its new eastern ports, Russia announced construction of the Trans-Siberian Railway in 1891. The line widely was seen as furthering expansionist ambitions, as it could deliver troops relatively quickly to Manchuria, a land coveted by both Russia and Japan. Routing a railway through the difficult terrain of the Amur Valley caused Russia to suspend the original line's construction and search for a straighter route for a line through Manchuria. China grated a concession for just such a line, allowing Russia a shortcut known as the Chinese Eastern Railway. China's accommodation to the Russian request angered the Japanese and amplified tensions that had been rising since at least 1890, when Crown Prince Nicholas II was nearly killed in Japan on his way to lay the cornerstone for the railway station at Vladivostok. The assassination attempt, by a fanatical police officer, may have influenced the future tsar's opinions about Japan. Further intrigue arose when Russia began the South Manchurian Railway, connecting its Chinese Eastern Railway with all of the Liaodong Peninsula. That line linked northern and southern Manchuria and granted overland access to Port Arthur and Dalny. Russia's growing presence in East Asia gave Korea the courage to protest against its longtime Japanese adversary, which since 1874 had dominated Korean politics and economics. As a result of civil unrest, the Korean king fled his palace for the Russian Legation in Seoul. To Japan, these actions meant one thing: Russia posed a challenge for supremacy in Manchuria and Korea. Japan countered by seeking and winning an alliance in 1902 with Britain, which had substantial commercial interests in China to protect and which historically opposed Russian expansion. The Anglo-Japanese Alliance and other diplomatic moves led Russia to agree, under pressure, to a phased withdrawal of its armed forces from Manchuria. But Russia did not keep the schedule of the withdrawal, stalling while it bargained with Korea to build a railway line through its territory. Japan saw this as a duplicitous threat and began preparing its army and navy for war. Russia's failure to comply with the terms of the treaty requiring a third phase of withdrawal by October 8, 1903, likely committed both nations to war.[9]

Parallel to these military and political developments, Japan opened a campaign to influence public opinion in the West and at home. Thomas F. Millard, who had covered the Spanish-American War and Boer War and eventually embedded with Russian troops fighting Japan in Manchuria, underscored the necessity of Japan winning the battle for goodwill. In a conversation, Millard asked a longtime foreign diplomat to name the most significant force that would readjust the balance of power after the conflict in East Asia. "'Public opinion in America and England,' the diplomat replied without hesitation," Millard wrote.[10] Millard said that without "the approval and consent of the British and American people," diplomatically and financially, Japan could not fight.[11]

Uchida Yasuya, head of the Political Affairs Bureau of Japan's Ministry of Foreign Affairs, had reached that same conclusion in 1898. He and his aides began systematically examining portrayals of their nation in foreign newspapers and magazines. "Wild," "dangerous," and "untrustworthy" were common themes, as was a lingering characterization of aggressiveness held over from the Sino-Japanese War—as if Japan were a young bully flexing his muscles.[12] Japan decided to launch a public relations blitz (although the term in vogue at the time was "publicity campaign") through the world press to try to make those impressions more favorable, in case Japan needed foreign aid. In 1900, it opened a press bureau in London with branch offices in Europe and telegraph cable connections to the United States. The bureau provided a steady stream of ready-to-print articles sharing Japan's views of current events to newspapers and magazines in the British Isles, continental Europe, and the United States. In East Asia, Japan provided telegraphic news at no charge to newspapers operating there and hedged its bets with subsidy payments to "a number of papers," according to Millard. He wrote, "Practically the whole of the British press in the Far East continues to be rabidly and unreasonably pro-Japanese." An unnamed Japanese correspondent on the Asian mainland working for a prominent London newspaper, "whose special service is widely used and opinion much quoted in America," published a newspaper that quietly received subsidy payments from the Japanese government in return for good press. Russia quickly countered by establishing and openly subsidizing two English-language papers in East Asia, but according to Millard they lost effectiveness because readers knew they were official organs and thus propaganda outlets.[13]

After examining ways to manipulate American public opinion through the press, Japan concluded it did not need to do anything radical. The Japanese Legation in Washington already distributed news to American newspapers, which printed much of what they received. "[I]f we give them news, we can always give it in such form as to retain their sympathy," the Japanese minister in Washington wrote to Chargé d'Affaires Nabeshima Keijirō, "and unless we keep in touch with them by such means, we shall be unable, when need arises, to make use of them to our advantage." In contrast to its methods in Europe, Japan decided against directly subsidizing any American newspapers. It reasoned that shaping opinion in such an expansive country would require cultivating influence in a great many newspapers, and that proof of any subsidy payments would leak and create negative publicity.[14]

Japan intensified its public opinion efforts in December 1903, two months before the attack on Port Arthur, by dispatching two special envoys to curry the favor of the English-speaking world in person. Suematsu Kenchō, a newspaper journalist, politician, and law graduate of St. John's College, Cambridge University, went to Europe while Kaneko Kentarō, a Harvard University graduate who had served as personal assistant to Japan's prime minister, went to the United States.[15] Suematsu, son-in-law of Prince Itō Hirobumi, gave interviews to papers such as *Le Temps* of Paris and wrote articles for European journals beneath titles such as "How Russia Brought on the Russo-Japanese War." He collected his articles in a 1905 book *The Risen Sun*.[16] Kaneko took a more forceful approach. Kaneko, knowing from his Harvard days that Americans would doubt the word of a "kept" press, continued the policy of not buying newspaper support in the United States. Instead, he traveled the country, making speeches, sending articles to newspapers for publication, and sitting for interviews—including one with the Sunday edition of the *New York Times* and a separate one with the Sunday *Los Angeles Times*. He also gave press conferences, including one on March 19, 1904, in New York City with seventeen journalists to explain why Japan felt it had been forced into war.[17] His mass mailings targeted newspapers from coast to coast, and scores of them printed the free, laudatory biographies of Kaneko and Foreign Affairs Minister Komura Jutarō, who would most directly shape Japan's image in the West. These articles included a ringing call for an American-Japanese friendship that greatly would benefit both countries economically—a vision no doubt intended to bolster the prospects of loans and investments. In an interview, Kaneko stressed the same message to prepare for expanded, amicable relations. After the war, he said, "[T]here will be a rush of commerce to the Far East unprecedented in the history of the trade of the world. And America, which is to have the lion's share of this trade, cannot handle it to advantage without Japanese assistance."[18] Notably, Kaneko placed "The Secret of Japan's Success" in *Collier's Weekly*, a popular magazine in the United States, after Japan's initial victories in 1904.[19] The publicity campaign focused on three themes: that Japan only seemed to be aggressive because it acted in self-defense; that the "yellow peril" (a term coined by Kaiser Wilhelm II) posed no threat to the world but that the "white peril" from Russia did; and that Japan desired equal status with all advanced, civilized nations, both politically and economically.[20]

While the Ministry of Foreign Affairs orchestrated an attempt to shape public opinion abroad, officials in the Japanese home islands targeted the domestic crowd. As public opinion already favored war with Russia, they needed only to stoke the flames.

Japan's press traditions differed significantly from those of the United States, and those differences would inform the eventual press coverage of the Russo-Japanese War. American papers began in the colonial era as commercial and political organs, and by the early nineteenth century political parties and newspapers openly supported each other. Those papers had relatively small circulations and cost too much for working-class Americans to buy. Newspaper content often appeared in the form of vitriolic commentary pointed at political enemies. A free exchange of newspapers among editors via Benjamin Franklin's continental postal service ensured that all thirteen colonies read of events and opinions that Franklin believed would coalesce into a common desire for independence from Britain.[21] He was correct. "In establishing American independence, the pen and the press had a merit equal to that of the sword," wrote David Ramsay in his 1789 history of the revolution. "As the war was the people's war, and was carried on without funds, the exertions of the army would have been insufficient to effect the revolution, unless the great body of the people had been prepared for it, and also kept in a constant disposition to oppose Great Britain."[22] Colonial public opinion decided the outcome of the Revolutionary War, and the press won the battle for public opinion. Given the important role of an independent press in the establishment of the United States, it is not surprising that press freedom became a foundation of the nation's new government as laid down in the First Amendment of the Constitution. Historian Arthur Schlesinger Sr. argued that the second most profound result of the Revolutionary War, after independence, was "the rooted conviction that freedom of utterance ranks unique among human rights as the protector and promoter of all others."[23]

The dominant partisan and commercial press gave way to a new paradigm in the 1830s with the introduction of the "Penny Press" in the United States. These one-cent newspapers, beginning with the *New York Sun* in 1833, printed thousands of copies that were sold on the streets. This fresh economic model changed the dynamics of profit: instead of selling a few expensive copies to a wealthy audience narrowly defined by business or political interests, the Penny Press newspapers sold many cheap copies to the widest possible audience—nearly all who could read. With the introduction of the double-cylinder rotary press in the 1840s, newspapers could produce tens of thousands or even hundreds of thousands of copies, further enforcing economies of scale.[24] Content changed too, as publishers began seeking news that would appeal to the middle and lower classes—crime, sports, features, and so on. The number of American newspapers exploded from two hundred in 1800 to three thousand in 1860, the eve of the Civil War.[25] French aristocrat Alexis de Tocqueville, visiting the United States in the 1830s, linked the large number of news journals to America's widely scattered settlements and to the distribution of power among the federal, state, and local levels, making each state and municipality protective of its own interests. No one paper could speak for everyone because Americans thought of themselves not only as Americans but also as Georgians, Pennsylvanians, Bostonians, New Yorkers, miners, farmers, factory workers, and so on. De Tocqueville wrote in his monumental *Democracy in America*:

> The extraordinary subdivision of administrative power has much more to do with the enormous number of American newspapers than the great political freedom of the country and the absolute liberty of the press. If all the inhabitants of the Union had the suffrage, but a suffrage which should extend only to the choice of their legislators in Congress, they would require but few newspapers, because they would have to act together only on very important, but very rare, occasions. But within the great national association lesser associations have been established by law in every county, every city, and indeed in every village,

for the purposes of local administration. *The laws of the country thus compel every American to co-operate every day of his life with some of his fellow citizens for a common purpose, and each one of them requires a newspaper to inform him what all the others are doing.* (Emphasis added)[26]

De Tocqueville considered an independent press to be a mixed blessing. Its power was second only to the power of the people, he wrote, but in order to enjoy the press's "inestimable benefit," Americans had to accept its "inevitable evils,"[27] a theme that would echo throughout the news coverage of future wars in which nations balanced the need for news with the risks posed by such news. By the mid-1800s, the newspapers of the United States spoke with many voices, which often opposed authority at various levels of government. Most significantly, they were free to do so, supplying news content that ranged from responsible, accurate accounts of events and ideas to sensationalism and reckless gossip.

The Civil War cemented the newspaper's crucial role in American life and set off major changes in papers' structure and content. The costs of sending telegraphic news from the sites of battle pressured war correspondents in the field to keep their stories short, leading to a terse, facts-based style of reportage. The rising expense of doing journalism on a national scale stimulated interest in sharing the cost of stories, cementing the widespread reliance on the Associated Press newsgathering cooperative that had been born in the 1840s. Delivering a single reporter's story by wire to an array of newspapers of various political leanings spurred an increasing demand that such stories be free of political bias and opinion—presenting "just the facts," as David T. Z. Mindich titled his history of the rise of the journalistic norm of objectivity beginning in the 1860s.[28]

Objectivity would not become the nearly universal standard for American journalism until the 1920s. The first industry code of ethics, adopted by the American Society of Newspaper Editors in 1922, detailed norms such as responsibility, accuracy, impartiality, and lack of conflict of interest.[29] Nevertheless, the norms we recognize today in the United States had begun much earlier. A wave of professionalization swept the developed world in the nineteenth century as doctors, lawyers, engineers, and others established rules governing their professions and qualifications for membership.[30] Journalists in the United States never took this step formally because of their guaranteed independence declared in the First Amendment. Nevertheless, norms emerged organically as the press matured and editors demanded concrete skill sets, resulting in the creation of the first American journalism course at Cornell University in the mid-1870s and first curriculum at the University of Pennsylvania in 1893.[31] Lessons focused on reporting facts and doing so accurately and quickly.[32] In the late 1800s and early 1900s, most correspondents, whether in combat zones or elsewhere, expected to witness events for themselves and write accounts that were free of obvious slant. But news does not exist in a vacuum. Advertising had replaced political subsidy as the dominant source of American newspaper income by the end of the nineteenth century, and advertisers wanted to connect with large audiences. Newspapers in big cities such as New York and Chicago relied heavily on street sales instead of home delivery, and therefore encouraged the development of stories that delivered big headlines and big audiences. The best stories had exclusivity, freshness, significance, and sensation. Stories both true and sensational, such as the destruction of the battleship USS *Maine* in Havana harbor and bloody battles in Cuba in 1898, resulted in increased newspaper income. The downside, as de Tocqueville warned, arose when reporters cut corners or fabricated stories for the sake of a sensational scoop.

Japan's press history developed quite differently. The first newspapers appeared in the pre-Meiji era. Townspeople in Kyoto and Osaka, and later in Edo, printed and distributed single-sheet fliers without government authority. Mostly these *kawaraban*, or "tile impression" papers, followed the human desire for sensation that appears to be universal, focusing on events such as earthquakes, fires, battles, and love affairs. The feudal government, known as the Tokugawa Shogunate, set up its own newspaper in 1862 and sent copies to all prefectures. This kept the samurai apprised of news of the West as well as from throughout their small nation—which, unlike the United States of that era, was compact enough to be served by national newspapers. Content of the shogunate papers included government decrees and articles encouraging the development of a modern civilization.[33]

Economic and political upheaval toppled the feudal shoguns in 1868 and restored a nation-state under Emperor Meiji the Great. For a brief time between the capitulation of the shoguns and the enforcement of imperial power on all Japanese citizens, twenty newspapers existed in Edo, the capital soon to be renamed Tokyo, and many freely published political criticism. That changed when Edo Castle, heart of Tokugawa power for nearly three centuries, surrendered to imperial forces in April 1868. The new regime issued orders abolishing press criticism of the government. Pro-Tokugawa newspapers fell silent or fell in line.[34]

Japanese newspapers of the late 1800s mostly extolled the new leadership, helping to give birth to the fierce nationalism that would fully blossom during World War II. "In Meiji Japan the national religion became Japanism," a tool the elites used to mobilize citizens to embrace their aims, according to historian Susan Cheryl MacDermid.[35] The Meiji aimed to reshape Japan into something like a family, with the emperor as unquestioned but loving father. Historian Andrew E. Barshay observed that the Meiji state "controlled the boundaries of legality in public discourse by administrative, judicial, and legislative means." It also attempted to define national values and identity.[36]

As in America, Japanese newspapers by the late 1800s required advertising revenue to remain profitable. Stories or editorials that upset advertisers and readers would result in a loss of advertising and a decline in single-copy sales, which almost totally were made through face-to-face transactions in shops and on street corners. The Sino-Japanese War of 1894 greatly boosted sales and readership, when the typical purchase price fell to levels affordable by laborers of limited education and income. Readers vicariously sharing in Japan's successes on the field of battle helped construct a sense of *kyokoku itchi*, or national unity, beyond anything Japan had experienced. Competition became fierce among papers based in big cities that sought to tap into the nationalistic public. Tokyo had about twenty dailies in the early 1900s producing hundreds of thousands of copies on newly installed rotary presses.[37]

To cut costs in an effort to gain a competitive edge, newspaper owners increasingly relied on official sources of information. This created symbiosis: the Japanese press got a steady source of free or cheap news that it could print without fear of government retribution, and the government got a legitimizing voice that spoke directly to the people. The peculiarly Japanese institution of the *kisha*, or press club, reinforced close links between reporters and government officials. The first *kisha* formed in 1890 to push for journalistic access to the newly formed Diet and to resist acts restricting the press. However, then, as now, journalists realized they could not produce proper news without reliable access to sources. Over time, reporters and editors developed close, family-like relationships with high-ranking officials, going so far as to view important issues from the government's point of view. *Kisha* clubs formed rules to govern themselves that had more bite than America's ethics codes.[38]

In addition to the nationalistic, economic, and structural forces that pressured Japanese newspapers to practice self-censorship and follow a pro-government line, new laws provided for punishment of the recalcitrant. A bill approved by the Diet in 1897 made it a crime to insult the dignity of the emperor. This law also gave the judiciary the authority to censor and close newspapers, which it did by shuttering the pacifist and socialist *Heimin Shimbun* in 1904. Four weeks after the attack on Port Arthur, police began visiting *Heimin*'s subscribers and advising them to choose another newspaper. Police also intimidated news dealers and tried to get them to stop making the paper available on the streets. One month after those actions, the government jailed editor Sakai Toshihiko and temporarily shut *Heimin* for opposing higher taxes brought on by the war.[39] The government closed *Heimin* for good after it published the complete *Communist Manifesto* of Karl Marx and Friedrich Engels in the issue of November 13, 1904. Lead writer Kōtuko Shūsui received a five-month prison term and the courts confiscated the printing presses, marking the newspaper's demise on January 29, 1905.[40]

"A free Press were as much a marvel in Japan as a mastodon in Hyde Park," observed British journalist Douglas Story in Tokyo in early 1904. "Comment is crushed, criticism is killed in Japan."[41]

Japanese papers remained divided about the need for war during the spring and early summer of 1903, as the government had not announced a clear stand on the issue of whether to fight or negotiate the complete withdrawal of Russian troops from Manchuria. Clarification began in June of that year when a group of seven professors, including six from Tokyo Imperial University's Faculty of Law, petitioned the prime minister and other high officials to make a "final determination" against Russia. They called for war. Their outspokenness resulted in a rebuke from Tokyo Imperial University, but the seven professors continued to protest. They found their arguments gaining traction with politicians and the press. Public debate forced Japanese newspapers to announce whether they favored or opposed total war against Russia. Most, including the largest-circulation *Asahi Shimbun* and *Hochi Shimbun*, supported war, with the former giving one of the professors the space for an opinion column headlined "Let's Definitely Begin the War."[42] Twenty-five hundred delegates representing Tokyo and Osaka newspapers attended a rally in Osaka on November 22 to foster unity in the press for immediate war against Russia. Major speakers included journalists from the *Osaka Asahi Shimbun* and the *Yorozu Chōhō*. Nearly all who spoke advocated for the war minister's resignation for his not moving swiftly enough against Russia. The next day a second rally, on the same topic, led journalists to resolve, "A peaceful solution of the Manchurian question through indecisive diplomatic measures and humiliating conditions is meaningless. This is not what our nation wants."[43]

Other than *Heimin*, newspapers that opposed the war joined the pro-war press by year's end, as Russia reneged on a portion of its promised withdrawal and international hope for negotiation ceased. By that point, the populace screamed for war and Tokyo newspapers published extra editions every half-hour.[44] Arriving in Japan before the attack on Port Arthur, British war correspondent Bennet Burleigh observed the effects of war fever:

> Patriotism swelled with every heart-beat, and their intense race pride, which had been sorely ruffled at the brusque nature of the Russian progress in Manchuria, fretted at the patient forbearance of their own Government. In certain quarters they denounced their own ministers as traitors, and threatened them with death. And all because these officials hesitated, and strove to avert war. I had at times doubts whether the authorities would be able to hold their own people's hands, if there should be no campaign against Russia.[45]

Frederick Arthur McKenzie, war correspondent for the London *Daily Mail*, saw many examples of war fever in January 1904, one month before the opening of hostilities. A young boy and girl swayed and sang a made-up song, "Kill! Kill! Kill! Kill until the sword breaks." An old woman in Hiroshima, visiting her grandson in a mobilization camp, told him, "Don't be satisfied with killing one Russian before you die. Kill six, and then you will have proved yourself worthy." And a popular song intoned, "Don't mind whether you die or not. Obey the emperor and go ahead."[46]

The correspondents often interpreted expressions of Japanese character through racist lenses. To Western eyes, their apparently uniform adoration of the emperor, desire for war, and devotion to honor cast them more as automatons than fully human. Willard Straight, representing the Associated Press and Reuters, confided to his diary that he found the Japanese "less human" than other races. "They are a great mass and not an aggregate," he wrote. "One cannot feel the individuality of the men themselves. That may be on account of the difference of race, but at any rate the feeling is there."[47]

Once the war began, Japan's people grew even more outwardly unified and the nation's press fell under even heavier censorship. A law passed during the conflict with China in 1894 had given the government absolute control over news related to war. This precedent led to a supreme effort to dominate the press in 1904. The twin tools were censorship and propaganda, although the government had little need for the former. A rare example occurred when Japanese economists agreed that the nation lacked the resources to defeat Russia. Such fear had concrete roots. No Asian nation had ever defeated a European one in war, and a comparison of the two nations did not bode well for Japan: Russia's standing army and economy dwarfed those of its rival, and its navy also was far larger, although its Pacific Fleet and Japan's navy were of roughly equal strength. The Japanese government suppressed the economists' forecast to avoid damaging public morale. As for propaganda, the cabinet turned for advice to Tokutomi Sohō, influential editor of the right-wing *Kokumin Shimbun* newspaper. Following his roadmap toward building even more vociferous support for the war, Japanese officials encouraged newspapers to play up stories of individual heroism and sacrifice. Meanwhile, they censored news of extreme violence from the public.

Such violence was unprecedented in 1904 because of the introduction of machine guns, mines, and other modern weapons of war. American war reporter Frederick Palmer noted that Japanese troops used French-made Hotchkiss machine guns and barbed wire so effectively in an assault on Port Arthur that gunners had to take breaks so that piles of Russian corpses could be removed. They had obscured the line of fire.[48] Japanese troops suffered similarly from Russian attacks. Veteran war correspondents felt revulsion at the sight of Japanese corpses on the flanks of 203 Meter Hill after the successful siege of Port Arthur, defended by British-made Maxim machine guns. Correspondent David H. James of the London *Daily Telegraph* wrote: "The sight of those trenches heaped up with arms and legs and dismembered bodies all mixed together and then frozen into compact masses, the expressions on the face of the scattered heads of decapitated bodies, the stupendous magnitude of the concentrated horror, impressed itself indelibly into the utmost recesses of my unaccustomed brain."[49]

Japanese reporters were given prime accommodations from the armed forces, being first among observers into the front lines and given exclusive access to warships. They also had permission to send their stories by wire after commanders had sent their official communiqués to the press in the home islands and abroad.[50] The result of this arrangement was to have war correspondents' stories, both from Japanese and eventually from Western reporters, act as independent confirmation of the military accounts, boosting public confidence in the armed forces and the government. Burleigh said, "I have regarded it as unfortunate that the bulk of the information transmitted from Japan for home publication has been, and is, in the hands of those who directly or indirectly have official connection with the Mikado's Government, or by local association have become more Japanese than the Japanese."[51] Uchimura Kanzō, whose pacifism as a Christian evangelist worked to shield him from the excesses of the national unity movement, accused the Japanese press of lies. "No newspaper reported the truth," he wrote. "They all covered up any unfavorable news about Japan and reported small events unfavorable to the enemy in the most exaggerated way."[52] A more poetical description of the situation came from veteran war correspondent Melton Prior. He observed in Tokyo in March 1904, "The local papers are only allowed to publish everything *couleur de rose*."[53]

The well-orchestrated publicity campaign, censorship, and propaganda had a powerful effect that no doubt was much admired in the Japanese government. Only one major element appeared to remain outside government and military control.

"The Japanese were absolutely prepared for this war and all possible contingencies save one," a Western envoy in Tokyo told Palmer. "They overlooked the coming of a small army of correspondents representing the public opinion of two great friendly nations, whose goodwill it is to Japan's special interest to court."[54] More than one hundred of these correspondents, most of them from Britain and the United States, converged on Tokyo early in 1904 to seek access to expected fronts in Korea and Manchuria. Japan did not know how to achieve two competing goals: keeping the war correspondents from reporting anything that might damage battlefield security or national unity, and keeping them happy so they would write stories that would inspire Western admiration and sympathy. It is no wonder a clash of wills occurred. Ever since the first war to be covered by professional war correspondents, Western reporters operated under a set of traditions, cultures, and laws at odds with their Japanese counterparts.

The Mexican-American War of 1846–1848 was the first to feature reports from battlefields by professional war correspondents. It also imposed the fewest restraints on the press. The U.S. Army imposed no censorship and did not issue accreditation or passes. Soldiers and officers had not previously seen newspaper reporters in their midst and had no protocols in place to deal with such strangers.[55] Nevertheless, as correspondents were fellow Americans who shared war's dangers and who posed no risk to military plans, soldiers and officers generally welcomed them. Reporters examined all facets of camp life and witnessed battles from within the ranks. Couriers took their handwritten dispatches from the interior of Mexico to ports such as Veracruz. From there, steamboats ferried them across the Gulf of Mexico to printing presses in New Orleans. Competition to be the first to get a paper on the streets pushed journalists to extremes. En route across the gulf, some newspapers took the extra step of having war dispatches typeset so that pages would be ready for inking upon arrival. The public demanded more and more of this new sensation: war news delivered within days of battle. The 1848 painting *War News from Mexico* by Richard Caton Woodville captures the excitement: a man slack-jawed with amazement reads a broadsheet filled with war news from Mexico, no doubt delivered by steam and the brand-new system of telegraph wires to his hometown. A crowd surrounds him—some stealing a peek over his shoulder, others locked in conversation upon the latest from the front. The long delay in the return of such publications to the war zone made it virtually impossible for them to damage operational security, and so the army accepted the arrangement without question. Newspapers printed on mobile presses and distributed within the army camps were another story. President James K. Polk happily allowed military commanders in the field to suppress as many as five battlefield newspapers, even though the army's authority over civilians in foreign territory was questionable.[56]

The rise of literacy, the increased distribution afforded by a growing network of railroads and steamships, the introduction of the telegraph in 1844, and the popularity of low-cost newspapers printed on high-speed rotary presses combined to increase newspaper readership to unimagined heights in the mid-1800s. More newspapers meant more reporters in the field, filing to telegraph terminals that had expanded across the country. The presence of reporters and telegraph lines meant a greater potential threat to military commanders in the field, and so censorship began to take root during the American Civil War of 1861–1885 despite—or because of—the rising demand for news. The war made the newspaper indispensable as readers clamored

Figure 1.1 Kaneko Kentarō headed a media blitz in the United States before and during the Russo-Japanese War.
Source: Library of Congress.

to learn details of the conflict that threatened the future of their nation, to say nothing of the lives of their loved ones. "Only the press could provide information about the course of the war, policy, and potential outcomes of the conflict—and hence, some sense of whether the nation might endure," wrote Hazel Dicken-Garcia, historian of the nineteenth-century press. "It was indispensable in providing information needed by a whole nation."[57]

About five hundred correspondents took the field for the Union and a fraction of that for the Confederacy, as the number for the South is difficult to pinpoint. They rode with armies and wandered nearly unobstructed, as did photographers in wagons. Restrictions did exist, but nothing like those of what was to come. In the North, after newspapers went to press too soon and reported the First Battle of Bull Run as a Union victory, U.S. Secretary of

War Simon Cameron issued an order placing reporters in war zones under military discipline. They were issued press passes and subjected to penalties ranging from eviction from camp to execution (thankfully, never performed) if they published anything that damaged the Union cause.[58] Cameron's replacement, Edwin Stanton, insisted that telegraph-borne news of the war be routed through his office for screening; acting as censor he sometimes lowered Union casualty figures before they appeared in print and jailed or otherwise restricted the movement of offending reporters.[59] Southern correspondents also contended with military censors, but mostly exercised self-censorship because of their consensus of support for the continuation of slavery and the independence of the Confederacy. They enjoyed the freedom to point out incompetence, drunkenness, and other weaknesses that might weaken Confederate forces but were prevented from publicizing obviously detrimental facts such as troop movements. Nor could they criticize slavery.[60]

Amid the fierce competition to publish a scoop, newspapers sometimes resorted to sensationalism, puffery, and fakery.[61] Union General William Tecumseh Sherman treated reporters as "pests" and blamed them for leaking battle plans. However, on the whole, the *New York Times* argued, the good posed by independent, civilian observers reporting the war outweighed the bad. The *Times* said any attempt to expel the press would cause the Union more harm than any stories reporters might write about military blunders and incompetence.[62]

For the first two years of the war, correspondents generally wrote anonymously. After a news leak angered Union General Joseph Hooker, he issued General Order No. 48 in the spring of 1863. It required all reporters with the Army of the Potomac to "publish their communications over their own signatures."[63] This held them accountable, but it also was a step toward turning correspondents into literary stars. Readers who recognized excellence learned to look for specific bylines. By the time the United States entered its next war, in 1898, newspaper and magazine publishers paid handsomely to engage the services of the nation's best-known writers so they could cash in on their bylines. Popular novelists such as Richard Harding Davis, Stephen Crane, and John Fox Jr. joined the press corps in Cuba.

In some respects, war in the Spanish territory of Cuba mirrored the conflict in East Asia six years later. When the battleship USS *Maine* blew up in Havana harbor on February 15, Spanish authorities invoked a censorship as strict as that of the Japanese. They allowed only two messages about the explosion to be cabled to the United States: an official notification to the Navy by Maine Captain Charles D. Sigsbee and about one hundred words written by a correspondent for the Associated Press. A correspondent for the *New York World*, Sylvester Scovel, tricked the Spanish censor into sending a third dispatch, Scovel's eyewitness account, by writing it upon a blank form containing the censor's stamp of approval that he had earlier stolen.[64] In the ensuing weeks, the continuation of Spanish censorship prompted many reporters on the island to hire dispatch boats to carry them outside Spain's jurisdiction—particularly to the nearest American town, Key West, Florida—to file their stories freely.[65] The same occurred in the Far East in 1904 and 1905 as journalists embedded with the Japanese and Russians sometimes made their way to China to send their stories over the telegraph wires.

The United States began hostilities by executing a blockade of Cuba, bottling up the Spanish fleet in the harbor of Santiago much like the way the Japanese had contained the Russian warships at Port Arthur. Cuba remained in contact with the outside world via underwater telegraph cables, but the navy and army placed censors at the cable companies on the receiving end of messages at Tampa and Key West, Florida, and in New York City, the nation's press headquarters.[66] Once journalists began gathering news on the island, they had three choices: submit censored stories to be sent via military-controlled telegraph lines once those lines were free of official traffic; sail to an uncensored port beyond American control, such as Port-au-Prince, Haiti, to send a cable; or mail their dispatches. The last method was common among reporters in the penny-pinching chain of newspapers owned by E.W. Scripps, anchored by the *Cincinnati Post* and *Cleveland Press*. Delays inherent in the latter two choices drained any potential risk to military security as well as most news value for stories that rival reporters had already cabled to competing newspapers.[67]

Initial censorship, as presented to correspondents by the U.S. government, was reasonable and soft: "Cipher [encoded] messages were forbidden to the West Indies [and Spain and her possessions]," as were "any messages in plain text which conveyed important information concerning military operations or such as were detrimental to the interests of the country."[68]

News of ship movements was not strictly forbidden at first, an oversight that led to the press leaking news of the army's attempt to supply Cuban rebels with food and ammunition by sneaking the steamer *Gussie* to an isolated section of coast. Advance newspaper stories alerted the Spanish, preventing the landing. After that incident, censorship regulations grew tighter. The armed forces would not allow any information of ship or troop movements to be cabled without approval.[69] It was a logical and appropriate rule, and one that would be followed in later American wars.

A correspondent who wanted to accompany the American armed forces in Cuba or Puerto Rico had to apply for credentials at the War or Navy Department with a letter of recommendation from the editor of his or her publication (one woman received accreditation). Secretary of War Russell A. Alger then signed a pass that journalists accompanying the army were expected to carry. It said:

> This is to certify that _____ has been duly accredited to the War Department as a correspondent of the _____.
>
> Military commanders are requested to permit him to pass freely, so far as in their judgment it is proper and expedient to do so, and to extend to him such aid and protection, not incompatible with the interests of the service, as he may require.

Alger also presented a similar pass for the correspondent to show to a quartermaster in order to arrange transportation by ship to the war zone.[70]

The total number of correspondents covering the war is difficult to assess, but historian Charles H. Brown's detailed study pegs it at about three hundred.[71] That is a staggering number for a shooting war lasting a little more than three weeks in Cuba.

The correspondents complained of censorship, but they remained free to witness war as closely as they dared and to share their views—eventually, in full—with their readers. Davis and Crane, popular novelists, were riding with the Rough Riders when fighting broke out at Las Guásimas. They crouched amid the heaviest shooting, surrounded by dense brush, and tasted war as deeply as any soldier. Crane wrote, "Our people advanced, deployed, reinforced, fought, fell—in the bushes, in the tall grass, under the lone palms—before a foe not even half seen." Davis received praise from Colonel Theodore Roosevelt for spotting Spanish snipers and pointing them out to the Rough Riders so they could return fire.[72] According to the romantic notions about warfare common at the time, many correspondents found the experience splendid and exhilarating. Even William Randolph Hearst, owner of a large chain of newspapers, got into the act. He joined his correspondents, numbering about fifty, in the field and helped a wounded James Creelman get his dispatch to Hearst's flagship paper, *The New York Journal*. "'I'm sorry you're hurt, but . . . wasn't it a splendid fight? We must beat every paper in the world," Hearst said to Creelman, lying dazed on the grass. Creelman recalled Hearst's face as being radiant with enthusiasm.[73]

News that lacked official approval did little discernible damage to security. In fact, some unapproved stories proved beneficial in the long run. In May, reporter Poultney Bigelow exposed inadequacies at army training sites in southern Florida, including poor food, winter-weight uniforms for a summer invasion, and an underprepared officer corps. The *Harper's Weekly* story outraged the army, but it drew needed attention to serious problems. It also cost Bigelow his accreditation; he missed the invasion.[74] In another example at war's end, the press got permission to report an outbreak of typhoid, malaria, yellow fever, and dysentery among American troops in Cuba. The topic previously had been forbidden for publication by censorship, but the death rate grew so high that military officials changed their minds. The War Department reacted by ordering a partial withdrawal of troops from the Cuban city of Santiago. Brigadier General William R. Shafter wired in response that he expected a yellow fever epidemic and that the evacuation needed to be accomplished as quickly as possible. The press obtained a copy of the letter and printed it. Public outrage at thousands of deaths angered President William McKinley but ultimately sped demobilization and saved lives.[75]

Styles of war reporting changed, albeit slowly, toward the turn of the century. War correspondence historian Phillip Knightley wrote that in one of the first wars covered by professional war correspondents, the Crimean War of 1853–1856, dispatches fell into two competing styles. One school, led by William Howard Russell, summarized the strategy and tactics of a battle, trying to say how and why it had been won or lost. The other, led by E. L. Godkin, focused on war's effect on individuals. While both types gained readers in England, Russell's style "carried more weight" because of his publishing in the *Times* of London, compared with Godkin's *London Daily News*. Reporters interested in writing about individual men and women caught up in war were in the minority. But toward century's end, there arose a few fresh and talented voices. According to Knightley, "two or three" reporters in the five decades between the American Civil War and World War I had the courage to report honestly about war's impact. He named Luigi Barzini of Milan's *Corriere della Sera*; Januarius MacGahan of New Lexington, Ohio, whose reports on Turkish atrocities for the *New York Herald* and *London Daily News* helped split the nation of Bulgaria from the Ottoman Empire; and James Creelman of the Hearst press.[76] Barzini and American novelist Jack London were among the reporters of the Russo-Japanese War who turned to creating pen portraits of ordinary people in harm's way. That particular template of war story would become far more common in later conflicts, thanks in part to talented, accredited female reporters who turned to it after being denied access to battlegrounds by chauvinistic generals.

Contemporary with the changes in war correspondence was a movement in the United States to invigorate newspapers with journalism based on action rather than reaction. According to historian W. Joseph Campbell, "journalism of action" had links to Britain's "new journalism" during the 1880s and 1890s and the idea expressed by *Review of Reviews* editor William T. Stead that an activist press could promote "government by journalism." Writing in 1885, Stead envisioned the power of the press as shaping public opinion by framing issues to excite or suppress emotional and intellectual responses.[77] Japan would carry out those ideas in the extreme by coupling censorship with activism in the cause of promoting a war.

If journalists were to have the most impact while covering the biggest stories, they had to have access to newsworthy events. A year after Spain's defeat, the Hague Convention of 1899 considered the status of journalists in its monumental report, *Laws and Customs of War on Land*. In concert with the Geneva Conventions, the Hague document spelled out rules defining civilized warfare, war crimes, and treatment of those taken prisoner. While the convention, which had been called by Tsar Nicholas II of Russia, did not define prisoners of war, Article XIII of its final version said:

> Individuals who follow an army without directly belonging to it, such as newspaper correspondents and reporters, sutlers, contractors, who fall into the enemy's hands, and whom the latter think fit to detain, have a right to be treated as prisoners of war, provided they can produce a certificate from the military authorities of the army they were accompanying.[78]

The right to grant such certificates of passage rested with the commander in the field. Thus, unless given specific orders by higher-ranking officers, the commander would be authorized to define the rules that correspondents must follow and by implication had the authority to exclude from the battlefield any who lacked proper documentation or violated the terms of their certification.[79] The treaty's signatories consisted of the United States, the United Kingdom, Germany, Italy, France, Japan, Russia, and nineteen other nations. The treaty went into effect in September 1900 for most nations and April 1902 for the United States.[80]

Formal procedures for handling accreditation of war correspondents got their first large-scale test during the Boer War in southern Africa (1899–1902). According to historian Donal P. McCrachen, the rules governing the issuance of licenses proved to be "chaotic and inconsistent." The rules called for the War Office in London or any of several army bases in South Africa to issue licenses to journalists, but many correspondents arrived in Cape Town without them. "It was proposed that no more than two licenses be granted to any particular paper, that licenses only be granted to dailies with a circulation above 20,000, and that no foreigners be granted licenses [for fear they could act as spies]," McCrachen wrote. "None of these proposals was imposed."[81] It appears no British correspondent was refused accreditation.

When the war broke out, British censorship was so light that the rules for correspondents fit on the back of the license card. By 1900, telegraphic communication became the main concern of British censors, as Boers could tap or cut the lines, but commanders in the field exercised much flexibility over journalistic use of the telegraph and mail. A guide for censors early that year said "[n]o hard and fast" regulations could be implemented. Field Marshal Lord Frederick Roberts, who curried favor with the press, encouraged this absence of rules. At one point, he ordered that letters (as opposed to telegrams) written by British journalists to their home papers go entirely uncensored.[82] Journalists rode with the troops, ate military food, fed military hay to their horses, and watched the British army in action; in return, being mostly sympathetic to the United Kingdom's cause against the Dutch-descended Boers, they produced generally supportive stories.[83]

Eventually, censorship rules became codified. The War Office produced a ten-page "Rules for the Guidance of Press Censors in South Africa," printed in Pretoria and issued in May 1901. Journalists in previous wars would have considered these rules to be wise. They included the logical requirement for vetting telegraphed stories and gave the censor the power to block transmission of those that posed a threat to the army in the field. But they also said journalists' letters to the United Kingdom "as a rule [were] to pass unopened," and censors were not to edit stories for accuracy.[84]

War correspondents anticipated the next major war before it broke out. Rising tensions between Russia and Japan signaled a near certainty of conflict months in advance of the first shots. The Associated Press contracted with twenty-nine journalists in Japan and the East Asian mainland for war coverage.[85] Tokyo was the center of the beehive. One hundred and twenty correspondents from Britain, the United States, Germany, France, and Italy began arriving in the Japanese capital in January 1904. Most congregated at the Imperial Hotel and Grand Hotel to await the outbreak of war and the expected presentation of credentials to go to the front. In Russia, reporters including Luigi Barzini initially waited in Saint Petersburg.

Burleigh, representing the London *Daily Telegraph* and keen to report from the Japanese side, recalled:

> We were to have press permits to follow the army, but not until war was declared. I had a notion that the first fight would be a naval one, but it was soon apparent that no foreign correspondents would be allowed to go on board any of their men-of-war. I had tried to get passage, but, as an American friend said, "Why, you may as well hope to make snowballs in August in South Carolina as to get that permission."[86]

Japan began mobilizing an army that would top more than one million men, but it looked to the sea for its first engagement. An island nation, it could not ferry troops to Korea and Manchuria until it controlled the lanes where many Russian warships patrolled. Nor could it guarantee protection to its many unfortified harbors, mostly fishing villages, until it neutralized the threat of the Russian fleet. The first move, a naval surprise attack at Port Arthur and Incheon, would maximize the damage inflicted on the enemy and set up Japan's land offensives.

In conjunction with the torpedo attack and shelling of Port Arthur, Japanese transports began unloading soldiers of the First Army on the night of February 8 at the port of Incheon on the west coast of neutral Korea. Robert

L. Dunn of *Collier's Weekly* lighted the harbor with magnesium flashes as he photographed the nearly three thousand soldiers coming ashore. Nobody bothered to hinder his work, neither Japanese nor Russian. A Japanese torpedo boat captain said the Russians "behaved with utmost unconcern" as the adversary's warships arrived. "Their washing was hanging out to dry and their swinging booms [were] out as if they were wholly indifferent to the great drama about to be enacted." After the transports left, the crews of the gunboat *Koreets* (Korean person) and cruiser *Variag* refused to surrender to a much larger Japanese squadron and scuttled their ships in Incheon harbor.[87]

The disembarked troops marched east and then north from Incheon to engage Russian soldiers in skirmishes at Seoul and Pyongyang, en route to the Yalu River that separates Korea from China. (The first significant land battle would occur at the river on April 30 despite Korea and China holding neutral status in the conflict.) As the First Army started transmitting official communiqués from Korea, Tokyo-based Western correspondents stepped up their requests for access. They were told that passes to accompany the armies would be issued only by the Ministry of War on the recommendation of the legation representing the correspondent's home nation. Without such endorsement, a correspondent could not hope to see battle. Consequently, journalists immediately hailed two-passenger rickshaws at their hotels and sped off to their legations.[88]

Once the correspondents had their letters of recommendation, they visited "scores of government officials," according to William H. Brill, an American representing the Associated Press. These included Foreign Minister Komura; Field Marshal Oyama Gentarō, the commander in chief; General Fukushima Yasumasa of the General Staff; and Admirals Yamamoto Gonnohyōe, minister of the navy, and Itō Sukeyuki, head of the Navy General Staff, for those still holding out hope for appointment to a warship.[89]

"'Passes will be issued very soon,' we were told every day, 'and very soon after that you will be allowed to proceed to the front,'" Brill wrote in an unpublished manuscript. "'We are very sorry but we cannot allow you to go at once. Very soon we will let you know the plans.'"[90]

When the passes finally arrived from the Foreign Office, the lobby of the Imperial Hotel became as "cheerful as a garden party," Palmer, representing *Collier's Weekly* magazine, recalled. Each pass was labeled "Certificate of Permission to Accompany the Army," and said that the named person was permitted to follow a division, with a blank inserted for the number of that division. A slip of rice paper attached to the pass read: "The bearer is requested to inquire at the Military Staff Headquarters as to the name of the division to which he is to be attached and the date of departure, and to request the name of the division to be entered upon this certificate." Each recipient of the pass immediately visited General Tanaka Giichi of the General Staff, soon to become chief aide to General Kodama Gentarō on the Asian mainland. Palmer found Tanaka somewhat surprised by the deluge of visitors but adept at disappointing them without creating rancor—at least, at first. Palmer asked if it might be two or three weeks before the correspondents departed; if not, he said he would like to roam the islands and visit some temples. Tanaka laughed and said, "Two *or* three weeks! That is a long time." When Palmer suggested that two or three days might be more likely, Tanaka laughed again and said, with a mischievous lilt, "Perhaps! You must be patient."[91]

The correspondents discovered a defining characteristic of the Japanese: a cultural aversion to the rudeness of saying "no" to an unwelcomed request. "When a Japanese has to refuse your request, courtesy forbids that he should reply with a direct negative," war correspondent McKenzie observed. "He points out to you the difficulties involved in your plan; he fears you may suffer if you obtain what you want; he expresses the cordial wish that if you still desire it, it may be possible to grant it in a day or two." Western correspondents, unaccustomed to Japanese ways, took such dissemblance to mean "yes" and became increasingly disappointed and angry with each passing week.[92] Several correspondents remarked in memoirs written after the war that they would have better appreciated the truth—that passes to the front would not be honored for several months, if honored at all.

To placate the war correspondents, give them something to do, and curry favor, the Ministry of Foreign Affairs arranged for entertainment. The journalists visited the opening of the Diet, attended by the emperor; viewed a sumo wrestling match; and ate many ceremonial dinners. They called themselves "Cherry Blossom Correspondents."[93] Some wandered the islands, sightseeing while thumbing copies of *Murray's Guidebook for Travellers in Japan*. They set about "collecting atmosphere, writing laudatory accounts of Japanese character, and describing Japanese gardens, street scenes, personalities," said Lloyd Griscom, the U.S. consul in Tokyo.

Willard Straight said the fêtes and parties did little to ease the tension. He described the air at the Imperial Hotel as "blue" from the curses of famous correspondents who found themselves figuratively "bound hand and foot by the dapper little Orientals." He found it unique that a government would isolate and censor journalists with one hand, while wining and dining them and "patting them on the back" with the other. The Japanese plan, he said, was to deaden their sense of duty to get into the field. It didn't work.[94] Brill observed that such experiences made nearly all correspondents pro-Japanese people but anti-Japanese government.[95]

Some correspondents skipped the festivities to travel through the country. Restrictions followed them everywhere.[96] Their letters leaving Japan were opened unless the correspondents carried them to Yokohama and placed them aboard outbound ships flagged by other nations.[97] Before war broke out, the

Figure 1.2 *War News from Mexico*, an 1848 painting by Richard Caton Woodville, captures the telegraph's impact on combat journalism.

Japanese government had established rules forbidding the snapping of photographs of anything related to the war. Several journalists had their cameras confiscated or their undeveloped film ruined. A French correspondent for *Le Figaro* hit upon the idea of clicking the shutter of his empty camera in prohibited areas in order to be arrested and irritate the authorities as recompense for their strictness. He explained his odd behavior by saying that he merely had been learning how to operate the camera's dials and buttons.[98]

Journalists found themselves followed as they wandered. Spies also read their mail and telegrams, eavesdropped on private conversations, and pawed through their belongings when they went outside their hotel.[99] Most journalists spoke little, if any, Japanese and so relied on translators or on having brief conversations with the few army or staff officers who could speak English. Translators and servants often eavesdropped and shared information they gathered with military and government officials.[100]

Japan distrusted not just correspondents but apparently all Occidentals wandering Tokyo in the weeks immediately before and after the outbreak of war. Consul Griscom heard many complaints from war correspondents that their baggage had been ransacked and that they had shadows tailing them as they roamed. Griscom learned that the British journalists had similar problems. In his memoir, Griscom recalled speaking with a representative of Scotland Yard who had traveled to Japan to learn the art of single stick, a martial art that, like the Japanese art of *kendo*, uses a sword-length cudgel to incapacitate an opponent. The Briton lost control of his stick during practice exercises one morning and smacked his Japanese instructor across the left cheek, leaving a purple welt. At dinner that night at the British Legation, he recognized his wine steward by the very same welt.[101]

While waiting for approval to travel with the armies, journalists staying at the Imperial Hotel found ways to occupy their time. George Lynch and Frederick Palmer organized them to collaborate on a book in which everyone shared a story of some significant event he had covered, with the profits to be turned over for war relief. *In Many Wars by Many War Correspondents* contained forty-nine stories. Published in Tokyo, it had a limited press run and never was intended for broad circulation. Original copies remain extremely valuable, as each article ended with the original, inked signature of its author—popular novelists Richard Harding Davis, John Fox Jr., and Jack London among them.[102]

They also set about assembling their war kits to be ready for call-up at a moment's notice. It was cold in Japan in February and March, and the Ministry of Foreign Affairs kept saying the journalists would depart soon. Winter clothes, horses, and other items had to be purchased. Brill recalled that the Imperial Hotel crawled with tradesmen seeking to make a sale. "If a correspondent left his room he was accosted by a half a dozen Chinamen who in pidgin English, argued the superiority of the tailoring establishments which they represented." He said "literally thousands"—surely an exaggeration—jockeyed to demonstrate the superior quality of their particular folding beds, camp chairs, tables, tents, stoves, and lanterns. Crowds of boys surged around each wayward journalist, begging to be hired as a personal servant. "It was as much as a correspondent's life was worth to venture on the street alone for he was sure to be accosted by dozens of men who desired positions as interpreters, men, most of whom could speak more or less Japanese and some of whom had a few words of English," Brill said. Employment seekers even invaded hotel rooms booked by the war correspondents at all hours of the day and night. Brill wrote:

> In the morning the court yard of the hotel resembled a county fair, for here were assembled hundreds of horses which were offered to the correspondents. Such a collection of horses as greeted the prospective purchaser when he entered the courtyard had seldom been seen before. There were all sorts, conditions and colors of horses, and most of them were lame, halt or blind. They had spavins and

sprung knees, epizoodic and saddle galls, cracked hoofs, swollen hocks—every disease and ailment that horse flesh is heir to. What to do with these horses was a simple problem—we sent them all away and resorted to private stables where most of us secured f[a]irly good tough little Japanese or Chinese ponies at not more than three times their actual value.[103]

Despite the correspondents' inability to report eyewitness accounts of warship encounters and the transportation of armies to Korea during the first two months of the war, their home magazines and newspapers continually demanded actual news of the war and not just features and travel pieces. The General Staff office distributed official communiqués from navy and army officers two to three times per day. The calls by the Ministry of War to the hotels at first sent journalists running, hoping that their passes finally would be endorsed for travel. Instead, for the first two months, the phone calls merely signaled the arrival of another bare-bones account of battles and skirmishes that no Western reporter had seen. Eventually everyone except the wire service reporters quit replying to the summonses.[104]

Correspondents took the initial communiqués and turned them into proper stories in the style of Western newspapers, which they then could send home by mail or telegraph. The mail option was much slower. Palmer posted a dispatch on March 15 about Japanese affairs in Korea that did not appear until the April 23 issue of *Collier's Weekly*. He noted rampant political speculation among Tokyo citizens about Korea's future under Japanese occupation and observed that censors struck certain words from telegraphed stories about the relationship of the two countries. "The censor does not allow use of that naughty word 'protectorate,'" he wrote. "If no Japanese will say that the arrangement is a protectorate, none will say that it is not." Invading soldiers turned independent Korea into a vassal state to Japan's suzerain, he said, but the Japanese papers virtually ignored that particular issue other than to reprint the "nicely worded" euphemisms of the Ministry of Foreign Affairs. "Yesterday Korea was Korean; to-day it is Japanese," Palmer observed in language that censors certainly would have stricken from a telegram. "The Korean Emperor becomes what the Khedive is to Egypt" under British rule.[105] Korea and Japan signed a treaty in 1905 that officially made Korea a protectorate, and five years later, again by treaty (never signed by the Korean regent emperor during the five-year puppet regime), Japan annexed Korea. Japanese rule in Korea did not end until Japan's surrender to the Allies in 1945. The role of propaganda in the takeover of the peninsula can be appreciated by terms commonly used by the two countries to describe the same thing. The 1905 treaty is known in Japan as the "Second Japan-Korea Agreement" and in Korea as "Eulsa Neukyak" or "Eulsa Coerced Government Treaty," taking *Eulsa* from the Korean calendar. The Korean ministers who signed it are the "Five Eulsa Traitors."[106]

Some journalists flagrantly embellished Japan's official communiqués in February and March. Luigi Barzini of *Corriere della Sera* said his counterparts created war news or sensationalized the military handouts to compete for readers. At night, they swapped stories in the billiards room of the Imperial Hotel. "For two months they know of no other field than the green carpet of the billiard table, no other projectiles than ivory billiard balls, no other weapons than billiard cues," Barzini wrote. In addition, Barzini said, some Americans—"They could only be Americans!"—agreed to tell the same lies so their editors would not question them:

> They have created a "trust" for "stunning" news. You know, news that appears in a single newspaper is "doubtful"; if it is reported by two newspapers it is "subject to being accepted"; three is "trustworthy"; four is "confirmed"; more than four is "irrefutable." A trust of five journalists can impose on posterity, can create the truth without being true, can win battles immemorial without visiting the site. Such is the strength of modern journalism![107]

Edward F. Knight of the London *Morning Post* suggested embellishment also occurred once a dispatch arrived in the correspondents' hometown newsrooms. Once when the press corps complained to the army about the restrictions under which they operated, Japanese authorities invited the journalists to attend a juggling exhibition in order to cajole them. Knight had lost an arm in 1899 while covering the Boer War but volunteered that he too could juggle. He held up a dispatch "as sent out from a correspondent," measuring eighteen inches long. Then he showed the same dispatch after it had gone through the censor's office, manipulating the strip of paper so it appeared to be a half-inch. "But here," he said, "here is the dispatch as it appears in the paper," and triumphantly produced an article several times longer than the original that had left the reporter's hands. Echoing Barzini, he added, "Of course, it was an American paper!"[108]

Japan apparently did not mind a bit of fudging of the facts in its favor, especially by the British and American newspapers whose support it cultivated. Because all outgoing telegrams suffered heavy-handed censorship, through a process the journalists could not observe or question, their reports could not threaten army and navy security. Correspondents in Tokyo who tried to file wire dispatches that winter had no way to learn whether censors had passed their stories, of if they had, what they had cut or how they might have garbled the news. "No one knew who the censor was or the location of his office," the *New York Herald* reported, "and it was useless to try to find out anything about it from any of the telegraph people."[109] Once reporters began filing from the mainland in spring, the censorship grew even more byzantine; censors could change a cabled story at every telegraph junction between the front and Tokyo. To reach the United States from the Chinese coast or from terminals controlled by Japan, a message from Korea or Manchuria had two possible routes. One route, used primarily by the British correspondents filing to the United Kingdom and beyond, traveled to Nagasaki, Japan, and from there an operator forwarded it under the ocean to Shanghai, China. The next stops were Hong Kong; Saigon; Singapore; Labuan, Borneo; Penang, Malaysia; Madras, Bombay, India; Aden; Alexandria, Egypt; Malta; Lisbon, Portugal; London; and across the Atlantic to New York.[110] The other route to the United States opened at the start of the war thanks to the intervention of Melville E. Stone, the general manager of the Associated Press. He arranged access through Japanese and Chinese ports to San Francisco via the trans-Pacific cable, which eliminated three-fourths of the number of relay stations required to send a message by the alternative route. However, Stone had to rely heavily on news from the Russian side of the war, given Japan's censorship, and thus continued to make use of Russia's overland cable route through Asia.[111] The cable press rate began at sixty-five cents per word and rose higher than one dollar per word for swifter priority.[112] Wires from Incheon could be transmitted only at the normal rate, about three times higher than the standard rate for the press. *Collier's Weekly*, which had nine correspondents reporting from and photographing Tokyo and the war on the mainland, spent $50,000 on war correspondence by mid-April 1904—the equivalent of $1.4 million just over a hundred years later.[113] Given their expenses versus their meager returns, it is no wonder that editors and publishers screamed for stronger news stories and the need for fewer restrictions on the press in order to receive them.

News from the mainland was subjected to a nearly total blackout in the war's early weeks, Griscom said, and reporters often complained to him about censorship of their dispatches.

The Japanese government owned all telegraph companies and lines on the home islands, so it easily held back bad news to avoid upsetting the public. Before it was shut down, the socialist *Heimin* newspaper criticized the government's control of news and war correspondents, saying "[G]ood reports always come through the censors so the majority of Japanese do not know how the war is going."[114] In mid-May 1904, for example, Russian mines sank two of Japan's six battleships, the *Yashima* and *Hatsuse*, and the cruiser *Yoshino* sank after a collision in the fog with the cruiser *Kasuga*. Since the Russians had not seen the *Yashima* go under, Japan's navy announced only the loss of *Hatsuse* and *Yoshino*. To fool the enemy about its strength, the navy suppressed news of the *Yashima* for more than a year, all the time keeping the families of its crew in the dark about their fate.[115]

Protests from the war correspondents reached Washington and London. Editors of the affected British papers complained to Viscount Hayashi Todasu, Japanese minister to Britain. He released a statement to the press defending total censorship in a war for the existence of one's country, without saying how a potential loss to Russia would spell the "death" of Japan:

Figure 1.3 Richard Harding Davis, right, talks with his friend, Lieutenant Colonel Theodore Roosevelt, during the Spanish-American War. *Source*: Library of Congress.

I have had numerous representations from English and other newspapers upon this subject, but I believe that our position in this case is not only right, but will be admitted to be such by those who look carefully into the circumstances.

We are fighting against numerical odds which are quite out of proportion to the odds against any combatant in recent wars. We are fighting for our existence and our only hope of maintaining it is to strike swiftly and secretly at the beginning. To get in the first blow means more to us than, I think, it has ever meant to any belligerent, and to insure this it is vital for us to demand a degree of secrecy which had not been necessary in any recent warfare. Even at the risk of alienating temporarily the friendship of the press of the world we must prevent even a whisper of our real intentions reaching our powerful enemy.

Before war was declared I knew that our military authorities had decided that our censorship must be more rigid than ever before attempted. One line might have ruined our first attack on Port Arthur, one line might ruin our projected land operations.

When we fought China we gave the war correspondents free latitude, and in many cases they took advantage of this to predict our future movements. That did not matter much when China was our enemy, but against a Power like Russia, so immensely superior in eventual resource, it might turn the scale. When you fight for your life everything else becomes of minor importance.[116]

Despite his public endorsement of strict censorship, Hayashi's sympathies lay elsewhere. The Ministry of Foreign Affairs and the armed forces disagreed on the extent of censorship required for Western correspondence, and in that fight the military initially reigned supreme. The Ministry of War believed that its early victories had been directly related to stiff censorship and would not allow journalists to accompany troops in the field "until the proper moment" presented itself. Minister of Foreign Affairs Baron Komura said it was "quite impossible" for the civil branches of government to dictate to the military during wartime.[117] It took multiple events in late February and March to persuade the Ministry of War that the moment for accepting journalists in the war zone had arrived. First, foreign war correspondents threatened a news strike in protest of the censorship.[118] Second, most American and British correspondents continued their boycott of the ceremony of news handouts at the Ministry of War, which caused a loss of face. Third, the correspondents and their consuls kept up their protests against General Komura, with Griscom pointing out that favorable Western opinion demanded objective reporting from the front.[119] Fourth, Russia announced it would accredit war correspondents and send them to the front. Fifth, editors of British newspapers, "growing weary of the enormous expenses which the Eastern war is costing them," protested to the Japanese minister in London. According to a wire dispatch, they pointed out the danger to Japan from "a bad policy of a reticence so extreme."[120] Sixth, *Indianapolis News* war correspondent Hector Fuller, aided by a letter of introduction from U.S. senator Albert Beveridge of Indiana, obtained an advantageous interview with Prime Minister Katsura Tarō on March 22. Dressed in frock coat and silk hat, Fuller elicited a promise from Katsura, an acquaintance of Beveridge's, to speak directly to the minister of the army about placing American journalists in the war zone in order to provide sympathetic news accounts to the United States.[121] And finally, Japan had enjoyed an unbroken winning streak, never losing any engagement on land or sea to the Russian enemy. That meant Japan's worst fears had been unrealized and that perhaps some leeway could be allowed as it pressed its advantages. Slowly, in London, Hayashi decided to confront the obstinate Ministry of War. In a telegram to Komura on March 31, Hayashi said representatives of the major British papers had approached him. While they reluctantly agreed to the initial censorship, they had begun to show "irritation," he wrote, especially given Russia's relative freedom.

> Therefore, if too strict censorship and detainment of correspondents continue long, I fear that it will exasperate the press and may possibly cause revulsion of feeling against us. Accordingly I think it advisable for us to grant early permission to correspondents to go to the front, arranging censorship within reasonable limit of necessity.

Komura replied the next day to say that such permission had already been granted, although it is not clear if he meant he had agreed to the change before hearing from Hayashi.[122] The accord would give journalists nominal access to the battlefields while controlling what they saw and reported.

When the American correspondents read the press regulations published by the Ministry of War to govern their actions, Griscom saw jubilation turn to gloom. The war correspondents would be "chaperoned as closely as children at kindergarten," he wrote, their movements banned except in the company of escorts, and everything they wrote subject to censorship at the source.[123]

The complete text of the regulations read as follows:

Japanese Regulations for War Correspondents, 1904

ART. I. Newspaper correspondents who wish to follow the army are required to make application to the department of war, together with a sketch of their antecedents and a document of personal guaranty signed by the proprietor of the newspaper to which they belong.

In case of foreign correspondents, their application shall be sent through their respective ministers or consuls and the department of foreign affairs. Foreign correspondents need only mention in their application the name of the newspaper to which they belong and dispense altogether with the presentation of sketches of antecedents and papers of personal guaranty.

ART. II. The applicant must have been engaged in journalistic work for not less than a year as a member of a newspaper staff.

ART. III. Foreign correspondents who cannot understand the Japanese language may take with them one interpreter each into the field. Any correspondent requiring an interpreter may engage one himself and present an application on the interpreter's behalf accompanied by a paper of personal guaranty for the same.

ART. IV. A foreign correspondent, in addition to his interpreter, may engage one or more servants when circumstances demand it, the procedure of engagement to be in accordance with the foregoing article.

ART. V. The authorities, when they consider it necessary, may cause the selection of one person to act as joint correspondent for several newspapers.

ART. VI. In case any person is allowed to accompany the Japanese forces an official permit shall be given him.

ART. VII. The applicants allowed as stated shall be attached to a "Kōtō shireibu" (higher commanding officer).

ART VIII. Correspondent shall always wear foreign clothes, and to their left arms shall be attached a white band, measuring about 2 inches in width, on which the name of the newspaper offices which they represent shall be written in Japanese with red ink.

ART. IX. Correspondents shall always carry with them the official permit, and shall, when asked, show it to officers and officials belonging to the Japanese forces.

ART. X. Correspondents shall always observe the rules and orders to be issued by the Kōtō shireibu, so long as they remain with the Japanese forces.

In case they disregard the above rules and orders, the authorities of the Kōtō shireibu may refuse to allow them to accompany the Japanese forces.

ART. XI. The war correspondent will not be allowed to dispatch his communications (whether they be correspondence for publication or private letters or telegrams, etc.) until after the examination by the officer appointed for the purpose by the higher commanding officers. No communication containing cipher or symbols will be permitted to be despatched [sic].

ART. XII. The army and its officers will accord, as far as circumstances permit, to the war correspondents suitable treatment and facilities, and, when in the field and in case of necessity give him food, etc., or, at his request, give him transportation in vessels or vehicles.

ART. XIII. In case the war correspondent is guilty of violation of the criminal law, military criminal law, law for the preservation of military secrets, etc., he may be adjudged and punished by the court-martial according to the military penal code.

ART. XIV. Art. VI. to XIII. are applicable to interpreters and servants.[124]

The contrast between the Japanese regulations and those of the Russians, published that spring, served only to highlight the differences. Correspondents at the Russian front moved freely with the troops and had their stories and photographs lightly censored. Douglas Story, a Scotsman accredited on behalf of the Newspaper Enterprise Association, the American syndicate founded by E.W. Scripps to distribute news-features, dedicated his memoir of the war to the Russian censors. Story found them sympathetic to journalists' needs and understanding of the difficulty of their work. He even befriended the chief censor, Colonel E. F. Pesteech. The Russian regulations given in April 1904 to Story, the first accredited non-Russian correspondent, were brief. They prohibited correspondents from boarding ships or entering dockyards, publishing falsehoods or news that could be misinterpreted, and criticizing officers. A separate set of censorship rules distributed at the port of Yingkou (Newchwang, Liaodong Peninsula), at about the same time was "extremely" reasonable, according to James F. J. Archibald of *Collier's Weekly* magazine. Archibald, the only American among seven correspondents receiving accreditation at that time, found the Russian rules more lax than those of the British in the Boer War.[125] Archibald shared the regulations with the readers of *Collier's Weekly*:

> The first rule for war correspondents says that they must not interfere in any way with the preparations for war, or the plans of the staff, or divulge military secrets of advantage to the enemy, such as actions in which forts are damaged or guns lost.

Rule two forbids the criticism of members of the General Staff, Corps, or Division Staff, and limits the report of an engagement to a simple statement of fact.

Rule three forbids the transmission of unconfirmed information about the enemy, such as rumors of victory or threatening movements, which may cause public uneasiness in Russia.

Rule four commands the correspondent to obey all orders received and to be careful in fulfilling instructions to the letter.

This manifesto orders the higher military authorities to turn back all correspondents without credentials. Those given permission to join the forces are in honor bound to observe the regulations, with the penalty of expulsion without warning for any violation. They can go anywhere in the field, and are barred only from the Russian fleet.[126]

While Russia was formalizing its rules governing war correspondents, Japan finally agreed to provide 16 of the 120 foreign war correspondents in Tokyo with permission to travel with the Japanese First Army. The journalists boarded a train at Tokyo's Shimbashi Station on the afternoon of April 1 as a crowd at the platform cheered their departure for the port of Moji.[127] From Moji, they crossed the Korea Strait on the steamer *Suminoye Maru*, moved up the west coast of the Korean Peninsula, embarked at Nampo (Chinampo), Korea, and moved inland. Eight of the sixteen represented British newspapers. The remainder were six Americans, one Frenchman, and one German. The organizer of the corps of correspondents was William Maxwell of the London *Standard*. The other Britons were Robert Joseph MacHugh of the *Daily Telegraph*, Frederick Arthur McKenzie of the *Daily Mail*, David Fraser of the *Times* of London, Robert Moore Collins of the Reuters news service, Walter Kirton of the Central News Agency (a competitor of Reuters), M. H. Donohoe of the *Daily Chronicle*, and Edward F. Knight of the *Morning Post*. Knight had the most experience covering combat; he also would have the distinction of having the *New York Times* mistakenly report him killed two months after leaving Japan for the front.[128]

The American journalists comprised Frederick Palmer of *Collier's Weekly* magazine, who had covered every major war beginning with the Greco-Turkish conflict of 1897 and would continue to be a war correspondent through World War II; Oscar King Davis of the *New York Herald*, a war correspondent in the Philippines who would join the *New York Times* to cover the Theodore Roosevelt White House; William Dinwiddie of the *New York World*, who had covered the Spanish-American War for *Harper's Weekly* and served as a provincial governor in the Philippines; John Bass of the *Chicago Daily News*, who had covered the Boxer Rebellion of 1900 in China and would go on to report from the Russian-German front in World War I;

novelist Jack London of William Randolph Hearst's chain of publications; and photographer James L. "Jimmy" Hare of *Collier's Weekly*.

The two continental Europeans left the front soon after arrival. The German, identified only as von Gottenburg, became ill and had to be evacuated during his first days ashore. The Frenchman, Charles Victor-Thomas of *Le Temps* of Paris, drew the suspicion of Japanese officers in the field because of France's close military ties to Russia. He departed after two months at the front.[129]

The Japanese Ministry of War offered to feed the correspondents standard field rations at no charge. As the correspondents hoped for something better, the ministry allowed them to hire an independent contractor to provide a "canteen" stocked with food. They had to pay for the service, which transported and cooked their meals in the war zone.[130] No doubt the army approved of such an arrangement because the cooks and sutlers could keep watch on the press corps and report on them to headquarters. The correspondents' avoidance of field rations proved to be an unexpected blessing; many Japanese soldiers developed beriberi, a debilitating thiamin deficiency, from a diet based primarily on white rice.[131]

The war correspondents' ship stopped briefly at Incheon before traveling along the west coast of Korea to land at the port of Nampo on April 12. From there, the correspondents traveled overland toward the First Army headquarters at Pyongyang.

Japan would go on to land three more armies—plainly enough, they were designated as the Second, Third, and Fourth. One group of war correspondents accompanied the Second and another group the Third. The Japanese strategy was to surround Port Arthur by land and sea, besieging it until it submitted to starvation, assault, or both. Other detachments would land in Korea and Manchuria and link up in a northward march. Three united armies would cut the railway lines supplying the Russians and engage the troops sent to relieve Port Arthur. This strategy proved most effective; Japan never lost a battle on land or sea. The Japanese Second Army completely isolated Port Arthur by capturing Nanshan Hill at the neck of the Liaodong Peninsula, opening the way for the Third Army to advance southwest and tighten the ring around the Russian outpost. The invaders penetrated four series of Russian defenses one at a time until they came to the outskirts of Port Arthur itself on August 12. A nearly constant assault lasting four months and nineteen days led to Port Arthur's capitulation on January 1, 1905, touching off a weeklong street party in Tokyo: demonstrations, flag-waving processions, band concerts, and everyone from shopkeepers to homemakers giddily congregating outdoors to throw their hands in the air and shout "Banzai!"[132]

What may have been the world's largest land battles to that time, at Liaoyang, China, in August-September 1904, and Shenyang, China, (known as the Battle of Mukden) in March 1905, sealed Russia's doom on land. The Russian admiralty risked one last gamble in the spring of 1905 by dispatching the Baltic battle fleet, pride of the Russian navy, around Africa's Cape of Good Hope and Singapore and northward into the Pacific in an attempt to neutralize the Japanese navy. When the two fleets met in the Tsushima Strait on May 27 and 28, too late to save Port Arthur, Admiral Tōgō's warships destroyed the Russian vessels. Although the two fleets possessed roughly comparable firepower, the Japanese ships outmaneuvered the enemy through a tactic known as "capping the T." The line of Japanese ships crossed in front of a perpendicular line of Russian ships, just as the top bar of the letter "T" crosses the letter's upright. This allowed Japan's warships to fire all of their guns while the Russians could fire only those facing forward. Russia lost all of its battleships and Japan took nine thousand prisoners including the commanding admiral, Zinovii Petrovich Rozhestvenskii. No Western journalists were on hand to witness the final Russian embarrassment, but the sea battle became a footnote in journalism history when a twenty-three-year-old H. L. Mencken, decades before becoming the celebrated "Sage of Baltimore," elaborated on the briefest Associated Press dispatch from Tokyo that arrived in the *Baltimore Evening Herald* newsroom. He fabricated a lengthy account of the Battle of Tsushima that was surprisingly close to the facts.[133]

Japan could not press its advantages. The further it fought from its home islands, the longer stretched its supply trail over roads that were poor at best. Furthermore, it had no more reserves to commit to the war, having had 88,000 die in battle or of sickness. Straight observed in March 1905 that troops remaining in Tokyo were "either very old or very young," and those most recently called to arms included many who appeared to exceed the conscription age limit of thirty-seven.[134] Russia also was exhausted, having its death toll reported variably at 43,000 to 71,000,[135] and lacked enough naval firepower after the Battle of Tsushima to prevent Japan from dominating Korea and Manchuria. Furthermore, Russia needed its troops in its European region to deal with revolution that had broken out in winter and spring 1905, partly in response to its loss of the war but also in support of better working conditions, wages, and power-sharing reforms.

At the end of its resources, Japan threw one last, defiant punch by invading southern Sakhalin Island, off the coast of Russia, in July 1905. The two nations, unable to bring sufficient resources to continue the war effectively, accepted President Theodore Roosevelt's offer to negotiate peace. Roosevelt met with envoys of both nations at Portsmouth, New Hampshire, and reached a settlement in September, earning himself the Nobel Peace Prize.[136] Russia ceded to Japan the Liaodong Peninsula, the southern portion of the South Manchurian Railway, and the southern half of Sakhalin Island; accepted

Japan's fait accompli in Korea; and acknowledged Japan's fishing rights in the Sea of Okhotsk and the Bering Sea.

As Western war correspondents accompanied the Japanese toward their final goals in 1904 and 1905, the rules of engagement between press and army changed—sometimes slowly, sometimes dramatically. Some of the most famous war reporters, including Richard Harding Davis and John Fox Jr., left the front in frustration in midsummer 1904 after becoming convinced that the Japanese armies would never let them see any significant engagement. Their complaints, published abroad, threatened to prevent any future war loans to Japan from the United States and the United Kingdom. That shook the Japanese government to its core, loosening some of the rules in the war zone that benefited those who had decided to stay no matter what happened. Other correspondents evaded the army and attempted to report without military supervision or assistance. And still others forged secret deals with the combatants that later generations of journalists would deem unethical conflicts of interest, creating unseen influences over the supposedly objective content they presented to their readers.

Their stories, and the censorship that shaped them and the wars to come, appear in the following chapters.

NOTES

1. "Has the War Correspondent Seen His Last Fight?" *The American Review of Reviews*, April 1913, 487.
2. Denis Warner and Peggy Warner, *The Tide at Sunrise: A History of the Russo-Japanese War, 1904–05* (London: Frank Cass, 2002), 20.
3. Francis McCullagh, *With the Cossacks: Being the Story of an Irishman Who Rode with the Cossacks throughout the Russo-Japanese War* (Uckfield, UK: The Naval and Military Press Ltd., 2004), 46.
4. Charles à Court Repington, *The War in the Far East, 1904–1905: By the Military Correspondent of the* Times (London: John Murray, 1905), 47.
5. Richard Connaughton, *Rising Sun and Tumbling Bear: Russia's War with Japan* (London: Cassell, 1988), 38–41.
6. Rotem Kowner, "Becoming an Honorary Civilized Nation: Remaking Japan's Military Image during the Russo-Japanese War," *The Historian* 64, no. 1 (2001): 18.
7. Ibid.; and Rotem Kowner, *Historical Dictionary of the Russo–Japanese War* (Lanham, MD: Scarecrow Press, 2006), 5–6.
8. Connaughton, *Rising Sun and Tumbling Bear*, 11.
9. Ibid., 11–15; Kowner, *Historical Dictionary of the Russo–Japanese War*, 3–4; Kowner, "Becoming an Honorary Civilized Nation," 19–20; John Maxwell Hamilton, foreword to George Lynch and Frederick Palmer, eds., *In Many Wars by*

Many War Correspondents (Baton Rouge: Louisiana State University, 2010), n.p.; Susan Cheryl MacDermid, "Print Capitalism and the Russo-Japanese War" (master's thesis, University of British Columbia, 1982), 5; and Frederick McCormick, *The Tragedy of Russia in Pacific Asia*, vol. I (New York: The Outing Publishing Company, 1907), 12–13.

10. Thomas F. Millard, *The New Far East* (New York: Charles Scribner's Sons, 1906), 7.

11. "The Resources of Japan," *New York Times*, August 27, 1905.

12. Kowner, "Becoming an Honorary Civilized Nation," 21.

13. Thomas F. Millard, "The Fruits of Japan's Victory," *Scribner's Magazine* 38, no. 2 (August 1905): 243. "No long-established and influential publication anywhere in the world outside of Russia is swayed by Russian influence," Millard wrote, "which places the empire at a great disadvantage in this game of stimulating publicity."

14. Robert B. Valliant, "The Selling of Japan: Japanese Manipulation of Western Opinion, 1900–1905," *Monumenta Nipponica* 29, no. 4 (Winter 1974): 420.

15. Ibid., 415; and Kowner, "Becoming an Honorary Civilized Nation," 21.

16. Valliant, "The Selling of Japan," 423.

17. Ibid., 425; "Baron Kaneko on the Yellow Peril: Leading Legal Authority of Japan Says That Russia Alone Appears to Fear It," *New York Times*, February 21, 1904; and Alonzo H. Stewart, "A Talk with Baron Kaneko: Greatest Legal Mind of Japan on 'Open Door,'" *Los Angeles Times*, March 4, 1904.

18. "Baron Kentaro Kaneko, a Very Interesting Visitor," *Vicksburg* (MS) *Evening Post*, June 17, 1904; and "Japan's Peaceful Policy," *New York Tribune*, August 21, 1904. For an example of the Komura biography complete with photographic portrait, see "Baron Komura a Harvard Man: Japanese Foreign Minister, Early in Diplomacy, Who Has Risen Rapidly," *Boston Globe*, February 13, 1904.

19. Valliant, "The Selling of Japan," 422, 424–25; and Kentarō Kaneko, "The Secret of Japan's Success," *Collier's Weekly*, June 4, 1904, 7–8.

20. Valliant, "The Selling of Japan," 427–28.

21. Arthur M. Schlesinger, *Prelude to Independence: The Newspaper War on Britain, 1764–1776* (Boston: Northeastern University Press), 54–55.

22. David Ramsay, *The History of the American Revolution*, vol. 2 (Philadelphia: R. Aitken & Son, 1789), 319.

23. Schlesinger, *Prelude to Independence*, 300.

24. Frank Luther Mott, *American Journalism: A History of Newspapers in the United States through 250 Years, 1690–1940* (New York: Macmillan, 1941), 203.

25. Ibid., 216.

26. Alexis de Tocqueville, *Democracy in America*, vol. 2, trans. Henry Reeve (New York: The Colonial Press, 1899), 121.

27. Alexis de Tocqueville, *Democracy in America*, vol. 1, trans. Henry Reeve (New York: The Colonial Press, 1899), 189.

28. David T. Z. Mindich, *Just the Facts: How Objectivity Came to Define American Journalism* (New York: NYU Press, 2001).

29. Robert W. Desmond, *Windows on the World: The Information Process in a Changing Society, 1900–1920* (Iowa City: University of Iowa Press, 1980); Michael

Schudson, *Discovering the News: A Social History of American Newspapers* (New York: Basic Books, 1978), 152–53; and "American Society of Newspaper Editors Code of Ethics," PBS, https://www.pbs.org/newshour/extra/app/uploads/2014/03/mediaethics_handout6.pdf.

30. See Magali Sarfatti Larson, *The Rise of Professionalism: A Sociological Analysis* (Berkeley: University of California Press, 1977).

31. Jerry Lee Morton, "The History of the Journalism Program at Michigan State University," (PhD diss., Michigan State University, 1991), 6, 8.

32. The emphasis on speed is evident in the name of the first journalism course at Michigan State University, "Rapid Writing," in 1890. See ibid., 8.

33. Gregory Kent Ornatowsi, "Press, Politics, and Profits: The *Asahi Shimbun* and the Prewar Japanese Newspaper" (master's thesis, Harvard University, 1985), 7–8.

34. W. William Steele, "Edo in 1868: The View from Below," *Monumenta Nipponica* 45, no. 2 (Summer 1990): 135–38.

35. MacDermid, "Print Capitalism and the Russo-Japanese War," 52.

36. Andrew E. Barshay, *State and Intellectual in Imperial Japan: The Public Man in Crisis* (Berkeley: University of California Press, 1988), 14–15.

37. MacDermid, "Print Capitalism and the Russo-Japanese War," 11, 68; and Frederick Arthur McKenzie, *From Tokyo to Tiflis: Uncensored Letters from the War* (London: Hurst and Blackett, Ltd., 1905), 3.

38. Au, Pak Hung, and Keiichi Kawai, "Media Capture and Information Monopolization in Japan," Munich Personal RePEc Archive, 2010, 10, https://core.ac.uk/download/pdf/12027645.pdf; and MacDermid, "Print Capitalism and the Russo-Japanese War," 50.

39. MacDermid, "Print Capitalism and the Russo-Japanese War," 51, 7.

40. Shumpei Okamoto, *The Japanese Oligarchy and the Russo-Japanese War* (New York: Columbia University Press, 1970), 140.

41. Douglas Story, *The Campaign with Kuropatkin* (London: T. Werner Laurie, 1904), 43.

42. James Boyd, *Japanese–Mongolian Relations, 1873–1945: Faith, Race and Strategy* (Leiden, Netherlands: Global Oriental/Brill, 2010), 48; and Ornatowski, "Press, Politics, and Profits," 67.

43. Shumpei, *The Japanese Oligarchy and the Russo-Japanese War*, 87; and Marshall Everett, *Exciting Experiences in the Japanese-Russian War* (Chicago: The Educational Company, 1904), 277

44. McKenzie, *From Tokyo to Tiflis*, 1.

45. Bennet Burleigh, *Empire of the East: Or Japan and Russia at War 1904–5* (London: Chapman and Hall, 1905), 14.

46. McKenzie, *From Tokyo to Tiflis*, 1–3.

47. Willard Dickerman Straight, Diaries, reel 11, segment 2, March 26 to November 30, 1905, 63, Willard Straight Papers, Division of Rare and Manuscript Collections, Cornell University Library, Ithaca, NY.

48. Nathan Haverstock, *Fifty Years at the Front: The Life of War Correspondent Frederick Palmer* (Washington, DC: Brassey's 1996), 131.

49. David H. James, *The Siege of Port Arthur: Records of an Eye-witness* (London: T. Fisher Unwin, 1905), 195.

50. MacDermid, "Print Capitalism and the Russo-Japanese War," 78–79. For examples of official news communiqués from the front in Korea and Manchuria, see "Other Reports of the Fighting," *Times of London*, October 13, 1904; "General Oku Captures 25 Guns," *Times of London*, October 14, 1904; and "The War: General Kuropatkin's Defeat," *Times of London*, October 15, 1904. These stories contained disclaimers such as "Marshal Oyama Reports" and "Telegraphing Early to-Day, the Headquarters Staff in Manchuria Reports."

51. Burleigh, *Empire of the East*, 76.

52. Uchimura Kanzō, *Uchimura Kanzō Zenshū*, vol. 14 (Tokyo: Iwanami Shoten, Shōwa, 1932–33), 387–88, quoted in Shumpei, *The Japanese Oligarchy and the Russo-Japanese War*, 266.

53. Melton Prior, *Campaigns of a War Correspondent* (New York: Longmans, Green & Co., 1912), 323.

54. Frederick Palmer, "Off for the Front," *Collier's Weekly*, May 14, 1904, 10.

55. Some historians credit Henry Crabb Robinson of the *Times* of London with being the first war correspondent. He covered the Peninsula War in 1808–1809. However, Robinson was not a journalist and wrote his accounts as letters without ever witnessing battle. See Neil Ramsey, "The Grievable Life of the War-Correspondent: The Experience of War in Henry Crabb Robinson's Letters to the *Times*, 1808–1809," in *Emotions and War: Palgrave Studies in the History of Emotions*, ed. Stephanie Downes, Andrew Lynch, and Katrina O'Loughlin (London: Palgrave Macmillan, 2015), 235–50; Michael S. Sweeney, *From the Front: The Story of War Featuring Correspondents' Chronicles* (Washington, DC: National Geographic Press, 2002), 20; and "The Henry Crabb Robinson Project," University of London, http://www.crabbrobinson.co.uk/the-project/.

56. Michael S. Sweeney, *The Military and the Press: An Uneasy Truce* (Evanston, IL: Northwestern University Press, 2006), 17–18; and *Mexican News*, "The News Media and the Making of America, 1730–1865," http://americanantiquarian.org/earlyamericannewsmedia/exhibits/show/news-in-antebellum-america/item/22.

57. Hazel Dicken-Garcia, *Journalistic Standards in Nineteenth-Century America* (Madison: University of Wisconsin, 1989), 51.

58. Jeffery A. Smith, *War and Press Freedom: The Problem of Prerogative Power* (New York: Oxford University Press, 1999), 104–5; and J. Cutler Andrews, *The South Reports the Civil War* (Princeton, NJ: Princeton University Press), 48.

59. Smith, *War and Press Freedom*, 101–2.

60. M.L. Stein, *Under Fire: The Story of American War Correspondents* (New York: Julian Messner, 1968), 19; and Ford Risley, "Peter Alexander: Confederate Chronicler and Conscience," *American Journalism* 15, no. 1 (Winter 1998): 35–50.

61. J. Cutler Andrews, *The North Reports the Civil War* (Pittsburgh: University of Pittsburgh, 1955), 640.

62. "Army Correspondents," *New York Times*, August 25, 1862.

63. Ford Risley, "Birth of the Byline," *New York Times*, April 22, 2013.

64. Charles H. Brown, *The Correspondents' War: Journalists in the Spanish-American War* (New York: Charles Scribner's Sons, 1967), 115–19.

65. F. Lauriston Bullard, *Famous War Correspondents* (Boston: Little, Brown and Co., 1914), 413.

66. Paul L. Aswell, "Wartime Press Censorship by the U.S. Armed Forces: A Historical Perspective" (master's thesis, Louisiana State University, 1978), 40.

67. Ibid., and Michael S. Sweeney, Paul Jacoway, and Young Joon Lim, "Weighing the Costs: The Scripps-McRae League Reports the War in Cuba," *American Journalism* 31, no. 2 (Spring 2014): 213–35.

68. U.S. War Department, *Annual Report of the War Department for the Fiscal Year Ending June 30, 1898. Report of the Chiefs of Bureaus* (Washington, DC: Government Printing Office, 1898), 215. Brackets in original.

69. Aswell, "Wartime Press Censorship," 40–41.

70. *Correspondence Relating to the War with Spain and Conditions Growing out of the Same: Including the Insurrection in the Philippine Islands and the China Relief Expedition, April 15, 1898, to July 30, 1902*, vol. 2 (Washington, DC: Government Printing Office, 1902), 300.

71. Brown, *The Correspondents' War*, 446.

72. Ibid., 317–322.

73. James Creelman, *On the Great Highway* (Boston: Lothrop, Lee & Shepard Co., 1901), 211–12; and Sweeney, Jacoway, and Lim, "Weighing the Costs," 216.

74. Brown, *The Correspondents' War*, 230–32; Joyce Milton, *The Yellow Kids: Foreign Correspondence in the Heyday of Yellow Journalism* (New York: HarperCollins, 1989), 279–81; and Poultney Bigelow, "In Camp at Tampa," *Harper's Weekly*, June 4, 1898, 550.

75. "On This Day: Who Is the Criminal," *New York Times*, http://movies2.nytimes.com/learning/general/onthisday/harp/0813.html; and [No title], *Harper's Weekly*, August 13, 1898, 786–87.

76. Phillip Knightley, *The First Casualty: From Crimea to Vietnam; the War Correspondent as Hero, Propagandist, and Myth Maker* (New York: Harcourt Brace Jovanovich, 1975), 46.

77. W. Joseph Campbell, *The Year that Defined American Journalism: 1897 and the Clash of Paradigms* (New York: Routledge, 2006), 80.

78. "Convention (II) with Respect to the Laws and Customs of War on Land and Its Annex: Regulations Concerning the Laws and Customs of War on Land," The Hague, Netherlands, July 1899, https://www.loc.gov/law/help/us-treaties/bevans/m-ust000001-0247.pdf.

79. Sakuyé Takahashi, *International Law Applied to the Russo-Japanese War with the Decisions of the Japanese Prize Courts* (New York: The Banks Law Publishing Company, 1908), 391.

80. "Convention (II) with Respect to the Laws and Customs of War on Land."

81. Donal P. McCrachen, "The Relationship between British War Correspondents in the Field and British Military Intelligence during the Anglo-Boer War," *Scientia Militaria: South African Journal of Military Studies* 43, no. 1 (2015): 104.

82. Ibid., 107–8.

83. Ibid., 111.

84. Ibid., 107.

85. J.A. Edgerton, "Task of the War Correspondents at the Front," *The Marion (OH) Star*, April 2, 1904.

86. Burleigh, *Empire of the East*, 70–71.

87. Connaughton, *Rising Sun and Tumbling Bear*, 191–92.
88. William H. Brill, "Chapter II—Weary Weeks of Waiting," unpublished manuscript, box 11, "Manuscripts and Dispatches, 1898–1922," MS P813, Hascal Russell Brill and Family Papers, Minnesota Historical Society, Saint Paul.
89. Ibid.
90. Ibid.
91. Frederick Palmer, "Japan Is Prepared for a Long War," *Collier's Weekly*, April 9, 1904, 7.
92. McKenzie, *From Tokyo to Tiflis*, 18.
93. Earl Albert Selle, *Donald of China* (New York: Harper, 1948), 22, quoted in Hamilton, foreword, *In Many Wars by Many War Correspondents*, n.p.
94. Herbert Croly, *Willard Straight* (New York: The Macmillan Company, 1924), 125–26.
95. Brill, "Chapter II—Weary Weeks of Waiting."
96. Lloyd Griscom, *Diplomatically Speaking* (Boston: Little, Brown and Company, 1940), 245.
97. Hector Fuller, "Japan Has Set the Pace in Secrecy: Wily Ways of Keeping the Most Astute Correspondents in Check," *Indianapolis News*, April 6, 1904.
98. Burleigh, *Empire of the East*, 114.
99. Ibid.; and Brill, "Chapter II—Weary Weeks of Waiting."
100. Robert L. Dunn, "Ways That Are Dark, and Tricks That Are Vain," *Collier's Weekly*, July 23, 1904, 9–10.
101. Griscom, *Diplomatically Speaking*, 244.
102. Lynch and Palmer, eds., *In Many Wars by Many War Correspondents*.
103. Brill, "Chapter II—Weary Weeks of Waiting."
104. Ibid.
105. Frederick Palmer, "War Correspondence from the Two Capitals," *Collier's Weekly*, April 23, 1904, 22.
106. Park Pae-Keun, "Discussions Concerning the Legality of the 1910 'Annexation' of Korea by Japan," *Korea Journal* 50, no. 4 (2010): 16, 19; Christine Kim, "A Chaotic Prelude to Korean Subjugation," *Korea Joongang Daily*, August 26, 2010, http://koreajoongangdaily.joins.com/news/article/article.aspx?aid=2925134; and Han Wan-Sang, "Preparing for the Next Hundred Years under the Mindset of the March First Independence Movement," Korea.Net, February 25, 2019, http://korea.net/NewsFocus/Column/view?articleId=168221.
107. Luigi Barzini, "La guerra russo-giapponese: Corrispondenti di guerra; guerra e carambola—aspettando di partire par il campo," *Corriere della Sera*, May 9, 1904.
108. McKenzie, *From Tokyo to Tiflis*, 114.
109. "Japan, Smiling, but Bitterly Hating Russia, Long Ready for War," *New York Herald*, February 16, 1904.
110. Everett, *Exciting Experiences in the Japanese-Russian War*, 399.
111. "Task of the War Correspondents at the Front."
112. Ibid., and Everett, *Exciting Experiences in the Japanese-Russian War*, 399.
113. "Good Things to Come in *Collier's*," *Collier's Weekly*, April 16, 1904, n.p.; and "How the War News Comes," *The Danville* (KY) *News*, April 1, 1904.

114. MacDermid, "Print Capitalism," 80.

115. Everett, *Exciting Experiences in the Japanese-Russian War*, 400; Griscom, *Diplomatically Speaking*, 249; and Warner and Warner, *The Tide at Sunrise*, 282–83.

116. "Rigid Censorship Vital to Japanese: Count Hayashi Fears That Latitude Allowed in Chinese War Would Be Fatal," *New York Herald*, February 29, 1904.

117. Valliant, "The Selling of Japan," 431–32.

118. Burleigh, *Empire of the East*, 78. Burleigh said the correspondents briefly executed the strike but gave neither details nor a date.

119. Griscom, *Diplomatically Speaking*, 245.

120. "They Want More News," *Los Angeles Times*, May 7, 1904.

121. Hector Fuller, "Prime Minister Is the Joy of Japan," *Indianapolis News*, April 23, 1904.

122. Hayashi Todasu to Komura Jutarō, March 31, 1904, "United Kingdom No. 1," and Jutarō to Hayashi, April 1, 1904, in folder "Nichirosen eki no sai senkyo shisatu no tame gaikoku shimbun kisha jugun ikken," Nihon Gaimusho hozon kiroku [Records of the Ministry of Foreign Affairs, The Diplomatic Record Office of the Ministry of Foreign Affairs], Japan Center for Asian Historical Records, National Archives of Japan, Tokyo.

123. Griscom, *Diplomatically Speaking*, 249.

124. Sakuyé, *International Law Applied to the Russo-Japanese War*, 393–96.

125. Rotem Kowner, ed., *Rethinking the Russo-Japanese War, 1904–05*, vol. I: *Centennial Perspectives* (Leiden, Netherlands: Global Oriental/Brill, 2007), 321; Story, *The Campaign with Kuropatkin*, n.p.; and James F. J. Archibald, "Russia Makes Rules to Govern War Correspondents," *Collier's Weekly*, April 30, 1904, 13.

126. Archibald, "Russia Makes Rules to Govern War Correspondents," 13.

127. "Japan Modifies the Censorship," *Daily New Era* (Lancaster, PA), April 1, 1904.

128. McKenzie, *From Tokyo to Tiflis*, 113–15; and "Noted Correspondent Slain?" *New York Times*, June 29, 1904. McKenzie gives the first name of Kirton as "William," but the correspondent signed his given name as "Walter" in the book *In Many Wars*. McKenzie also misspells MacHugh. For the name of the transport ship, see "Scribes Not Permitted to Land at Chemulpo: Japanese Preserving Censorship on All Paper Reports," *Reno* (NV) *Gazette-Journal*, April 8, 1904.

129. McKenzie, *From Toyko to Tiflis*, 114–15.

130. War Department, "Note-Verbal to Messrs. The Foreign War Correspondents," March 1904, file "1. general section No. 1," in folder "Nichirosen eki no sai senkyo shisatu no tame gaikoku shimbun kisha jugun ikken," Nihon Gaimusho hozon kiroku [Records of the Ministry of Foreign Affairs, The Diplomatic Record Office of the Ministry of Foreign Affairs], Japan Center for Asian Historical Records, National Archives of Japan, Tokyo.

131. William H. Brill, "With the Army at Last," unpublished manuscript, box 11, "Manuscripts and Dispatches, 1898–1922," MS P813, Hascal Russell Brill and Family Papers, Minnesota Historical Society, Saint Paul.

132. Richard Barry, *Port Arthur: A Monster Heroism* (New York: Moffat, Yard & Company, 1905), 15; Straight, Diaries, reel 11, segment 1, November 9, 1901, to March 15, 1905, 207, Willard Straight Papers.

133. Edward A. Martin, "On Reading Mencken," *The Sewanee Review* 93, no. 2 (Spring 1985): 248–49.

134. Straight, Diaries, reel 11, segment 1, November 9, 1901, to March 15, 1905, 235, Willard Straight Papers; and Kowner, *Historical Dictionary of the Russo–Japanese War*, 80.

135. Kowner, *Historical Dictionary of the Russo–Japanese War*, 81.

136. An excellent day-by-day calendar of major events of the Russo-Japanese War can be found in Murat Halstead, *The War between Russia and Japan: Containing Thrilling Accounts of Fierce Battles by Sea and Land* (S.l.: s.n., 1904), 651–56. An account of Mencken's fabrication can be found in "Flying Shells Strike Rojestvensky; Five of the Fugitives Elude Togo," *Baltimore Evening Herald*, May 30, 1905; and in Marion Elizabeth Rodgers, *Mencken: The American Iconoclast* (Oxford, UK: Oxford University Press, 2005), 97–98.

Chapter 2

Lionel James and Stanley Washburn

He had a wonderful experience, having escaped death miraculously.

—Excerpt from editor's note atop
Stanley Washburn interview, 1905[1]

Several reporters frustrated by Japanese restraints on their freedom evaded the rules and managed to gather and distribute uncensored news. While some escaped their confinement in Japan to move about the Korean Peninsula unfettered, others took to the open sea to observe the coastline, the Russian naval base and garrison at Port Arthur, and any ship movements or battles that might occur as they watched.

One of the oceangoing correspondents, Lionel James, made the Russo-Japanese War the first conflict to be reported by radio. His accounts were unlike radio news as it came to be defined later in the century—not the propaganda broadcasts of the 1936–1939 Spanish Civil War, the first conflict in which radio contributed significantly,[2] nor independent news and commentary such as the broadcasts of Edward R. Murrow in England and William J. Dunn in the Pacific during World War II.[3] More than sixteen years before radio news made its first foray into American consciousness when Pittsburgh's radio KDKA announced the presidential election returns of 1920, James helped radio take its first baby steps as a point-to-point, invisible communication through the air. Like a telephone call or telegram without the copper circuitry, radio communication became known as "wireless."

Several other correspondents, notably Stanley Washburn and Bennet Burleigh, also attempted to get around censorship by chartering ships to sail the Yellow Sea. James, Washburn, and Burleigh had varying levels of success. All ran afoul of the combatants and quit their seagoing work before war's end. Their unsolicited presence in a war zone drew suspicion, and suspicion brought danger. Radio went to its first war, and while it stumbled from time to time, it made a start upon which later correspondents could build. Radio dispatches, keyed and received by Morse code, reliably brought the news at the speed of light although the newsworthiness of the messages varied considerably.

James worked jointly for the *Times* of London and *New York Times*. He chartered the dispatch boat *Haimun* and equipped it with the latest radio communication equipment. His confederate from the London *Times*, a soldier of the Boer War named David Fraser, set up a receiving station to transcribe James's dispatches so they could be forwarded to land-based telegraph lines. This made their operation the first to file news by radio from a war zone, giving a competitive advantage through the speed with which their dispatches reached Western audiences. However, to achieve freedom of movement, James cut a secret deal with the Japanese admiralty: in return for Japan turning a blind eye to his observing its naval movements, James agreed to accept the presence of a spy on board the *Haimun* and to share all news he gathered with Japanese intelligence. This arrangement gave him the closest access to the Japanese navy of any journalist in the war, at a cost of making him a quasi-agent of the emperor. And yet, the operation never worked as planned. Radio brought novelty to war reporting but did not approach its full potential.

Figure 2.1   S.S. *Haimun*, leased by Lionel James, reported the war by radio.

James was well suited to cover the war in the Far East. As a young man, he took risks, prepared for life as a soldier, and acquainted himself with the workings of an army. Born in 1871, James grew up in a military family and entered journalism only by accident. His father was an artillery officer who joined the Indian army in Bengal in 1858, and James hoped for a career as a soldier in the British army. After completing public school in England, Lionel James settled for ten years in India, where he grew indigo. In 1895, he lost nearly all of his indigo profits on a horse race. Desperately in need of income, James agreed to become a war correspondent for Reuters and the *Times of India*, covering an outbreak of violence on the Indian frontier. He took quickly to the job, learning journalism and the skill of working with army authorities in his early assignments. James considered his most important lesson to be that a war correspondent "must depend upon himself and his own individual efforts absolutely for any service of news that is to be of value to his employers." James's work came to the attention of the *Times* of London, which made him its chief war correspondent from 1899 until his resignation in 1913.[4]

In late 1903, *Times* of London manager Charles Moberly Bell told James to prepare to sail for Japan to cover the expected outbreak of war. James thought of the possibilities of using radio to increase the speed of communication and end the complete reliance on land-based telegraph lines. A few weeks earlier, he had been in New York City's harbor, where he witnessed radio pioneer Lee de Forest's attempt to broadcast news of the America's Cup yacht races. De Forest had placed radio equipment aboard a British yacht to give updates during the races. James believed a similar shipboard radio set would be useful in any war between Russia and Japan, as much of the fighting would likely occur on the Yellow Sea near Port Arthur. If so, the fundamental qualities of naval warfare at the time, in which ships could fight only if they could see each other (and an adventurous journalist could observe the battle from a safe distance), would provide wireless telegraphy with "special facilities for the application of this new adjunct [radio] in the rapid transmission of news." As luck would have it, de Forest was in England at the end of 1903, making an ultimately unsuccessful sales pitch to the British General Post Office. De Forest had hoped to develop commercial radiotelegraphy, in which a sender transmits a telegram in Morse code via radio from one station to another; the receiver then translates the code back into the English alphabet and delivers the decoded message as a telegram on paper. When De Forest bought a ticket on a steamship to return to the United States, James arranged to sail with him in order to solicit his help in reporting war from a ship at sea.[5] De Forest told him that he would need a mast 180 feet high on the coast of China to pick up a radio message from a boat within 160 miles if the boat's crew could expose at least 120 feet of transmission wire.[6]

The *Times* of London and the *New York Times* agreed to jointly finance James in his effort to be the first to broadcast war news from the ocean. According to the deal, de Forest would supply, at cost, the radio equipment he had failed to sell to the British Post Office, as well as two operators trained to send and receive Morse code. The newspapers would pay expenses and salaries of the two operators.[7] De Forest would gain valuable publicity for his idea of commercial telegraphy that might someday yield a profitable business.

James's assistant, newly recruited *Times* of London correspondent Fraser, hired workers to erect a reception tower at Weihai (Weihaiwei), a British-leased town on China's Shandong Peninsula. The location was ideal, as it was near to expected battles and the harbor remained free of ice all year. As a bonus, the British lease provided the crown's protection for those who lived there.[8] The Eastern Telegraph Company at Weihai provided cable service west from Weihai across Eurasia to London.[9]

Japanese warships would have to pass through the neck of water between the Shandong and Liaodong peninsulas to access seaborne invasion routes on the Chinese coast. About ninety miles to the north of Weihai lay Port Arthur near the tip of the Liaodong. To the east were Incheon (Chemulpo), Seoul, and Nampo (Chenampo), all strategic Korean cities. To the west lay Yantai (Chefoo), home of a British legation. Given the 160-mile radius of a radio signal from a ship bearing the de Forest equipment, James could file live war reports from Port Arthur and beyond to the radio receiver in Weihai.

Fraser arrived at Weihai on February 6 on board the SS *Siberia*. In his pocket he carried a cable from de Forest describing the optimal construction: a mast 180 feet high and 30 feet from the water's edge. Leery of competitors and spies, he told no one about his intentions. Fraser hired an engineer and set about finding a particular site and gathering lumber to lash together for the radio mast. Their work provoked much comment among the English residents, including speculation that the poles would serve as a flagstaff. As they prepared the wooden transceiver tower, Fraser received a cable from James in Tokyo. "Expedite forestry scrap imminent." Fraser and James had agreed to describe their venture as *forestry* as an inside joke about Lee de Forest. The rest of the message anticipated the opening shots of the war and urged Fraser to hurry.[10]

The work on the radio tower concluded none too soon. War began on the night of February 8–9 as Japan commenced surprise attacks on Russian warships in Port Arthur and Incheon. Japan then attempted to isolate the Russians in Port Arthur and to muster and land enough troops to defeat expected relief operations in Manchuria.

The *Times* of London chartered the 1,200-ton Chinese steamer *Haimun* at Hong Kong. It sailed February 14 to Weihai. De Forest's wireless operators,

Pop Athearn of Brooklyn and Harry Brown of Manhattan, fitted the boat with a Morse key, antenna, radio tower, and other equipment. The latest technology came from de Forest's drawing board: the "electrolytic detector," which allowed long-distance, high-speed Morse code signal traffic for the first time.[11] The fully equipped boat sailed to Nagasaki, where James boarded March 8. Athearn, twenty-one years old, stayed at Weihai to work the receiver, and Brown, thirty, went aboard the *Haimun* to transmit.[12]

News of James's intentions leaked to the press. He said he felt jealousy from fellow correspondents who were confined to Tokyo while awaiting permission from the Ministry of Foreign Affairs to go to the expected fronts in Korea and Manchuria. Some told him the Japanese navy had plans to sink the *Haimun*, claiming an accident, if its crew witnessed anything authorities did not want publicized. What James did not tell them—or anyone else publicly, until he wrote a memoir in 1929—was that he had no fear of retaliation. He had secretly obtained the Japanese navy's consent for his sailing in contested seas, in return for allowing Japan to place an agent on board who would serve as spy and censor.[13] The arrangement sprang from the British-Japanese treaty of alliance signed in 1902, which resulted in Britain sharing with its new ally the latest radio technology.[14] James's espionage agreement was acknowledged in a document signed by the minister of state for the navy, Vice Admiral Ijuin Gorō. He wrote:

> I take this opportunity to thank you for your cordial offer to place, if required, your telegraphic apparatus and expert operator at the service of the Imperial Forces and at the same time I hope you will consider that we shall be happy to give you any such assistance as you may require and which is possible for us under the present circumstances.[15]

When James took control of the *Haimun* in Nagasaki harbor, the Japanese spy, naval commander Tonami Kurakichi, was on board. Tonami had been Japan's leading radio expert since 1899. The *Haimun* also had six European officers and a crew of forty Chinese sailors and four Malay quartermasters.[16] James took the boat on a cruise to test the radio equipment at sea.

The first radio dispatch sent from a war zone contained little hard news, hinting only at expected violence, but the *Times* of London and *New York Times* printed it with a view to the historical significance of radio's introduction to war: "I am at sea on board the *Times* steamer *Haimun*, en route to Chinampo," James wrote. "The military developments foreshadowed in my previous telegrams should be taking place very soon, as, according to later information, the ice is disappearing fast."[17] The message was a safe one, intended to check the radio equipment and win the endorsement of Tonami, who could find nothing objectionable in it.

Meanwhile, a second news boat made a brief appearance off the coast of Korea in early March. The London *Daily Mail* had sent its representatives to sea in the chartered steamer *Chefoo*. Soon after learning of its existence, the Japanese consul in Nampo on the northern Korean coast informed Foreign Minister Baron Komura Jintarō that the boat had been caught sending news by wireless and asked for the transmissions to be stopped. Komura told the consul to give the *Chefoo* an ultimatum: halt transmissions or be seized. The *Chefoo* complied.[18] Another vessel, the *Industrie*, chartered by the *Chefoo Daily News*, suffered a worse fate. Japan charged that it had attempted to gather naval secrets for the Russian government and had been subsidized its operations. A Japanese court declared the *Industrie* to be an enemy ship and confiscated it.[19]

The *Haimun*'s arrival at Nampo harbor on the northern Korean coast provided a more substantial news story. On March 15, James's crew sailed into a beehive of activity, as Japanese transport ships hurried to unload thousands of troops of the First Army—the first wave of soldiers aiming to cut off Dalny and Port Arthur from Russian reinforcement via land, and to also confront any Russian assault aimed at relief. A Japanese cruiser halted the *Haimun* long enough to check James's authorization. An eyewitness radio dispatch that James filed the next day described pontoon jetties, landing barges, and chunks of ice in the harbor. His story added, "I cannot give the numbers and designation of the various troops which have been disembarked, as that would be unfair to the Japanese."[20]

James sent several similar dispatches of four hundred to two thousand words that week, some by Morse code radio transmission and some that he filed after the *Haimun* returned to a neutral port where he could put the story directly, uncensored, on a telegraph wire. One story recounted how the *Haimun* crew sailed into Nampo harbor and witnessed Japanese workers dismantling two Russian warships, the aging gunboat *Koreets* and cruiser *Variag*, both badly damaged and scuttled February 9 in the Battle of Chemulpo. The Japanese had surprised and attacked the two Russian ships in a naval action coordinated with the attack on Port Arthur, which lay 300 miles to the northwest. James described workers removing the Russian dead.[21]

Afterward the *Haimun* itself became news in two separate incidents.

The first occurred April 6 as the boat sailed slowly back and forth about five or six miles from Port Arthur, hoping that a rumor of the emergence of the Russian fleet to engage the Japanese would turn out to be true. Without warning, a cannon shot exploded in the water not far from the boat. The *Haimun* dropped anchor. The Russian armored cruiser *Bayan*, having slipped through the Japanese mines at the harbor mouth, pulled alongside and two Russian officers clambered aboard. They searched thoroughly, examining the ship's papers and its radio equipment, but found nothing worth making an arrest. Tonami, the Japanese spy, had disappeared the moment the Russians approached the *Haimun*. Brown, the radio operator, recalled that the crew explained his absence by saying he was a coolie who was mortally afraid of Russians. The Russian officers laughed and declined to have Tonami brought to them. After they left, Brown found Tonami in his cabin. "He had disrobed, and was standing, knife in hand, ready to commit hara-kiri if any attempt had been made by the boarding party to make him prisoner." Tonami, Brown, and James relaxed after the *Bayan* steamed back to the safety of Port Arthur before the Japanese fleet arrived.[22] The explanation of the *Bayan*'s risky foray into the open wasn't clear, but James thought of one possibility: the air had been alive with Japanese radio signals that morning, interspersed with dispatches from the *Haimun*, and the Russians likely believed that the Japanese navy and James's boat had been in communication.

The second incident occurred on April 15. Admiral Evgenii Ivanovich Alekseev, viceroy of the Far East region and commander of all Russian armed forces in the East at the start of the war, warned of the arrest of any correspondents found aboard radio-equipped ships in the war zone. In a circular memo shared with the foreign offices of various world powers, Alekseev said:

> In case neutral vessels, having on board correspondents who may communicate news to the enemy by means of improved apparatus not yet provided for by existing conventions should be arrested off Kwangtung [*sic*; Kwantung Leased Territory, formal name for the Russian-occupied southern tip of the Liaodong Peninsula], or within the zone of operations of the Russian fleet, such correspondents shall be regarded a spies, and the vessels provided with such apparatus shall be seized as lawful prizes.[23]

If found to be acting as a spy, a journalist would face dire consequences. The Hague Convention of 1899 defined a spy as an individual who, "acting clandestinely, or on false pretenses . . . obtains or seeks to obtain information in the zone of operations of a belligerent with the intention of communicating it to a hostile party." The definition contained a loophole for civilians if they acted "openly" and had been "charged with the delivery of dispatches destined either for their own army or for that of the enemy."[24] According to a contemporary Japanese legal scholar, the mere presence of a radio on board a neutral ship in a war zone would not be enough to justify its seizure or its operator's arrest. However, if the journalist were to act like a spy, as defined by the Hague Convention, then seizure of the ship and arrest of the journalist would be warranted. The penalty for espionage, as approved by the 1899 convention, to which Russia and Japan subscribed, was for the accused to stand trial by military court and, if convicted, be executed by hanging.[25] James did not act "openly" by choosing to conceal Tonami aboard the *Haimun*, and thus could have faced the ultimate penalty if found out. Small wonder that he kept the secret for two-and-a-half decades.

Although the Russian edict caused a brief diplomatic stir, it faded from significance without incident. The Russian fleet, nearly totally captive in Port Arthur, had little means to carry out its threat. And even if it could do so, the seizure of a non-belligerent nation's ship would have had serious diplomatic consequences unless the Russians could uncover, and prove, the presence of the Japanese operative aboard *Haimun*.[26]

As there was only one radio-equipped boat consistently in the war zone, James knew his reporting had touched a nerve and that Alekseev's warning had been meant for him. The story most likely to have angered the Russians had been filed three days earlier. Acting on a tip from Tonami about an expected naval engagement, the *Haimun* sailed to the waters off Port Arthur. James witnessed the Japanese navy laying mines and shelling the garrison, apparently in an attempt to draw out a full-scale battle with the Russian fleet. He reported in a fourteen-paragraph radio dispatch that began:

> OFF PORT ARTHUR, on Board the *Times*'s Steamship *Haimun*, April 13—
> The Japanese torpedo craft attacked Port Arthur early this morning and the fleet later shelled the forts. The bombardment began at 9:45 o'clock.
>
> Last night we ran into dirty weather. At 4:30 this morning, amid rain and squalls, we made out a squadron of warships in the line ahead, steering a course similar to our own.
>
> As the light increased it became manifest that it was a Japanese squadron of six battleships, followed by a first-class cruiser squadron of six ships in line, the third and fourth being the *Kasuga* and *Nisshin*, which were making their first appearance....
>
> Although I went closer to the approaches to Port Arthur than ever before, yet I saw no sign of Russian shipping. I could, however, make out a lighthouse. The shell which fell nearest us was exploded by impact with the water.[27]

The Russians never did rise to the bait and engage the Japanese fleet. However, James was on hand when the Russian battleship *Petropavlovsk* struck a mine that touched off the shells in its magazine. It sank with the loss of hundreds of lives, including the commander of the Russian Pacific Fleet, Admiral Stepan Osipovich Makarov.[28]

James and Brown had managed to send a radio dispatch within one minute after the Russian shore batteries opened up on the Japanese fleet on April 13. James said that day remained the most successful experience of his long journalism career.[29]

The story of the shelling marked the height of the *Haimun*'s role in gathering war news. On April 21, while taking on coal at Nagasaki, James learned that Japan had placed restrictions on the boat's movements despite Tonami's continuing presence. It could not go north of a line drawn from Yantai to Incheon, placing the northern reaches of the Yellow Sea and all of Port Arthur and Dalny off limits. That effectively prevented the *Haimun* from witnessing the long-expected landing of the Japanese Second Army. Tonami investigated and learned that Japanese army generals had raised security objections about the *Haimun* to the government, and had managed to override the navy's secret espionage mission. They may have been afraid that Russian ships might seize the *Haimun*, its spy, and its valuable radio equipment. The restriction remained in effect until May 10, when the line was shifted northward but not eliminated. James set sail again from Nagasaki aboard the *Haimun* and ran into a typhoon 100 miles after leaving Japan. The winds tore off the ship's topmast and the radio equipment attached to it. Although he was able to repair the damage within thirty-six hours, the *Haimun* never again gained permission to sail into what James called "the real theater of war."[30]

Japan's fear of news leaks from the sea turned out to be valid; secrets of extreme sensitivity did exist. During his confinement to a Japanese port, James missed the landing of Japan's Second Army on the southern coast of the Liaodong Peninsula, northeast of Dalny and Port Arthur. Admiral Hosoya Sukeuji began unloading troops there on May 5. The water along the shore was so shallow that no boats of any substantial size could land, and the soldiers of the Second Army had to wade two-and-a-half miles to reach dry land. According to war correspondent George Lynch of the *London Daily Chronicle*, "If that spot had been indicated, Russian troops could have been sent there, and 500 of them could have kept 5000 men at bay."[31] One secret that did come James's way occurred when a Russian spy who identified himself as "Baron Lubavin" of Shanghai visited him. After the Japanese armies cut off Port Arthur by sea and land, Lubavin approached James and asked to rent his radio operation to send a message to the officers in the besieged port. In return for sending a few hundred cipher groups, Lubavin promised to hand over £20,000—the equivalent of $2.5 million in the early twenty-first century—which he produced from his pocket. James, who recorded the conversation in his diary, replied, "Baron, you have made a mistake. You are trying to buy the *Times*. The *Times* is not to be bought. . . . I bid you good evening!"[32] James did not disclose that he already was acting as an accomplice to Japanese espionage.

In leaving the open sea, James felt considerable frustration, as he believed he had cooperated by eliminating all potential issues of national security from his dispatches and had declined the Russian spy's lucrative offer. Tonami, who compared James's news dispatches with the official reports of engagements issued by the Japanese navy, considered James to have been "more careful" in his descriptions than the navy's top admiral. Having had its value as a newsgathering machine compromised, the *Haimun* sent its last wireless dispatch June 6. James abandoned its charter twelve days later and switched to becoming a land-based, accredited reporter.[33] George Morrison, the London *Times*'s bureau chief in China, attempted to get Japanese permission to take over the ship, but he was refused.[34] The adventure of the *Haimun* had cost its sponsors about £1 for each word it transmitted.[35]

Months later, James wrote a eulogy for radio reporting of the Russo-Japanese War in the London *Times*. "I maintain that *The Times* has amply demonstrated the value and possibilities of wireless telegraphy in conjunction with journalistic enterprise; in fact, I am inclined to think that it has demonstrated its uses too well, and that the success of the system has assisted in its downfall," he wrote. He was convinced, he said, that his paper not only was the first but also would be the last to use radio to report naval warfare. Its risks to belligerents were so significant that he foresaw international laws evolving to control radio news about military and naval operations.[36]

Another attempt to gather and transmit news by ship merits mention. Bennet Burleigh of the London *Daily Telegraph* chafed at Japan's official refusal to send reporters to the front in the winter and early spring of 1904. According to *Indianapolis News* war correspondent Hector Fuller, Burleigh balked at the Ministry of Foreign Affairs asking him "most politely" to remain in Tokyo while awaiting permission to embed in an army unit. Burleigh announced he would find a way to visit the war zone in Korea on his own. "He got along well as far as Nagasaki," Fuller recounted, "but there, strange to relate the health officers met him, remarked that he was looking pale, had him medically examined and pronounced him to be suffering from some mysterious malady which justified them in putting him in quarantine for an indefinite period."[37] Burleigh eventually was released to embed in the Second Army in July, but that experience must have proved less than satisfying. In October 1904, he took to the sea to operate a newsgathering boat named the *Samson* between Yantai and Port Arthur, drawing close attention from the Japanese consul in the neutral port of Yantai. A lawsuit in 1905 elicited unusual details about how Burleigh obtained the ship. Burleigh had gone to Shanghai, where he suggested to Alexander Pavlov, the head of Russian espionage operations in the Far East, that Burleigh obtain a ship to gather information. A Danish intermediary received money from Pavlov for the purchase and gave it to Burleigh; the suit arose from Pavlov attempting to get the money back. Their arrangement called for Burleigh to have the steamer registered with the British Consulate with him as owner. Burleigh insisted that nothing in writing connect him to the Russian government for fear of arousing Japanese suspicions and, one suspects, clouding any claim to objectivity. Burleigh operated under the cover story of attempting to carry medical supplies to Port Arthur. Burleigh's operation was exposed by a colleague from his paper who, not wanting to be involved with anything illegal, revealed that secret messages had been buried amid the medical supplies. The *Samson* never docked at Port Arthur; the *Daily Telegraph*, informed of the secret mission, wired Burleigh to abort his plans. It is unclear whether secret documents intended for the Russian garrison actually had been stowed aboard.[38]

While the work of the *Samson* and *Chefoo* crews was being criticized, James and his radio operators earned the respect of the American press. Brown and Athearn, James's radio operators, returned to New York to work for de Forest's radio company.[39] In interviews with the *New York Times*, Brown said he had little trouble sending messages from aboard the *Haimun* and Athearn rushed to get them to Western audiences. They agreed the radio equipment had worked "perfectly." Athearn said the radio link between land and sea gave them no trouble except one time when a typhoon briefly knocked out the receiving pole at Weihai. On a good day, messages could be heard at Weihai from as far away as 240 miles, he said. "Every day the news came right from where things were happening," Athearn said, "and as fast as I took it [off the receiver] I chased it over to the office of the Eastern Extension Telegraph and Cable Company, a mile and a half over the hill, by a Chinese runner whom I had employed."[40]

The *Haimun*'s day-to-day news "circled the world," the *Times* said. It was this speed-of-light quality of radio news, rather than the content it provided, that most strongly impressed the editors of the *New York Times*. In an April editorial, before the *Haimun*'s troubles with the Russians and its confinement to port by the Japanese, the *Times* urged readers to appreciate the technological triumph of receiving news from the ship's radio. "To consider such a feat as this is," the *Times* said, "in the course of man's conquest over nature, to consider what it implies, is to be astonished, enlightened, and to be put in the way of making useful reflections upon the progress of the human species."[41]

The *Haimun*'s technical accomplishment also drew praise from an unexpected quarter. William Preece of the British General Post Office—ironically, the agency that had rejected de Forest's pitch for radiotelegraphy—said, "The *Times* transmitted much news to Printinghouse Square by Eastern Telegraph Cable: 2,000 uncensored words were one day sent across 180 miles of sea at a mean speed of 30 words a minute, and thence 14,010 miles to London, where they were printed in the *Times* the next morning with marvelous accuracy."[42]

James's coverage of the Russo-Japanese War was one of many highlights in his career. He had begun covering war in the Sudan in 1898 with General Sir Herbert Kitchener, who sought revenge against the Mahdists for the death of Major General Charles George "Chinese" Gordon at Khartoum. He worked as the *Times* of London's chief war correspondent from 1899 through 1913. After the Russo-Japanese War he covered conflicts in India, Persia, Turkey, the Balkans, Morocco, Albania, Tripoli, Bulgaria, and Thrace. During World War I, he served as an officer in the British Army on the Western

Front, earning the Distinguished Service Order for his actions at the Battle of the Somme. He died at age eighty-five in 1955.[43] Within weeks of his death, a syndicated newspaper trivia column put his name before millions of readers across the United States. The anonymous columnist asked: "Who was the first reporter to cover war by radio?" The answer, printed under headlines such as "Test Questions" and "Q's and A's," was: "Lionel James of the *Times* of London. He chartered a ship and equipped it with a radio system and covered the Russo-Japanese War at the turn of the century."[44]

Of all of the *Haimun*'s competitors on the high seas, Stanley Washburn of the *Chicago Daily News* proved the most effective. Washburn's youth had prepared him more for politics than for journalism. His father, William Drew "W. D." Washburn, was a newly elected Republican Congressman representing Minneapolis when Stanley was born in 1878. Stanley's father took him at the age of two to the Republican National Convention in Chicago, which nominated presidential candidate James Garfield. W. D. Washburn served three terms in the U.S. House of Representatives and then was chosen by the Minnesota Legislature to serve as a U.S. senator. The Washburn family moved to Washington, DC, in 1889. Stanley grew up keenly interested in politics and eavesdropped when his father had prominent political guests. Among them were Secretary of State James G. Blaine, who had lost the 1884 presidential race, and powerful U.S. House Speaker Thomas B. Reed.[45] A few years later, through his father's connections, he met Benjamin Harrison and William McKinley.

Washburn graduated from a military school in Pennsylvania and Williams College in Williamstown, Massachusetts, where he studied history and economics. Upon his father's insistence, he entered Harvard Law School in fall 1901 but dropped out to pursue journalism as a reporter for Minneapolis newspapers. He learned how to report and sometimes "create" news, once going so far as to goad the city's police chief to raid an illicit gambling house so he could write about it. Washburn appeared to grow restless with local news and in fall 1903 urged his father and the *Minneapolis Times* to send him to the Far East, where he expected war to break out. His hometown paper and the Portland *Oregonian* agreed to pay $10 for a story each week from the war zone, and Washburn's father kicked in a gift of $1,000 if his son would stay away for six months, "by which time I think he hoped my interest in journalism would have evaporated," the younger Washburn said.[46]

Washburn sailed on January 25, 1904, from Vancouver on the RMS *Empress of Japan*, which also transported war correspondents Melton Prior and John Bass. The latter, representing the *Chicago Daily News*, asked Washburn to file dispatches for his paper in return for the *Daily News* paying Washburn's expenses. Washburn agreed. Shortly after landing in Japan, he received a telegram from Bass asking him to charter a boat to cover the expected war from the vantage point of Liaodong Bay and other regions of the Yellow Sea. With money from the *Daily News*, Washburn rented a salvage boat from an English company and hired a crew.[47] Boat and crew covered the war during thirty-three voyages from mid-March through mid-July 1904, when the boat's charter was purchased by Japan to deprive Washburn of his ability to sail freely in contested waters.[48]

After that, Washburn covered the siege of Port Arthur and witnessed close fighting. The experience left him numb and perhaps longing to be back at sea. "I must have seen 10,000 wounded men in all conditions of dismemberment," he told a Minneapolis reporter upon returning home. "Men blown to pieces by shells, wounded, sick and hurt in a thousand ways."[49]

Washburn preferred seeing the war's opening moves from his boat. Like other correspondents covering the war, he found the Japanese authorities reluctant to assist Western journalists in witnessing land battles. "The government is giving out almost no news at all," he wrote, "and is censoring what does leak out."[50] By chartering a boat, he figured he could witness naval warfare from neutral waters and file his stories from neutral ports, free from the interference of land-based censors.

The boat was the *Fawan*, which Washburn said was Chinese for "Good Luck." The seven-year-old boat, registered at 300 tons, repeatedly merited its name: it sailed through mine fields and shallow waters between sandbars, and escaped close encounters when Washburn and his primarily Chinese crew feared the boat might be seized or sunk by hostile warships. "When I think of her my heart goes out as to an old and tried friend," Washburn recalled.[51]

Washburn based his operations at Yantai on the Chinese coast. There he established that he would have access to telegraph wires to send his stories to his newspapers in the United Kingdom and the United States. He also had his crew sworn before the British consul there because *Fawan* sailed under British flag.[52]

Early in the war, *Fawan* attempted to shadow ships of the Japanese navy ferrying troops to the Korean Peninsula, but after the Japanese army routed the Russians at the Yalu River and crossed into Manchuria, Washburn turned his attention to the garrison at Port Arthur. From May through July, scarcely a day passed when *Fawan* did not try to detect naval action somewhere near Port Arthur, although Japan by May had stopped attempting to lure the Russian fleet out of the harbor for a massive surface engagement. *Fawan* often made anchor in the Minotao island group, a few miles from Port Arthur on the Manchurian coast.[53]

Washburn's first task was to ferry the new Korean prime minister from Yantai to Incheon. Along the way, Washburn saw four Japanese transports carrying invasion troops bound for the mouth of the Yalu River. As he made the final approach toward Incheon harbor, he saw the remains of the Russian gun vessel *Koreets*, cruiser *Variag*, and transport *Sungari*, all of which were sunk on the first day of the war. The sightings gave him grist for news stories.[54]

His next major journey was to sail for the port of Yingkou (Newchwang), home to a Russian military outpost at the head of the Liaodong Gulf above Port Arthur. As *Fawan* approached, a launch arrived to deliver a cable: the harbor had been placed under Russian martial law, and all ships that sailed past Buoy No. 5 without proper authority would be sunk by mines or artillery at the fort. *Fawan* dropped anchor short of the buoy. At noon of April 1, a motorboat flying the Russian flag approached. "As she loomed up the decks could be seen alive with big, rough men in astrakan shakos and mud colored clothes, all carrying bayoneted guns and all apparently aching to stick those bayonets into someone," Washburn wrote in a dispatch. Despite Washburn's protest that *Fawan* was a British ship and could not be boarded under international law, a Russian officer, crew of marines, and half-dozen men in plain clothes came aboard and examined boat and crew. The search party found nothing of importance.[55] As *Fawan* waited for permission to move, the ice breaking up in the Yalu River tore off both of the boat's anchors, causing it to drift. When the Russians noted the boat's predicament, they told Washburn that if he attempted to leave the harbor, he would be shot. The Russians then placed *Fawan*'s crew, including Washburn and *Chicago Daily News* correspondent Richard Henry Little, under arrest as prisoners of war and shipped the boat's two Japanese servants to the interior of China for interrogation. Washburn reported that word had circulated among the Russian soldiers on shore that *Fawan* had been acting as a spy ship for the Japanese. Cossacks lined the nearest bank to keep an eye on the boat, making Washburn feel less than welcome if he should make for shore. The American consul-general to China came aboard *Fawan* on Easter Sunday to say that if the Japanese attacked the Russian garrison while the boat was in the harbor, *Fawan* would be immediately sunk.[56]

Washburn convinced the consul, Henry B. Miller, to wire the editor at the *Chicago Daily News* with a message that he dictated: "Our boys likely to be shot as spies. Our persons in danger. Wire Secretary of State to have Russian Government order us released."[57] Miller tried on his own at first to secure release, but Russian authorities refused him. Miller then took the matter directly to Washington. Twelve hours later, thanks to the intervention of Secretary of State John Hay with the Russian minister of foreign affairs at Saint Petersburg, and the minister's communication with General Aleksei Kuropatkin, *Fawan* was freed and told to sail within twenty-four hours. The Chinese crew ignited firecrackers in celebration as the boat slipped unmolested out of the harbor.[58]

The second time the Russians seized *Fawan*, it posed greater danger. The *Fawan* sailed from the Yalu River toward its base at Yantai. Washburn planned to stop briefly about seven or eight miles outside Port Arthur to check for signs of naval activity. On April 21, 1904, *Fawan* made a cursory inspection and then turned for Yantai across the bay. Suddenly, two Russian destroyers, steaming at twenty-five miles per hour, emerged from the port to approach *Fawan*. As Washburn tried to decide whether to halt or to make a run for it, one of the destroyers dropped an artillery shell twenty feet from the boat—"whereupon we stopped," he said.[59] The Russians towed *Fawan* through the hulks of damaged and scuttled ships into the besieged harbor, halting within 200 yards of a fort. The boat's crew and guests, including Army Colonel Webb C. Hayes, the son of former president Rutherford B. Hayes who carried State Department credentials to allow him to observe the war zone, were confined below decks while Russian sailors searched the boat. Washburn later learned they were looking for radio equipment, similar to the kind that James had placed upon *Haimun*; apparently the Port Arthur garrison suspected *Fawan* of transmitting sensitive military information directly or indirectly to Japan.[60] The Russian government had just published its order in Saint Petersburg declaring that any correspondent caught using a wireless transmitter was to be treated as a spy. *Fawan* had no such radio. Russians found nothing suspicious aboard, and at what Hayes described as a "tedious" trial they failed to establish that the *Fawan*'s crew had acted as spies or even belligerents. Frustrated, the Russians ordered the crew to clear out. That proved extremely risky. *Fawan* had entered the harbor with Russian help to avoid elaborate mine fields, but the Russians refused to provide a guide or a map for the return journey. *Fawan* sailed blindly at dusk through the mines. Washburn put his "trust in Providence" that the boat would not strike and detonate any hidden explosives.[61] The boat made it out unscathed, but Washburn said he was shocked to learn that a week later, one of the Russian ships that had intercepted *Fawan* struck a mine in the same vicinity and all aboard were "blown to pieces."[62]

Fawan had another close call in late June. Once it became clear that Japanese warships would not approach Port Arthur through the maze of Russia's electrically operated mines, the Russians began setting mechanical contact mines adrift farther offshore. On June 20, *Fawan* steamed within inches of one such contact mine.[63] At about the same time, the crew learned that a Russian destroyer had torpedoed the British-flagged bean-oil freighter *Hipsang*, sinking it and killing eight men. The *Hipsang* had refused to stop for inspection and the Russian sailors likely had mistaken it for *Fawan*, which it had targeted for sinking.[64]

Fawan also had a series of encounters with Japan. Four days after a Japanese warship struck a Russian mine and sank, the cruiser *Kosuga* spotted

Fawan between Dalny and Port Arthur. A Japanese lieutenant who spoke English boarded *Fawan*. He told Washburn that the *Kosuga* had initially considered *Fawan* to be a Russian minelayer, and if the boat had not stopped when hailed it would have been sunk.[65]

Such encounters became friendlier after mid-May, when the Japanese navy issued a permit to allow *Fawan* to observe the movements of its warships and dock at its military bases. Although Washburn's personal documents at the Minnesota Historical Society do not explain why the permit was approved, it is possible that the relative success of the Japanese army and navy had made them more willing to relax their relationships with foreign correspondents.[66]

Washburn reported some significant stories while at sea. These included the landing of Japanese troops north of the mouth of the Yalu River and several encounters with Japanese warships. He described the blocking of the harbor of Port Arthur by the hulls of twelve sunken Japanese and Russian vessels, some of whose identities he was the first to confirm. He reported, through inferences made in naval movements, that Russian troops had evacuated Yingkou. And he reported the movements of Japanese torpedo boats sent to patrol outside Port Arthur and to protect the landing of the Second Army's troops. His biggest scoop occurred one day when *Fawan* stood off the Korean coast. After hearing explosions in the fog, Washburn spotted Japanese destroyers pulling lifeboats from two battleships, the *Hatsuse* and *Yashima*, demonstrating that both had been sunk by mines—until World War II, the only two Japanese battleships sunk in that nation's history. He also hailed a Japanese cruiser, went aboard, and learned through an officer who spoke English that the navy was daily sending eight thousand soldiers of the Second Army onto the shore at Pitzuwo on the Liaodong Peninsula.[67] Thus, Washburn reported a story that James could not.

Despite his scoops, while Washburn heard an occasional shell fired from or at Port Arthur, he witnessed no actual naval engagements. *The Chicago Daily News* told Washburn not to risk taking *Fawan* under fire, although Washburn's temperament suggests he might have chosen to ignore the order under the right circumstances.[68] Instead of battle, his scrapbooks at the Minnesota Historical Society are dominated by accounts of his sailings on *Fawan* and his two arrests by the Russians.[69]

Although he failed to witness ship-to-ship combat, Washburn gleaned many details about life in Port Arthur by interviewing refugees who fled the Liaodong Peninsula in small boats, as well as Chinese merchants who sneaked into and out of the harbor to sell meat and vegetables. On July 30, from Yantai, he wrote:

> Many of the upper-class residents of Port Arthur are arriving here. They state that the Japanese are pressing close upon the fortress. . . .

Officials of the Russo-Japanese bank are among the refugees. The social status and intelligence of these people is a guaranty that their story that the fortress is being hard pressed is true. There is no doubt that there was serious fighting on July 25, 26 and 27, and it is highly probable that the Japanese are fighting their way over the last stages for a general assault on the inner citadel and its outworks.

According to the refugees, all the public buildings in the city, including the large hotel, are being utilized as hospitals. Rickshaws and all the public and private carriages are being used to transport the wounded into the fortress. Most of the deaths are from artillery wounds. It is impossible to estimate the number of wounded in the hospitals, but it is large.[70]

Washburn noted that sampans easily ran the Japanese blockade. From the returning boats, he learned that the Russian government in Port Arthur forcibly began collecting private stocks of food three months into the siege. "Rice, chickens, dogs, all go into their larder irrespective of how the rightful owner feels," he wrote. This left Chinese residents of the port on the verge of starvation, prompting many to leave by sea.[71] News of such a food shortage surely encouraged the Japanese invaders.

Washburn reflected philosophically on the risks and benefits of his time aboard *Fawan* during an interview with a Hong Kong newspaper after he left the war zone. "You like the life?" the unidentified Hong Kong reporter asked him. "Yes, I guess so," Washburn replied, adding,

> although sometimes I wonder whether all the risk we must take is justified by what we get.... There is nothing spectacular about Port Arthur engagements. At least, not the manoeuvres war correspondents are permitted to see. Boats run in and out, and then you hear a terrible bombardment taking place. The only way to know that a vessel has been sunk is by its total absence.[72]

Washburn joined General Nogi Maresuke's Third Army outside Port Arthur in May 1904 on behalf of the *Times* of London and stayed until September 1905, when the peace conference arranged by President Roosevelt ended hostilities. By the autumn of 1904, he found the Japanese willing to allow him to roam through its network of trenches and report with great freedom. *The Chicago Daily News* printed a two-page article and two photographs filed on October 21 in which Washburn detailed withering exchanges of fire. Washburn crept forward with the Ninth Division toward the center of the Russian defense. Miles of trenches, ten feet deep, spread to left and right in snaky and confusing zigzags that Washburn likened to the catacombs of Rome. As he approached the farthest trenches, he found some spots that had not been dug as deep, requiring him to duck and run to avoid sharpshooters' fire. All the while, artillery shells whistled overhead. "But as we creep up through the trenches toward the Russian position, we begin to hear a new sound, which is not so easily faced," he wrote. "It is the querulous whine of the rifle balls as they pass a few feet above our heads." The sharp report of a rifle indicated Russian sharpshooters who kept watch on gaps in the trench network for a chance to shoot a body dashing across to safety. One Japanese soldier raised his head to take a quick look at the Russian lines and was shot through the brain. "He was a fine fellow," an officer told Washburn as they removed the soldier's body. Washburn found the soldiers who were under the worst gunfire to be as "calm and cool as if on dress parade."[73] Furthermore, they welcomed war correspondents who agreed to share their risks and record their bravery: "The soldiers, I think, are glad enough to see correspondents in the trenches among them and are more than willing to have their photographs taken—willing even to pose in the very act of firing through the loopholes at the Russians over yonder."[74]

A popular perception persists that journalists who receive special access and privileges during wartime, such as those embedded for prolonged periods in military units, do so at some cost to credibility and accuracy. Accredited correspondents in World War II were subject to censorship, but they censored themselves as much or more than the officers who blue-penciled their dispatches. Through long periods of sharing the life of soldiers, correspondents developed empathy for them that colored their reports. Accredited correspondent and novelist John Steinbeck said journalists "carefully protected" the home front from the truest, grim accounts of war. They came to dwell on the positive rather than the negative. Similarly embedding of journalists in wars a half-century later tended to create an intimate relationship.[75]

This clearly was the case with Washburn. At war's end, a Japanese orderly handed him an envelope marked with characters identifying it as originating from the military telegraph office. "Return," said the message inside. Washburn noted in a memoir that the conclusion of his assignment left him feeling more warmly about the Japanese than his colleagues who had departed after a short stay. "So many of the correspondents left the 'front' with such bitter feelings toward their erstwhile hosts," he wrote. But those who abandoned the Third Army at war's conclusion "left with only the tenderest affection toward the commander under whose shadow we had lived, slept and thought these many months."[76] This détente likely was due not only to a general relaxation of press-military relations throughout the army in late 1904, as detailed in chapter 4, but also the role of the Third Army within the larger scope of war strategy. General Nogi's army had the assignment of encircling and besieging Port Arthur. Unlike the First, Second, and Fourth armies, it carried out its mission in full view of the Russians, lessening the need for secrecy. Sharing living space with the Third Army's officers for fourteen months naturally encouraged Washburn to identify with his hosts. He struck up a particular friendship with Nogi's chief of staff, Major General Ichinohe Hyōe. Ichinohe insisted on riding with Washburn as he departed for the coast to the tune of John Philip Sousa's *The Stars and Stripes Forever* played by the Third Army Corps Military Band. In parting, Ichinohe called Washburn his friend.[77]

It is somewhat incongruous that upon leaving Japan, Washburn expressed racist attitudes toward his former hosts. After stopping in Saint Petersburg to report briefly on the Revolution of 1905, Washburn went on to Rome. There he told the U.S. ambassador to Italy that the Japanese "do not care for whites, not even for the English and Americans, who are useful to them now, and they are working them for all they can." He called them "most untruthful and deceitful" as they played "a big game before the world."[78] Washburn also told a Minneapolis newspaper that "You cannot know a Jap very well. And too often you find him insincere, deceitful, and a . . . master at prevarication."[79] It is possible that his opinions shifted with the fortunes of the Japanese during the war. It was easy to root for an underdog, but when Japan dominated the Russians at sea and on land, they became a world power and a potential threat to American interests in the Pacific. While Washburn kept individual Japanese close to his heart, he could see the potential danger arising from their nation's awakening. Perhaps he appreciated individuals more than the nation as a whole.

Tucked in the clippings that make up Washburn's archive at Saint Paul is a short item that initially appeared to be of little consequence. Headlined "Explosions at Port Arthur," it told of the *Fawan* sailing on June 8 toward the garrison from its haven in the Minotao islands after the crew heard four loud blasts to the south. Outside Port Arthur, Washburn came upon a small, open boat sailing toward shore. In the boat, he noted, were two Chinese oarsmen and a man he identified as "Fuller," a war correspondent for the *Indianapolis News*. Fuller was trying to sneak into Port Arthur before the Japanese or Russians could halt him. A week later, after exchanging news with a Japanese cruiser and some Chinese junks, Washburn reported two items of interest: food was so scarce in Port Arthur that Russian soldiers were eating dogs, and that Hector Fuller—apparently having earned the right to a first name in print—had made his way inside the city.[80] Fuller's story is recounted in chapter 8.

James, Washburn, and their colleagues afloat all faced a choice that journalists covering war in the twenty-first century must make: to embed in a unit of the armed forces and be subject to its rules, or to freelance on their own as a "unilateral" correspondent. While such choices affected the kind of stories produced in the Russo-Japanese War, they did not necessarily affect the quality of journalism.

James, by virtue of his connections with the Japanese navy, got the scoop on the sinking of the *Petropavlovsk* and artillery duel of April 13, as well as the landing of First Army troops on March 15. Yet his obtaining official approval of the Japanese navy had its costs. James self-censored stories to win the support of Commander Tonami and his superiors, and thus did not report the numbers of invasion troops or other information beyond the barest of outlines. When he agreed to a Japanese rule restricting his movements, he missed his chance to see the landing of the Second Army, which his competitor, Stanley Washburn, unencumbered by obligations to the Japanese, was able to report independently. Washburn's freedom also allowed him to report the Russian evacuation of Yingkou, the sinking of two Japanese battleships, and the food shortages in Port Arthur. Yet, his reporting methods nearly cost him his freedom and his life in repeated encounters with hostile combatants.

Washburn continued his life as a war correspondent, covering the Russian army from 1914 to 1916 during the first years of World War I for *Collier's* and the *Times of* London. He later reported from the Romanian and French armies before joining the American Expeditionary Forces as a commissioned major in the cavalry in 1918. In later years, he ran unsuccessfully for a New Jersey seat in the U.S. House of Representatives and served in military intelligence. He died at age seventy-two in 1950, not long after providing an extensive oral history of his life to Columbia University.[81]

It is interesting to note that much of James's and Washburn's dispatches focused on *how* they reported, not *what* they reported. The novelty of covering war from the sea by radio and land-based telegraph wires captured much of the public imagination, as evidenced by the numerous stories describing the voyages of *Fawan* and the mechanics of the *Haimun*'s reporting system. This phenomenon of not reporting much war news, per se, day to day can also be explained in part by the pace of war. Pitched battles occur from time to time but are separated by periods of recovery, reinforcement, and movement. Many days, not much happens that could be classified as news. And yet major news outlets, such as the *Times* and Chicago *Daily News*, expected daily dispatches in return for their considerable expenditures.

What James and Washburn failed to report also is noteworthy. They missed the two most decisive elements of the conflict. First, the war's outcome depended in large measure on huge land battles in Manchuria, particularly at Liaoyang and Mukden, as the Russian army attempted to relieve Port Arthur and clashed with well-disciplined Japanese forces bent on establishing Japan's influence on the mainland. Those battles could only be reported by accredited correspondents working with the approval of the combatants, as any unapproved American or British reporters would quickly be removed after identification as outsiders by virtue of their light-colored skin and European features. Disgusted at the Japanese treatment of neutral correspondents, James left the Japanese army before the final battles, thus missing the turning point of the war—and not to mention the largest land battles up to that time.

Washburn, assigned to the Third Army, was on hand for the assault on Port Arthur, but he too missed out on Liaoyang and Mukden, as his accreditation did not allow him to switch from one front to another—a benefit of reporting as an unaccredited unilateral in later wars. Second, the decisive battle at sea and Russia's last hurrah—the unprecedented clash of the Russian Baltic Fleet and Japanese navy at the Battle of Tsushima Strait in 1905—occurred long after the correspondents had abandoned their boats.

No matter how much these reporters tried to plan in advance for the best news coverage, the war and the vagaries of Japanese press controls unfolded in unforeseen ways that kept them from consistently covering the most significant news.

NOTES

1. "Stanley Washburn Returns from Seat of Eastern War," *Star-Tribune* (Minneapolis), March 5, 1905.

2. For a thorough account of the uses of radio by the government, rebels, and other propagandists in the Spanish Civil War, see Alan Davies, "Broadcasting in the Spanish Civil War of 1936–1939," *Historical Journal of Film, Radio and Television* 19, no. 4 (1999): 473–513.

3. There are many excellent biographies of Edward R. Murrow. The most significant and detailed, in this author's opinion, are A. M. Sperber, *Murrow: His Life and Times* (New York: Fordham University Press, 1999), and Joseph E. Persico, *Edward R. Murrow: An American Original* (New York: McGraw-Hill, 1988). For a memoir of NBC's Dunn, see William J. Dunn, *Pacific Microphone* (College Station: Texas A&M University Press, 2009).

4. Jacqueline Beaumont, "The Making of a War Correspondent: Lionel James of the *Times*," in *The Impact of the South African War*, ed. David Omissi and Andrew Thompson (Houndmills, UK: Palgrave, 2002), 125; and Peter Slattery, *Reporting the Russo-Japanese War 1904–05: Lionel James's First Wireless Transmissions to the Times* (Folkestone, UK: Global Oriental, 2004), 3.

5. Slattery, *Reporting the Russo-Japanese War*, xi, 1, 11.

6. Ibid., 13.

7. Ibid., xii, 13.

8. David Fraser, *A Modern Campaign: Or War and Wireless Telegraphy in the Far East* (London: Methuen & Co., 1905), 1–4.

9. Bartholomew Lee, "Wireless—Its Evolution from Mysterious Wonder to Weapon of War, 1902–05," *AWA Review*, California Historical Radio Society, http://www.californiahistoricalradio.com/wp-content/uploads/2013/01/BartWirelessWar190205Lee.pdf.

10. Fraser, *A Modern Campaign*, 18, 23–24.

11. Lionel James, *High Pressure: Being Some Record of Activities in the Service of the Times Newspaper* (London: John Murray, 1929), 235–36; Slattery, *Reporting*

the *Russo-Japanese War*, xiv; and Lee, "Wireless—Its Evolution from Mysterious Wonder to Weapon of War, 1902–05."

12. Lee, "Wireless—Its Evolution from Mysterious Wonder to Weapon of War, 1902–05."

13. James, *High Pressure*, 237–38.

14. Lee, "Wireless—Its Evolution from Mysterious Wonder to Weapon of War, 1902–05."

15. James, *High Pressure*, 239.

16. Ibid., 242; and Lee, "Wireless—Its Evolution from Mysterious Wonder to Weapon of War, 1902–05."

17. Slattery, *Reporting the Russo-Japanese War*, 42.

18. Valliant, "The Selling of Japan: Japanese Manipulation of Western Opinion, 1900–1905," 436.

19. Takahashi, *International Law Applied to the Russo-Japanese War with the Decisions of the Japanese Prize Courts*, 397–401.

20. Slattery, *Reporting the Russo-Japanese War*, 47.

21. "Wireless Workers Back from the Scene of War," *New York Times*, August 21, 1904.

22. Ibid.; Fraser, *A Modern Campaign*, 60–61.

23. Sakuyé, *International Law Applied to the Russo-Japanese War*, 388.

24. "Convention (II) with Respect to the Laws and Customs of War on Land and Its Annex: Regulations Concerning the Laws and Customs of War on Land," Arts. 29–30, The Hague, Netherlands, July 1899, http://www.opbw.org/int_inst/sec_docs/1899HC-TEXT.pdf.

25. Sakuyé, *International Law Applied to the Russo-Japanese War*, 388–89.

26. "Correspondents as Spies," *New York Times*, April 16, 1904; and Slattery, *Reporting the Russo-Japanese War*, 73.

27. "Torpedo Attack Yesterday," *New York Times*, April 14, 1904.

28. Slattery, *Reporting the Russo-Japanese War*, 63; "Torpedo Attack Yesterday"; "How the *Times* Gets War News by 'Wireless,'" *New York Times*, April 24, 1904; and "Alexieff Admits Togo Sank Petropavlovsk," *New York Times*, May 1, 1904.

29. Slattery, *Reporting the Russo-Japanese War 1904–05*, 66.

30. "All Pe-Chi-Strait Is Sown with Mines: Russian Desperation Imperils the Ships of Neutral Powers," *New York Times*, May 22, 1904.

31. Sakuyé, *International Law Applied to the Russo-Japanese War*. 387.

32. James, *High Pressure*, 300–301.

33. Slattery, *Reporting the Russo-Japanese War*, 90–91, xvi.

34. Valliant, "The Selling of Japan," 436.

35. Ibid., 437.

36. "The *Times* and Wireless War Correspondence," *Times of London*, August 27, 1904.

37. Fuller, "Japan Has Set the Pace in Secrecy: Wily Ways of Keeping the Most Astute Correspondents in Check," April 6, 1904.

38. "The *Times* and Wireless War Correspondence"; and Sakuyé, *International Law Applied to the Russo-Japanese War*, 402–5.

39. Slattery, *Reporting the Russo-Japanese War*, 119.
40. "Wireless Workers Back from the Scene of War."
41. "Wireless," *New York Times*, April 15, 1904.
42. Lee, "Wireless—Its Evolution from Mysterious Wonder to Weapon of War, 1902–05."
43. United Press, "Lionel James Dies, First War Reporter to Use Radio," *Saint Louis Post-Dispatch*, June 1, 1955; and "He Wielded Pen and Sword," Northwood Village, July 25, 2011, http://www.northwoodvillage.org.uk/tchudsonarticles/he-wielded-pen-and-sword-by-t-c-hudson/.
44. "Test Questions," *The* (Eureka, California) *Times-Standard*, July 4, 1955.
45. "The Reminiscences of Stanley Washburn, 1950," 1–5, in the Oral History Collection of Columbia University, New York City.
46. Ibid., 30–31.
47. Ibid., 32.
48. Richard Barry, *Events Man: Being an Account of the Adventures of Stanley Washburn, American War Correspondent* (New York: Moffat, Yard & Company, 1907), 289.
49. "Indianapolis War Reporter Home," clipping from unidentified newspaper, Washburn Scrapbook, 101, "Washburn, Stanley" papers, Minnesota Historical Society, Division of Library and Archives, Saint Paul (hereafter Washburn Scrapbook).
50. Clipping from unidentified newspaper, Washburn Scrapbook, 15.
51. Barry, *Events Man*, 17, 19.
52. Ibid., 24–25, 37.
53. Stanley Washburn, "Floating Mines in Naval War: Evils Which the Hague Conference Should Attack," *Outlook*, June 8, 1907, Washburn Scrapbook, n. p.
54. Barry, *Events Man*, 37, 53.
55. Ibid., 75–80.
56. Clipping from unidentified newspaper, Washburn Scrapbook, 101
57. Barry, *Events Man*, 89.
58. Uchida [Yasuya] to Komura [Jutarō], Tokyo, telegram, April 8, 1904, "Nichirosen eki no sai Rokoku nioite Chicago Daily News tsushinin kosen o yokuryushi dosen norikumi honpojin inchi no ken," Nihon Gaimusho hozon kiroku [Records of the Ministry of Foreign Affairs], the Diplomatic Record Office of the Ministry of Foreign Affairs, Tokyo, Japan; "Hon. W. D. Washburn," telegram, April 14, 1904, Washburn Scrapbook, 16; and "Press Boat Is Released," *Boston Globe*, April 4, 1904.
59. Washburn Scrapbook, 101.
60. Ibid.; and "From Port Arthur: Adventures of an American War Correspondent," newspaper clipping identified in handwritten note as *Hong Kong Times*, Washburn Scrapbook, 57.
61. Washburn Scrapbook, 57; and "Imprisoned by Russians: Col. Webb C. Hayes Had Thrilling Experience in the Far East," *Arkansas Democrat* (Little Rock), June 30, 1904.
62. Ibid., 101.
63. "Floating Mines in Naval War."
64. Barry, *Events Man*, 287–88.

65. "Floating Mines in Naval War."

66. "Held Up by Japanese Ships," clipping from unidentified newspaper, Washburn Scrapbook, 34.

67. Barry, *Events Man*, 210–11, 169.

68. Ibid., 217.

69. Washburn Scrapbook, 24.

70. "Officially Denied That Fortress Has Fallen—Big Fight Has Begun at Haicheng," clipping from unidentified newspaper, Washburn Scrapbook, 39.

71. "Dangers on Open Sea: Daily News Dispatch Boat Fawan Has Narrow Escape from Electrical Mine," clipping from unidentified newspaper, Washburn Scrapbook, 38.

72. "From Port Arthur: Adventures of an American War Correspondent."

73. Stanley Washburn, "Under Iron Tempest: Stanley Washburn Sees Horrors of War in Trenches at Port Arthur," *Chicago Daily News*, clipping in Washburn Scrapbook, 49–50.

74. Ibid.

75. John Steinbeck, *Once There Was a War* (New York: Penguin, 1977), 7; and Bill Katovsky and Timothy Carlson, eds., *Embedded: The Media at the War in Iraq* (Guilford, Connecticut: Lyons Press, 2003), appendix. A U.S. Department of Defense policy statement during the 2003 invasion of Iraq defined an embed as "a media representative remaining with a unit on an extended basis—perhaps a period of weeks or even months." Embedded correspondents often came to identify with the troops they covered. Embedded journalist Rick Atkinson of the *Washington Post* told his readers, "In 20 years of writing about the military—including two previous stints as an embedded reporter, in Bosnia and Somalia—I had never seen a more intimate arrangement between journalists and soldiers." See Rick Atkinson, "Embedded in Iraq: Was It Worth It?" *Washington Post*, May 4, 2003.

76. Stanley Washburn, *The Cable Game: The Adventures of an American Press-Boat in Turkish Waters during the Russian Revolution* (Boston: Sherman, French & Company, 1912), 2–3.

77. Washburn, *The Cable Game*, 4–7.

78. Tyler Dennett, *Roosevelt and the Russo-Japanese War: A Critical Study of American Policy in Eastern Asia in 1902–05, Based Primarily upon the Private Papers of Theodore Roosevelt* (Garden City, New York: Doubleday, Page & Company, 1925), 310–11.

79. "Stanley Washburn Talks of War and Its Results," clipping from unidentified newspaper, Washburn Scrapbook, 104.

80. "Reduced to Eat Dogs," clipping from unidentified newspaper, Washburn Scrapbook, 30.

81. "Biographical Note," Stanley Washburn, Minnesota Historical Society Manuscripts Collection, Minnesota Historical Society, http://www2.mnhs.org/library/findaids/01250.xml.

Chapter 3

Jack London

I had run into a hive of blue uniform, brass buttons and cutlasses. The populace clustered like flies at doors and windows to gape at the "Russian spy."

—Jack London, 1904[1]

Japanese censorship of land engagements in the Russo-Japanese War astonished Jack London and his fellow journalists who were covering the First Army in 1904.[2] The censorship reached an unexpected magnitude and made little sense to them. "Practically everything" was a military secret, London wrote to the newspapers owned by William Randolph Hearst, and that included something as insignificant as a photograph he took of a Chinese blacksmith in Korea that he was forced to relinquish to military authorities.[3] The army did not allow correspondents representing friendly or neutral countries near enough to the front lines to witness actual combat and seldom left them free enough to send dispatches to the rear that contained significant news. The experience soured London and his fellow journalists on the future of war correspondence.[4]

According to the regulations, journalists had to have escorts at all times on the battlefield and agree to participate in an early form of press pools. Also, journalists had to submit all reports, private letters, telegrams, and other communications to military censorship, which would remove anything liable to disturb the public peace or to dispirit the troops. If London and the other reporters did not like these arrangements, there was little they could do. As guests of the Japanese, they were expected never to do anything disorderly, the code said.[5]

Japan controlled information partly out of suspicion that foreigners were spies[6] but mainly because it feared security leaks and the potential social and political consequences of uncensored news on the home front. One overriding political interest was harmony. News stories that disturbed morale or the public peace were unlikely to be released by military or government authorities. Japanese authorities feared that public morale would suffer, and thus the state would suffer, if news of the war were reported freely, said Tokutomi Sohō, president of the semiofficial *Kokumin Shimbun* newspaper. "Only the officials in the government knew of the various internal weaknesses and overall vulnerability of the nation. They kept their knowledge strictly secret lest it have an adverse effect upon the morale of the people," he said.[7]

The Russo-Japanese War was London's first foray into war correspondence although he had packed many rough-and-tumble adventures into his twenty-eight years. He was born in 1876 to a working-class family, his father never identified, in San Francisco. As a teenager, he stole and sold oysters from private reserves in San Francisco Bay, sailed to Japan on a sealing schooner, and marched and rode in one of the branches of Jacob Coxey's "Army" of the unemployed that converged on Washington, DC, in 1894 to demand federal jobs building paved roads as a way to end their poverty and stimulate the economy. As a Coxeyite, London often went door to door begging for food, which got him jailed for a month for vagrancy. He began writing fiction around that time. His first foray into publishing nonfiction was a short story, "Typhoon off the Coast of Japan." London prospected for gold in the Klondike in 1897 but did not get much in return for the effort except material for his 1903 novel *The Call of the Wild*, which made him one of the most successful and celebrated writers in the United States.[8]

London bought into the contemporary image of combat journalism as one of dashing heroism, drama, intrigue, and pageantry. He admitted as he returned home after the war in 1904 that he had gone to Japan with "gorgeous conceptions" of a correspondent's role. He had based his notions upon his reading accounts of the British reporters who died during Major General Charles George "Chinese" Gordon's defense of Khartoum against Mahdist Sudanese rebels in 1885, and of novelist-journalist Stephen Crane's description of being under fire in Cuba while reporting on the Spanish-American War for the *New York World*.[9]

At the end of 1903, London was determined to report on the conflict that he expected to begin soon; tensions between Japan and Russia had been building for months over the collision of their expansionist interests in Manchuria and Korea. At the time, despite being one of the most popular writers in the United States, London was nearly broke and emotionally exhausted by his relationships with his wife, Bess, and his mistress, Charmian Kittredge.[10] On January 7, 1904, five days before his twenty-eighth birthday, he dispatched the final pages of his novel *The Sea Wolf* to the *Century Magazine* and left his home in Oakland, California, bound for Japan via Hawaii.[11] He had agreed to cover the expected war for the Hearst newspaper chain, headed by the *New York Journal* and *San Francisco Examiner*. He chose to write for the lord of yellow journalism because Hearst paid more than *Collier's Weekly*, *Harper's Magazine*, and the *New York Herald*, which also had approached him with offers.[12] Orders from the Pacific Mail Steamship's New York office held the transport Siberia at its San Francisco dock for ten hours beyond its scheduled departure time to allow correspondents Frederick Palmer of *Collier's Weekly* and Oscar King Davis of the *New York Herald* to board. Their train from the East had arrived late. Joining them and Jack London on the ship were Lionel James of the *Times* of London and the *New York Times*, Percival Phillips of the London *Daily Express*, and photographers James H. "Jimmy" Hare and Robert L. Dunn of *Collier's Weekly*. The *Siberia* docked in Honolulu, where several more correspondents gathered aboard on January 14 and sailed with London for Japan. They arrived in Yokohama eleven days later.[13]

Western reporters in Japan in January and the first week of February 1904 requested permission to go to the sites of expected land battles. Instead, they were treated to dinners at Tokyo's Imperial Hotel, where most of them stayed. It was "the most ingratiating hospitality in the world," said fellow war correspondent Frederick Palmer. The Japanese Ministry of War did issue passes to battle zones, but no battles were in progress at the time, and the appropriate military officials refused to sign the passes.[14]

London was not content to wait for permission to leave for the Asian mainland. He wrote in an unpublished collection of notes that he "found that there were two ways of playing the game—either to sit down in Tokio [sic] as the Japs wanted me to and eat many dinners, or to go out on my own resources."[15] He left the capital without informing the proper authorities, seeking to book his own passage to Korea. He did not get far.[16]

London did not know that the Japanese armed forces had restricted the use of cameras. On February 1, a week before the Port Arthur attack, he wandered through the port of Moji and nearby Shimonoseki, the westernmost city on the main island of Honshu. He unknowingly entered a fortified area where martial law forbade photographing of "land or water scenery." Japan had turned the twin ports into what Canadian correspondent Frederick Arthur McKenzie, who observed military preparations there in January, called "one of the most strongly fortified spots on earth." But few signs of mobilization appeared in public, he said, and "[e]very trace of the gigantic naval and military preparations proceeding in the neighborhood was as carefully covered as possible." The hills bristled with artillery, yet no gun barrels presented themselves to the casual observer in the streets. On the day McKenzie visited, stevedores unloaded 1,000 junks of supplies destined for the army and navy, yet none of the workers wore a uniform—and, in fact, not one uniformed soldier or sailor appeared outdoors. As he wandered and took pictures, London had little reason to suspect the magnitude of the threat he appeared to pose as a non-Japanese defying the law.

London bought a ticket to Incheon (Chemulpo), the major port on Korea's western coast, at a steamship office. He stepped out the door. "Then came four coolies carrying a bale of cotton," London wrote in a letter to the Hearst syndicate.

> Snap, went my camera for five little boys at play; snap again. A line of coolies carrying coal—and again snap, and a last snap for a middle-aged Japanese man, in European clothes and in great perturbation, fluttered his hands prohibitively before my camera. Having performed this function, he promptly disappeared.
>
> "Ah, it is not allowed," I thought, and, calling my rickshawman, I strolled along the streets.
>
> Later, passing by a two-story frame building, I noticed my middle-aged Japanese man standing in the doorway. He smiled and beckoned me to enter. I was in the police station.[17]

"Japanese police 'very sorry,' but they arrested me," London wrote to Kittredge. "Of course I missed steamer. 'Very sorry.'" Police took London and his camera to a photography shop, drawing attention from bystanders curious to see the "Russian spy." A clerk developed the negatives and made prints, but it did London no good that they showed only simple street scenes. London was bundled off to the military prison at Shimonoseki, and then on to Kokura, where he was convicted of espionage at trial. The prosecution likely served as an attempt to warn other correspondents rather than to punish the world-famous writer. The court merely confiscated his camera, fined him five yen, and released him—forgetting in the process to actually collect the nominal penalty. Once free, London wired fellow correspondent Richard Harding Davis in Tokyo to ask his help in getting the court to release the camera, which he needed to take pictures to accompany his war stories. Davis asked American consul Lloyd Griscom to intercede.[18]

Griscom requested the camera's return during his next visit to Baron Komura Gentarō at the Ministry of Foreign Affairs. The exchange, as recorded by Griscom and repeated by London's and Davis's biographers, is worth quoting in full:

> He [Komura] was in a rather irritated mood, and said that he did not know how he could grant the request, but to make certain he would summon the legal counsel of the Foreign Office. I knew very well that when a Foreign Minister rang the bell for his legal adviser, it meant he needed support, and I would not get what I wanted.

Figure 3.1 Jack London, circa 1906, had never covered war before being hired by William Randolph Hearst. *Source*: Library of Congress.

The counsel arrived, an extremely clever lawyer, who, according to the quaint Japanese custom, had sat on the bench for many years to gain experience before being allowed to practise [*sic*] and have clients. As soon as the case was put to him he answered, "What you ask, Your Excellency, is absolutely forbidden. The statute declares that the weapon with which a crime has been committed becomes the property of the court."

"There you are," Baron Komura said to me.

"Does that apply to every crime?" I asked the lawyer.

"Yes, to every crime of every description."

I turned to the Foreign Minister. "If I can name a crime to which this does not apply, will you release the camera?"

Regarding me doubtfully for a few seconds, Baron Komura replied, "Yes, I will."

"Well, what about rape?"

Baron Komura's Oriental solidarity dissolved in a shout of laughter.

Komura repeated the story at the next cabinet meeting to much amusement. The court released London's camera.[19]

Undaunted, London set out again. He caught a steamer for Busan on the southeastern corner of the Korean Peninsula and there boarded another steamer that took him to Mokpo, on the southwestern tip. He arrived at Mokpo during the opening of hostilities at Port Arthur. Thereupon the Japanese confiscated London's ship.[20] He obtained passage aboard a Korean fishing junk on February 9. It took him up the coast to Incheon, where he arrived on February 16. The trip in an open boat in freezing weather (the air temperature plunged to ten degrees below zero Fahrenheit), contrary to the wishes of the government in Tokyo, was fitting for a war correspondent who had expected a life of intrigue and adventure. London devoted one dispatch to Hearst's newspapers about his adventures trying to find and equip his own expedition to the front without the help of the Japanese army. The *Examiner* apparently shared his sense of excitement about his journey, giving better display to the story of London's methods of evading authorities to enter northern Korea than to his dispatch printed the same day about what he saw after he arrived.[21]

"Buy everything in sight and get ready to start for Ping-yang," a Westerner in Incheon advised him. London hired an interpreter, whom he addressed as Mr. Yamada, and Korean houseboy who spoke good English and could run errands and cook meals. London stopped in a doctor's office to get vaccinated and ended up buying the doctor's horse before acquiring three ponies to carry his gear. "Everything was to be bought," he wrote. That included:

> saddles, bridles, blankets, hitching straps, nose bags, rope lashings, spare sets of horseshoes all around, horseshoer's tools, pack-saddles, extra girths, canned goods, rubber boots, mittens, caps, gloves, clothes, flour, cooking utensils, shoes, candles, and all the thousand and one articles necessary for a campaign which might extend into Manchuria. And it was [Chinese] New Years![22]

London set off with his little caravan. Hundreds of miles from the bureaucracy of Tokyo, he enjoyed a measure of freedom to report and to write. He found and followed the First Brigade of the First Army into northern Korea and stayed with it for about two months, "seeing what I could see and taking pictures. They didn't seem to have orders concerning me and let me follow along."[23] He rode a horse that formerly had belonged to a Russian diplomat at Seoul, Korea, northward to Pyongyang, which he spelled "Ping-yang" in his letters and dispatches. London had not learned to ride before arriving in the Far East, and he quickly developed saddle sores. However, according to a traveling companion, London never stopped smiling and laughing, nor did he desist from demanding to continue as far and as fast as necessary to keep up.[24] Upon arriving in Pyongyang, he lived in a Japanese hotel that was "crammed with soldiers," he wrote to Kittredge and was the only American reporter at the front. Three other correspondents—McKenzie, writing for the London *Daily Mail*, "Lewis" of the London *Daily Telegraph*, and the American Robert L. Dunn, a *Collier's Weekly* photographer—had managed on their own to get to Pyongyang before Japan had clamped down on travel from the home islands. McKenzie and Dunn guessed correctly that military and naval action likely would occur at Incheon and made their way there. As detailed in chapter 7, Dunn was on hand to photograph the night landing of Japanese troops. McKenzie, who had returned to Incheon after a visit to the Korean seat of government in Seoul, described the efficiency of the landing. The First Army had arranged for coolies to greet the invaders by holding paper lanterns to show pre-arranged routes to the Japanese homes in the city. Each home displayed a military lantern that had been given to the homeowner. Japanese officers holding lists of names directed soldiers to their appointed lodgings, where the host families were expected to provide food and places to sleep. McKenzie watched the invasion unfold in near silence; the plans had been crafted so thoroughly that few had the need to speak.[25]

London hired a valet and an interpreter and bought four more horses and two grooms. Thus equipped, he rode for the Yalu River, the border with Manchuria.[26] While in Korea, he wrote and cabled apparently uncensored dispatches to the United States. His freedom to do so stemmed from his being far from Japan and from the First Army's indifference to him.

His dispatches from northern Korea described the march of the First Army from Seoul; the excellence of the army's equipment, training, and composure; the difficult negotiations in which he obtained his horses; the river of mud upon which the army marched from Seoul to Pyongyang and then farther north; and the reaction of Korean villagers in Sunan-guyŏk to the occupying army.[27] With no combat to cover, London recounted quotidian details of warfare that nearly a century later still create vivid images in the mind's eye.

He turned his attention to war on a smaller scale: its impact on the people in harm's way. London mailed a particular story in this vein to San Francisco to avoid telegraph censors deleting his comments about the ethics of the Japanese occupation of Korea. He wrote of soldiers stealing chickens and eggs, as if such theft meant nothing to Korean farmers trying to scratch out a living. He described Koreans grumbling because the First Army requisitioned food and fodder from them without giving the farmers a fair price. He said the blame fell on the middlemen who took a large cut from what the farmers should have received. London wrote:

> The true inwardness of the situation is this: The Japanese military authorities requisition so much food and forage for which they pay a fair price. But the deal goes through the hands of the Korean officials. Now, the Korean official can give the Occident cards and spades when it comes to misappropriation of funds. The Oriental term for this is "squeeze." Centuries of practice have reduced it to a science, and in Korea there are but two classes—the "squeezers" and the "squeezees." The common people, of course, all the world over, are the "squeezees."[28]

Despite the color and life in these stories, London was dissatisfied with them, considering them dull. He itched to see real combat. He did not know when or where he would get the chance, but he suspected that his odds were diminishing. In his notes, he quoted an order that had aimed to prevent him from leaving Tokyo. He did not say how or when he had received the order, but he noted that if he had obeyed it, he would have been stuck in Japan with the scores of correspondents who heeded similar orders. He expected that news of his presence with the First Army north of Pyongyang would soon be made known to officials in Tokyo, who would limit his movements and impose censorship on his dispatches. "I am prepared . . . to be held up by Japanese scouts at any moment and be brought back to Ping-yang. But it's all in the game," he noted.[29] His choice of metaphor is revealing: He saw a war reporter's life as a sport in which the rules can be bent or broken.

In a dispatch on March 5, he reported the first skirmish between Japanese and Russian troops, near Pyongyang. The Seventh Company of the Forty-Sixth Infantry Regiment, Twelfth Division, opened fire at a distance of 700 meters upon a Russian scouting party sent to probe the Japanese defenses. The only casualties were two Russian ponies, and the scouting party withdrew. Although it was not much of a battle and no Westerner witnessed it, London gathered enough details—through interviews with Japanese officers and evacuees from an American mining concession who traveled briefly with the Russian scouts—to fashion a word picture. The Russians had crossed the Yalu River at Wiju, he said, and probed 200 miles into Korea, never knowing when they would encounter the enemy. Details about the Seventh Company's resistance were offered by Lieutenant Y. Abe, whom London entertained in his Pyongyang hotel room. Abe described the battle as they sat shoeless on the floor, drank saki and tea, and ate onions with chopsticks.[30]

Four days later, London's freedom to observe and to write as he pleased came to an end. He was detained by Japanese soldiers at Sunan-guyŏk, 16 miles north of Pyongyang, and ordered not to travel toward the front. "As I write this a thousand soldiers are passing through the village past my door," he wrote in frustration to Kittredge. Two days later, he added, "East, West, and South I may ride as far as I wish, but North, where fighting is soon to begin, I may not go." Guards with bayonets threatened him; to go north he would need the permission of a lieutenant general in Seoul, many miles away, but he never revealed in his letters whether he ever sought it.[31] Forty miles from Russian troops, the only journalist that far north, he raged at his having to miss the "fun."[32]

He moved into an abandoned house on the main street of Sunan-guyŏk, announcing in an article for the Hearst press that he had "taken possession" of it. His presence became a local curiosity. Korean houses, he wrote, were built so that doors and windows must be kept open to let in light and air. They also let in many glances from curious passers-by. London's daily routine became a kind of play in which the curtain never rang down, he said.

> I am certain that if I charged a penny a "look see," that I should more than clear expenses, and I am equally certain that a head charge of a nickle [sic] would yield a handsome dividend on the capital invested in this trip by Mr. Hearst. The first of the audience arrives before breakfast, and in wonder and amazement watches me turn out and wash. With the explanation that the Korean does not wash, his wonder and amaze will be understood.
> Each doing of mine is duly noted and before nightfall is spread to the remotest recesses of the hills. Some of my actions are greeted with shouts and explanations. There is a constant discussion going on as to why I do this or that, but my star performance is shaving. When [servant] Manyoungi brings the hot water and I lather my face the street blocks up. The marching troops have to force their way through; it is like a street in front of a metropolitan newspaper when the election returns are being posted.[33]

For exercise and entertainment, London saddled one of his horses and rode out to see the sights. He visited a temple and a Red Cross hospital and rode quietly among the deserted homes in the village, drawing the attention of roaming dogs. He snapped many photographs of the soldiers and Koreans, drawing a crowd curious about the workings of his camera. But always, he remained aware he lived within boundaries. The constant crunching of boots and sandals outside his door reminded him that the lifeblood of war flowed around him, and his small world was a glorified prison until some army officer far away decided what to do with him.

> In the middle of the day, when the sun tempers the bite of the wind which sweeps down from Siberia, it is my custom to go for a ride. First, I ride north, my alloted hundred yards for the pleasure of having my guards turn out and warn me back. Then I turn to the east, following the trend of the village, and ride to Captain Teshima's quarters. Captain Teshima is my jailer, and he is "very sorry" for me, as everybody has been "very sorry" for me ever since I struck Japan. I know half a dozen words of Chinook, and he speaks French, so I fall back on my interpreter in order to learn the state of Captain Teshima's feelings for me.
> He is constant, at any rate, for each day he is equally sorry for me, and he is as courteous as he is sorry. He gives me rations for my horses and rice and soy (sauce) and beef for my men—also any information he is at liberty to divulge.[34]

On March 16, the order for his removal arrived. He told Kittredge that he had been sent back to Seoul. The reason for his return, he wrote to the Hearst press and to his mistress, was professional jealousy. His exclusive dispatches and photographs had "raised a commotion" in the home offices of competing newspapers that he had scooped, he said. Those papers' angry telegrams to correspondents who were still stuck in Japan led to protests that London had been given preferential treatment. His description of his plight in the *Examiner* cast himself as the victim of his own rugged individualism in refusing to play the war correspondent's game by anyone's rules but his own: "The dining correspondents at Tokio said to their hosts: 'Here we are. We have been very polite. These other men are at the front, three of them. They are very impolite, yet see how their impoliteness has been rewarded. You must recall them. If you do not recall them, we, too, shall become impolite and dine no more.'" London had no recourse but to submit to authority. He told the *Examiner*, "A war is like a tea party—whoever gives it runs it."[35]

The animosity toward London among the Tokyo-based correspondence may have run deeper than London believed. Walter Kirton of Britain's Central News Agency and veteran of the Boer War[36] blamed Americans with no background in war correspondence for Japan's decision to keep reporters from the front throughout much of 1904. In interviews with reporters in Canada after leaving the Far East, Kirton did not name London or anyone else, but the implication was clear. Of the Americans following the First Army, only London and William H. Brill of the Associated Press had no experience covering war, although Brill had covered a skirmish with the Chippewa. Kirton did not object when a fellow correspondent, war artist J. Sheldon Williams of London's *The Sphere* newspaper, expressly praised the AP correspondents' work. That would appear to have ruled Brill out despite his relatively weak résumé. In contrast, London had no journalism background at all. *The Gazette* of Montreal said Kirton "declared with great emphasis" that responsible civil and military officials told him, not for attribution, that the blame for the restrictions fell entirely on ignorant, "irresponsible and sensational" American newspaper reporters "who knew nothing of war."[37]

London's reports from the front no doubt rankled Kirton, but they were far from being bad journalism. London's audaciousness in refusing to acquiesce to the Ministry of Foreign Affairs, as well as Tokyo's reaction, likely stung more deeply.

The Tokyo-based correspondents' protest helped bring about its desired result. On April 1, sixteen correspondents departed for northern Korea. Despite allowing journalists to enter combat zones, however, Japan had no intention of giving them the freedom to witness actual combat or report freely about it.

When the correspondents arrived in Seoul, London was freed from detention and told to stay with the rest of the press corps. He did so, but as he waited for his chance to return to the front he spent much of his time drinking in a bar.[38] "Eating [his] heart out with inactivity," he focused his anger at what he perceived as the deviousness and suspicion of his Asian hosts. "I'll never go to a war between Orientals again," he told Kittredge on April 1. "The delays and vexation are too great."³⁹

Japan's First Army then gave its permission for London and thirteen reporters remaining from the original sixteen permitted to accompany troops toward the Yalu, but under strict supervision. London said the arrangement "has all the appearance . . . of a [C]ook's tourist proposition."⁴⁰ This time, he noted, "we saw what we were permitted to see, and the chief duty of the officers looking after us was to keep us from seeing anything."⁴¹ A military censor named T. Okada who was assigned to the correspondents often told them little more than, "All is going according to plan." That once prompted London to retort, "Don't forget to tell us if it is not."⁴²

It was easy for the Japanese to monitor the movements of Western correspondents, as they had European features and almost none spoke Korean, Mandarin, or Japanese. The correspondents also had no control over the route or timing of their dispatches to the rear, and the subject matter of their dispatches was limited to information approved by censors. "Leakage" of news to Tokyo was strictly forbidden.⁴³ They were at the mercy of their hosts. Nevertheless, the First Army codified their expected conduct in a three-inch-by-five-inch booklet of regulations specific to that army, which differed slightly from the regulations printed and distributed in Tokyo.

The regulations, which London saved along with his war notebooks, consisted of fourteen articles ranging from the mundane, such as the quartermaster's responsibility for lodging the reporters, to a specific list of do's and don'ts. Article VII said, "Press correspondents shall not go about the battle field except at the time and place shown by the supervising officer or the detachment commander." Article VIII required an official inspection and censorship stamp for all outgoing communications. Most restrictive was Article XI, which said correspondents should not "disturb the public peace" nor dispirit the troops, nor print any details about troop deployment or possible future actions. Article XII required the correspondents to choose a representative to act as a liaison with military headquarters. War correspondent Palmer referred to this bureaucracy of control as "The Great System." Once each day, he said, the representative of the press (given the title "Intelligence Officer in Brigade Waiting"⁴⁴) approached the First Army headquarters to ask for fresh news, which, if he received any, he distributed to his colleagues, "This was like standing outside the inclosure and having a man on the fence tell you who has the ball on whose fifteen-yard line," Palmer wrote.⁴⁵ Not only did it promote a simple, sanitized view of the war, it also defeated the "scoop" system. With each journalist given exactly as much news of the war as his rivals, there was no reward for an adventurous or imaginative correspondent.

The message of the day sometimes contained details, such as an 800-word briefing shared by First Army's chief intelligence officer in early May. It described Chinese civilians looting the bodies of slain Russians after a fierce battle that included Cossacks and Japanese troops fighting hand to hand. Particular details carried the whiff of lies told to benefit Japan. Writing for the *Philadelphia Inquirer*, Oscar King Davis craftily hinted as much in a letter that had passed through Japanese censorship. Summarizing the battle as described by the intelligence officer, Davis noted that the assaulting Japanese force claimed to have suffered far fewer casualties than the entrenched defenders—which would have defied the logic that the offense, being exposed, suffers more gravely in such a situation than the sheltered defense. "The exact number of Russian dead found and buried by the Japanese was given to us as 1362," he wrote. "All reports and estimates of Russian wounded put together did not make a number greater than this." He considered that fact "extraordinary," given the usual ratio of wounded to dead of three to one. The Japanese put the number of their own dead at 165. "This shows how accurate and deadly the Japanese fire must have been," he concluded with a note of sarcasm that apparently got lost in translation.[46]

William Dinwiddie of the *New York World* elaborated on Captain Okada's routine for First Army correspondents. In a dispatch to the *Fourth Estate*, a weekly magazine for American newspaper publishers and advertisers, Dinwiddie wrote:

> We live by the clock. At 10 in the morning Captain Okada will receive one correspondent as a representative of all, and give out any news he may have. At 4 o'clock rations may be drawn for the day. At 5 o'clock food for the horses may be obtained. Between 4 and 5 Captain Okada will censor all telegrams and manuscripts which must first be read to him, line by line, and then he submits them to the higher officers. If they pass muster two red seals appear on the paper, covering the first and last word, and all letters are sealed and stamped with the censor's stamp in his presence.
>
> One correspondent spent two whole days in trying to have his horse's shoes tightened. There were something like ten men's hands through which the matter had to pass before the necessary permission could be secured, and each man had to write or see personally the man ahead of him before the important question could be settled. . . .
>
> One correspondent, particularly bitter against the commanding generals in Cuba and the Philippines [in the Spanish-American War of 1898], was heard to exclaim: "Say, Pussy Shafter and Grandma Otis were real saints in disguise to the Umpty Umps we're up against now."[47]

London felt anger at the restrictions and included in his private notebook various examples of censorship he considered absurd. Over a four-hour period one day, he wrote, reporters took turns trying to worm as much as they could from an intelligence officer, but all they got was, "At some place, not indicated," ten Japanese cavalrymen surrounded two Cossack squadrons and charged with drawn sabers, forcing a retreat. He added that Japanese censors refused to allow one journalist's dispatch to include the dateline "Wiju," apparently reasoning that its occupation was a military secret; however, they allowed the name in the body of a telegram, in which the correspondent described how the Yalu River looked from the town. In another episode that seemed like nonsense, London noted, "One correspondent could not say a bridge was being built—but did say: Japs are working with timbers in the [Yalu] river. I am not permitted to say what they are doing, but I can state that they are not digging a well."[48] These last two episodes, however, might have been attempts at disinformation. Photographer Jimmy Hare of *Collier's Weekly* said the Japanese army attempted to confuse the Russians by conspicuously preparing to build a bridge at Wiju. Under cover of darkness, they removed the timbers and reassembled them farther north, allowing the army across the Yalu with minimal opposition.[49] Perhaps the Japanese censors deliberately cleared for release the information that London had considered a tip-off to any careful reader. Under this scenario, censorship was not inept, but rather clever if rapid dissemination of news from Wiju actually reached the Russian army in a timely manner and was interpreted as indicating construction of a bridge where no bridge was being built.

Once the reporters had written up their versions of such news, the Japanese censors deleted and rewrote portions without allowing the journalists to see the final versions. Even then the censors seldom released the cables quickly for distribution to Western papers. Japan cut off communications with the world outside Korea from April 27 to May 6, London wrote in his war notebook, and he could not be certain that anything he sent to the Hearst press was printed in a timely manner, or even if it had been received at all.[50] A cable written at the front near the Yalu had to be censored, then sent by Korean runner to Pyongyang, where it would be telegraphed to Seoul and from there cabled again to Japan, where bureaucrats might or might not cable it again to the correspondent's paper.[51] Delays are evident in London's description of the first contact between Japan's and Russia's land forces, on March 5, which appeared in the *Examiner* on April 19. Other stories averaged a five-to-six-week delay. From Dandong (Antung, China), they took six weeks to get to New York.[52]

What angered London most was the army's refusal to expedite the release of news of the one major battle that he was close enough to hear and to examine the field after its conclusion. The Battle of Wiju lasted from April 26, when the sound of Japanese rifle fire awakened London at 5 a.m., to May 1, when the Japanese crossed the Yalu River. Not until May 9, seven days after the army's official communiqués of the battle were printed in Tokyo newspapers and cabled throughout the world, did the army share with London and his colleagues the details of the fight in which Russian field guns tried unsuccessfully to repulse a Japanese crossing into Manchuria.[53] London's report on the artillery duel at the Yalu appeared in the *Examiner* on June 4, five weeks after its conclusion. "If other nations in future wars imitate the Japanese in this, the 'cable' men would cease to exist," he wrote to the Hearst press. "The regular newsgatherers in the capitals of the contending countries would serve the purpose just as well and a great deal better."[54]

Nevertheless, London managed to sneak away on his own and crossed the Yalu on horseback. He arrived after a skirmish at Kulien Cheng and looked down upon multitudes of dead and wounded Japanese as well as four hundred Russian prisoners as he rode toward the town of Dandong. The First Army placed the number of Japanese battle casualties at one thousand, he said. He wondered whether any Western general would have ordered the frontal attack that had won the battle. The Russians could easily have been outflanked and forced to surrender; however, London speculated that the Japanese officers had ordered the assault knowing full well its cost. The patriotic press of the home islands demanded only victory, he said, and paid no mind the amount of spilled blood as a Western newspaper would have done. In addition, he said Japan likely had wanted to seize its first opportunity to show the world that face to face, it could whip the Russian army. At Dandong, an English-speaking Japanese man in civilian clothes seemed to confirm as much, telling London: "Your people did not think we could beat the white; we have beaten the white."[55]

In addition to delays, London's telegraphed dispatches faced rigorous, repeated censorship. At the Yalu River, he gave his stories to a runner, who took them to the next in a line of runners London and other correspondents had set up to connect with Pyongyang. The news was censored at the Yalu and at the Japanese army's field telegraph office in Pyongyang, which forwarded it to Seoul. From there, London recalled, "[i]t was censored and censored and finally reached Tokio [*sic*] by wire, where it was again subjected to censorship. Every censor who could take a whack at it did so. There wasn't much left of it by the time it reached my papers."[56]

London poured out his frustration in letters home. On May 6, he said, "Whatever I have done I am ashamed of. The only compensation . . . is a better comprehension of Asiatic geography and Asiatic character." And on May 8, he wrote, "The insane state of affairs I find myself in, the restrictions, the inability in any way to get in touch with things (& not my fault)—make my stuff the rot it is. It will require another war, & a white man's war, for me to redeem myself."[57] His letters reflected a change in his opinions of the Japanese—at least those opinions that he committed to paper—commensurate with the change in his degree of freedom. Whereas in early March he had reported that the Japanese were the most "peaceable, orderly" soldiers in the world, "a race of warriors" and "their infantry is all their infantry could possibly be,"[58] by May he privately was cursing them as "absurd," "ridiculously childish," "savages," and narrow-minded opportunists who adopt "our science, but nothing else."[59] Palmer quoted him as privately denigrating the bravery he once had extolled in print: the Japanese "may be brave, but so are the South American peccary pigs in their herd charges."[60] Although a socialist, London paradoxically was also a racist, believing in the moral superiority of white people. His initial contacts with Japan, during a seal-hunting voyage in 1893, had been positive, but his growing racism, fueled by his readings of Friedrich Nietzsche and Benjamin Kidd, drew strength from his experiences during the 1904 war.[61]

Like London, Frederick Palmer saw a group mentality, a manifestation of national unity, in the ordinary Japanese soldier, but without the mindless and mechanical reactions his fellow correspondent inferred. Instead, Palmer saw devotion to the nation and emperor as expressed through the modern interpretation of *bushidō*, the ancient code of the samurai that valued loyalty, courage, and honor unto death. Palmer said a Japanese officer always knew that his soldiers would stay where he ordered them—"alive or dead." That was true of a unit of any size, and of Japanese troops from any social rank or province. Soldiers were as alike as "peas in a pod," he wrote. "No special units; no Rough Riders; no King's own. . . . A commander may choose a unit at hand as a mechanic takes down any number of equally tempered tools from a rack. If you want a Horatius at the Bridge, take the nearest first sergeant."[62]

The First Army permitted London and the other correspondents to cross the Yalu into Manchuria in early May but further restricted their movements and access to information. At a camp at Fengcheng (Feng Hwang Cheng), the journalists found their movements limited to a circle with a radius of a mile and half surrounding a grove of trees and a temple. There was nothing for them to do, for days at a time, except to swim, play bridge, and protest daily to be allowed to see something worthwhile to report, London noted.[63] The Western correspondents composed a telegram to their employers that all signed; the text is preserved in the London archives at Utah State University. Addressed to wire services and newspapers in England, the United States, and France, it explained the impossibility of filing timely and independently reported stories and asked for instructions. Restrictions that prevented observation made them feel "useless," the correspondents said. But the telegram was never sent. It, like some of the journalists' news dispatches, was "sidetracked" by the censors, London said.[64] Another draft of the telegram appears in London's papers, although he did not record whether the correspondents ever attempted to send it as written to their editors. This second version, in London's handwriting, said the correspondents foresaw little chance of improvement in their ability to cover the war, blaming strict censorship, lack of independent observation, and the "fact that official information is furnished here after publication in Tokio."[65]

Disgusted, London decided he had had enough of Japanese censorship. There was nothing for him to see or write about except "the woes of correspondents, swimming pools and peaceful temple scenes."[66] He appealed to Hearst to allow him to transfer to the Russian side of the war, but he did not get the chance. Before his request could be considered, Japanese officers angrily arrested him again. His offense: punching one of his Japanese assistants in frustration.[67] He had accused the aide of stealing fodder meant for London's horse. His release came only after the personal intervention of President Theodore Roosevelt.[68] After being freed, London started for home.

London tried to blame what he perceived to be his failure as a war correspondent on the differences between Japanese and Westerners, as if the new censorship were a peculiarly Asian plot. Japan did not understand the workings of a war reporter's mind, "which are a white man's mental processes," he wrote in his private notebook. "The Japanese is of a military race. His old castle [sic] distinctions placed the fighting man at the top; next comes the peasant; after that the merchant; and beneath all the scribe."[69]

In fact, the new control was not uniquely Eastern. In previous wars, in which journalists were allowed more freedom to roam the battlefield, they still could not single-handedly observe and judge conditions of the big picture—strategy and tactics along a wide front. They relied partly on the expertise of others as well as their own analysis. The basic situation was the same in Japan; reporters at least traveled with the army and were housed close enough to observe the edge of the front and occasionally hear or glimpse the fringes of combat. The main difference in Asia was that the correspondents' supervising military officers were unwilling to provide facts, and the journalists were forbidden to speculate in the absence of such facts. Journalists could not attempt to covertly interview soldiers because of the language barriers. Forced to rely on second-hand information, reporters became, if not the allies of the Japanese war effort, at least not a threat to that effort.

Japan's censorship of the dispatches of Jack London and his colleagues demonstrated the power inherent in the control of access to information coupled with control of access to the channels through which information could be shared. Desiring war reports that would bolster the home front—and possibly deceive the enemy—Japanese military authorities shepherded foreign journalists near the combat zones but allowed them only to report on approved subjects, with approved phrasing, and at approved times. The result, in Japan, was to create the appearance of an ostensibly objective (foreign) news media whose dispatches corroborated the image of combat that previously had been selected for emphasis by Japanese authorities and distributed by government channels. That is, Japan tried to have its cake and eat it too:

to have the benefit of reporters reinforcing domestic harmony during wartime, without the potentially detrimental effects of unsupervised, uncensored coverage. It helped, of course, that Japan never lost a land battle during the war and that the most serious setbacks occurred on warships that had no Westerner observers on board.

Japan had taken censorship far beyond the mere negative function of preventing the escape of sensitive information to the enemy. The Japanese ministries of War and Foreign Affairs emphasized a constructive function of shaping war news from nongovernmental observers to fit governmental purposes.

Jack London's problems did not end when he boarded the SS *Korea* to take him home to Oakland. Before he could step onto the California dock, a lawyer handed him a summons to answer a bill of divorcement from his estranged wife, Elizabeth Madden "Bess" London. He read through the document until a group of his friends arrived bearing copies of newspapers containing accounts of what one paper called his "matrimonial complications." London indicated that he probably would not contest his wife's suit and then turned to answering reporters' questions about his experiences as a war correspondent. He told reporters that he probably would write a book about his experiences, although he never did.

"I am glad to be home. . . . You see I went out there on a vacation," London said. "I am not a journalist in any sense of the word, only a writer of books and stories."[70]

London underestimated the quality of his work. He chastised himself for not getting to see actual combat. But combat in a modern, mechanized war had reached a scale beyond the abilities of a single journalist to observe firsthand, much less distill into word pictures of valorous and heroic deeds. The world of wars between nations, and of the correspondents who covered them, had moved on from the romantic template London had expected. A new model would arise in the twentieth century, and it is fitting that Jack London, one of the greatest wordsmiths of his day, helped inaugurate it at the century's beginning. That model, still prevalent today, became common when women war correspondents of the Spanish Civil War and World War II turned to stories of people caught up in war because the female journalists were forbidden by the armed forces to cover combat itself. Their response to the restrictions was to focus on the lives of individuals, both in uniform and in civilian clothes, as they faced what war brought them. Staff officers can give the summaries of how many miles of territory were gained or lost and how many men were killed, captured, or missing. Only the journalist can put a human face on war, and London did that in his personal accounts of his travels, conflicts with censors, and life among the correspondent corps. His only failure was that he wished there was more "war" in his war correspondence. But that was beyond his power to make happen.

London wrote well about his life as a correspondent and about the people he met in Korea because that was his trade as a novelist. He had completed five novels and dozens of short stories before departing for the Far East. He would finish seventeen more novels upon his return to California, including the critically acclaimed *White Fang* and *Martin Eden*. In 1915, one year before he died of uremia at age forty, London wrote a most unusual novel. *The Star Rover*, known as *The Jacket* in the United Kingdom, tells of a prisoner trussed tightly in a jacket as a form of punishment. The prisoner learns to tap previously undiscovered mental powers to detach his spirit from his body and place it in other places and times. One of the eras he visits is medieval Korea, where he is mistreated and jailed. The protagonist learns Korea's language, music, and points of view, and nearly wins a fistfight single-handedly against a horde of Koreans, earning him the nickname "the Mighty." He rises to prominence only to be laid low and abused for forty years by an enemy he has made. The form of punishment reads remarkably like the journalistic torture that London felt in Korea: never permitted to escape, neither across the northern frontier into China nor by sampan across the sea. For most of his time in Korea, the protagonist of the story lived as a marked man.[71]

NOTES

1. Jack London, "Jack London Tells about His Arrest," *Pittsburgh (PA) Press*, February 28, 1904.

2. A version of this chapter appeared in *Journalism and Mass Communication Quarterly* 75, no. 3 (Autumn 1998), 548–59. This revised and expanded version is printed here with copyright permission of the Association for Education in Journalism and Mass Communication, Columbia, South Carolina.

3. Jack London, "Japanese Officers Consider Everything a Military Secret," *San Francisco Examiner*, June 26, 1904.

4. While Jack London's fiction and poetry have been the subject of much scholarship, little has been written about his war correspondence. For London's published correspondence, see Earle Labor, Robert C. Leitz, and I. Milo Shepard, eds. *The Letters of Jack London*, vol. 1 (Stanford, CA: Stanford University Press, 1993). For biographies, see Alex Kershaw, *Jack London: A Life* (New York, St. Martin's Press, 1999); Richard O'Connor, *Jack London: A Biography* (Boston: Little, Brown, 1964); and Andrew Sinclair, *Jack: A Biography of Jack London* (New York: Harper & Row, 1977). The best modern biography is Earle Labor, *Jack London: An American Life* (New York: Farrar, Straus, and Giroux, 2013). O'Connor's biography includes a chapter on the Russo-Japanese War based on four dispatches to the *San Francisco Examiner* and two books by war correspondent Frederick Palmer, *With My Own Eyes: A Personal Story of Battle Years* (Indianapolis: Bobbs-Merrill Company, 1933), and *With Kuroki in Manchuria* (New York: Charles Scribner's Sons, 1906).

5. "Regulations for Press Correspondents, the First Army Headquarters," box 20, folder 1, Jack and Charmian London Papers (henceforth JCLP), Special Collections, Utah State University, Logan. The regulations also appear in an out-of-print collection of London's letters and war correspondence: Jack London, King Hendricks, and I. Milo Shepard, *Jack London Reports: War Correspondence, Sports Articles, and Miscellaneous Writings* (Garden City, NY: Doubleday, 1970), 25–26. The Utah State collection of London's papers contains many original documents, including war notes and the above regulations, as well as photocopies of documents from the London archive at the Henry E. Huntington Library in San Marino, California. The California archive contains an extensive collection of photographs that London took during the war. These are available for viewing online through the Huntington Digital Library.

6. Knightley, *The First Casualty*, 61. Knightley notes that reporters for the *Times* of London occasionally served as government information agents.

7. Shumpei Okamoto, *The Japanese Oligarchy and the Russo-Japanese War* (New York: Columbia University Press, 1970), 126.

8. Jack London wrote several semi-biographical works of fiction, including *John Barleycorn* and *Martin Eden*.

9. "Japanese Officers Consider Everything a Military Secret."

10. Sinclair, *Jack: A Biography of Jack London*, 102.

11. Ibid.; and Jack London to George P. Brett, January 7, 1904, box 3, folder 3, JCLP.

12. Jack London to Cloudesley Johns, January 7, 1904, box 2, folder 8, JCLP.

13. "The Siberia Held for War Correspondents by Harriman's Order," *San Francisco Examiner*, January 8, 1904; Jack London to Charmian Kittredge, January 15, 1904; and London to Kittredge, January 28, 1904. Both letters are in box 2, folder 12, JCLP.

14. Palmer, *With My Own Eyes*, 237; and O'Connor, *Jack London*, 206–7.

15. Jack London, "July 1st [1904]," unpublished notes, box 22, folder 15, JCLP.

16. Jack London to Charmian Kittredge, February 3, 1904, box 2, folder 12, JCLP; and O'Connor, *Jack London*, 208.

17. Frederick Arthur McKenzie, *From Tokyo to Tiflis: Uncensored Letters from the War* (London: Hurst and Blackett, Ltd., 1905), 12; and London, "Jack London Tells about His Arrest."

18. Ibid.; Richard O'Connor, *Jack London: A Biography* (Boston: Little, Brown, 1964), 208; Jack London to Charmian Kittredge, February 3, 1904, box 2, folder 12, Jack and Charmian London Papers, Special Collections, Utah State University, Logan, Utah; and ibid., 245–46.

19. Griscom, *Diplomatically Speaking*, 246.

20. Jack London to Charmian Kittredge, February 9, 1904, box 2, folder 12, JCLP; and "How Jack London Went to the Front," *San Francisco Examiner*, April 17, 1904.

21. "How Jack London Went to the Front"; "Troubles of War Correspondent in Starting for the Front," *San Francisco Examiner*, April 4, 1904; "Royal Road a Sea of Mud," *San Francisco Examiner*, April 7, 1904; "How Jack London Went to the Front: The Novelist Took Great Chances Quite as a Matter of Course," *Pittsburgh Press*, May 7, 1904; and "How the Hermit Kingdom Behaves in Time of War," *San Francisco Examiner*, April 17, 1904.

22. "Troubles of War Correspondent in Starting for the Front."

23. London, "July 1st [1904]."

24. F[rederick] A[rthur] McKenzie, "The Little Brown Man Laughs at Trouble," *The* (Chanute, KS) *Sun*, July 19, 1904.

25. McKenzie, *From Tokyo to Tiflis*, 40. "Lewis" most likely was Lewis Etzel, an American who wrote for the London *Daily Telegraph* and was killed by Chinese soldiers three months later. The only war correspondent in the Far East with the last name of Lewis was Willmott Harsant Lewis, but he wrote for the *New York Herald*. See Bryna Kranzler, "The Accidental Anarchist: Eyewitness Account of the Russo-Japanese War," https://www.theaccidentalanarchist.com/eyewitness-account/.

26. "Troubles of War Correspondent in Starting for the Front"; and "Men Who Are at the Front," *The Hawaiian Star*, March 7, 1904.

27. Ibid.; Jack London, "Japan's Invasion of Korea, as Seen by Jack London," *San Francisco Examiner*, March 4, 1904; "Japanese Army's Equipment Excites Great Admiration," *San Francisco Examiner*, April 3, 1904; "Royal Road a Sea of Mud"; and "How the Hermit Kingdom Behaves in Time of War."

28. Jack London, "Troops in Korea Highly Praised," *San Francisco Examiner*, April 3, 1904. The story was datelined Pyongyang, March 5.

29. Jack London, notes appended to a letter, C. Chinjo to Jack London, March 9, 1904, box 2, folder 12, JCLP. It is unclear whether London sent Kittredge a copy of the letter from Chinjo, acting consul, or whether he shared with her his appended notes. Chinjo's letter appears amid the collection of London's letters to Kittredge.

30. Jack London, "Cossacks Eight Then Retreat," *San Francisco Examiner*, April 19, 1904.

31. Jack London to Charmian Kittredge, March 9, 1904; and Jack London to Charmian Kittredge, March 11, 1904. Both are in box 2, folder 12, JCLP.

32. Jack London to George P. Brett, April 3, 1904, box 3, folder 3, JCLP.

33. "How the Hermit Kingdom Behaves in Time of War."

34. Ibid.

35. Jack London, "'Examiner' Writer Sent Back to Seoul," *San Francisco Examiner*, April 25, 1904.

36. "Maj Walter Kirton," Find a Grave, https://www.findagrave.com/memorial/117027507/walter-kirton.

37. "From Seat of War: British War Correspondents on Their Way Home," *The Gazette* (Montreal, QC), July 13, 1904; and "Why Ban Was Placed on Correspondents," *Spokane* (WA) *Chronicle*, July 13, 1904.

38. O'Connor, *Jack London*, 214.

39. Jack London to Charmian Kittredge, April 1, 1904, box 2, folder 12, JCLP.

40. Jack London to George P. Brett, April 3, 1904; and London, "July 1st [1904]." A "Cook's tour" was a nickname for a group tour conducted by the British travel agency Thomas Cook & Son.

41. London, "July 1st [1904]."

42. Palmer, *With My Own Eyes*, 239.

43. Jack London, "Jap-Russ War Notes," (personal notebook), box 20, folder 4, JCLP.

44. Oscar King Davis, "Across-the-Yalu Conditions as Found by Japan's First Army under Kuroki," *Philadelphia Inquirer*, July 3, 1904.

45. Palmer, *With Kuroki in Manchuria*, 221.

46. Davis, "Across-the-Yalu Conditions as Found by Japan's First Army under Kuroki."

47. "The Woes of the Poor War Correspondents: They Are All Longing for the Good Old Days of Shafter and Otis," *The Fourth Estate: A Weekly Newspaper for Publishers, Advertisers, Advertising Agents and Allied Interests* 544 (July 30, 1904): 12. William Rufus Shafter and Elwell Stephen Otis were much-maligned generals in the Spanish-American War.

48. London, "Jap-Russ War Notes."

49. James H. Hare, *A Photographic Record of the Russo-Japanese War* (New York: P.F. Collier & Son, 1905), 81.

50. London, "Jap-Russ War Notes."

51. "Japanese Officers Consider Everything a Military Secret."

52. Frederick Palmer, "With the First Japanese Army in Manchuria," *Collier's Weekly*, May 28, 1904, 11.

53. Jack London, "Japanese in Invisible War," *San Francisco Examiner*, June 12, 1904; Jack London, "Jack London's Graphic Story of the Japs Driving Russians across the Yalu River," *San Francisco Examiner*, June 4, 1904; London, "Jap-Russ War Notes"; and London, "July 1st [1904]."

54. "Japanese Officers Consider Everything a Military Secret."

55. Jack London, "'Have Beaten the White': Race Question in the War as It Impressed a Correspondent," *Baltimore Sun*, June 13, 1904.

56. "Jack London Returns from the Battlefield," *The Pacific Commercial Advertiser* (Honolulu), June 24, 1904.

57. Jack London to Charmian Kittredge, May 6, 1904, box 2, folder 12, JCLP; and London to Johns, May 8, 1904, box 2, folder 8, JCLP.

58. "Japan's Invasion of Korea, as Seen by Jack London."

59. Jack London to Charmian Kittredge, May 22, 1904, box 2, folder 12, JCLP; Jack London to George P. Brett, June 4, 1904, box 3, folder 3, JCLP; and London, "Jap-Russ War Notes."

60. Palmer, *With My Own Eyes*, 241–42.

61. Joan London, *Jack London and His Times: An Unconventional Biography* (Seattle: University of Washington Press, 1939), 210–12; and O'Connor, *Jack London*, 121–22. Upon London's return from Japan, other Socialists called him to account for his espousing the seemingly contradictory philosophies of racial superiority and the international brotherhood of working people. London's response at an autumn 1904 gathering of Socialists in Oakland was to say, "What the devil! I am first of all a white man and only then a Socialist," according to eyewitness Edmundo Peluso. See London, *Jack London and His Times*, 284.

62. Palmer, *With Kuroki in Manchuria*, 167–68.

63. London, "July 1st [1904]."

64. Ibid.

65. "Next to Last Joint Telegram," May 14, 1904, box 20, folder 4, JCLP.

66. London, "July 1st [1904]"; and Jack London to George P. Brett, June 1, 1904, box 3, folder 3, JCLP.

67. London, *Jack London and His Times*, 285.

68. Rotem Kowner, *Historical Dictionary of the Russo–Japanese War* (Lanham, MD: Scarecrow Press, 2006), 212.

69. London, "July 1st [1904]."

70. "Jack London Returns from Orient but Says It Is Not to Fight Wife's Suite for Divorce," *San Francisco Call*, July 1, 1904.

71. Jack London, *The Star-Rover* (New York: McMillan, 1915).

Chapter 4

John Fox Jr.

Their predominating defect is their aptitude not to tell the truth; it runs in the people from the major-general down, excepting perhaps the private, for I have never been intimate enough with him to know.

—John Fox Jr., 1904[1]

After having traveled thousands of miles and waiting five months to go to war, John Fox Jr., his friend Richard Harding Davis, and a handful of other war correspondents reached the Chinese village of Haicheng, about five miles from the nearest Russian soldiers and a short march from the headquarters of Count Oku Yasukata, commanding general of the Imperial Japanese Second Army. They hoped to finally see battle as members of the second detachment of foreign war correspondents allowed into the war zone. However, restrictions placed on the correspondents did not encourage optimism. Japanese officers censored their letters and dispatches but did not return them or reveal what they might have removed. Wearing a white armband displaying Japanese characters in red to distinguish them from Russian soldiers, the Western reporters, artists, and photographers could wander freely within Haicheng's outer walls but could not leave the city without gaining approval via written application. Even then, three guards shadowed the correspondents' every movement and tried to keep them from seeing anything that might portray the Japanese in a negative light. But there was hope. Some managed to escape the guards for a short while and, Fox wrote, "testified that they received nothing but courtesy, kindness, and child-like curiosity from the Japanese Tommy always."[2]

General Oku welcomed the correspondents by sending them a gift no doubt designed to promote warm relations: one dozen bottles of champagne, four dozen bottles of beer, one package of fly paper, and a live sheep to be butchered for meat. The sheep died of natural causes before it could be butchered, but the drinks and flypaper "are all the heart could desire," Fox wrote. A short while later, the correspondents' three guards told them to prepare to visit Oku's camp. All dressed for the occasion, with Davis and two others placing ribbons on the left side of their chests and Fox, lacking such decorations, adorning himself with a Virginia volunteer policeman's badge. A lieutenant escorted the party to a grape arbor, under which sat two tables covered with cigars and cigarettes. An interpreter introduced them to Oku and another visitor to the front, Prince Nashimoto Morimasa, who served as a captain on Oku's staff.

Fox considered Oku to be "the most remarkable man I've seen thus far among the Japanese." His dress was simple—olive green serge augmented by a single star on his cap and three stars and three stripes on his sleeve. His face had the sadness of Abraham Lincoln's. And his eyes—mercurial, big, and black—made one think of "lightning and thunder-storms" when they moved. After the correspondents thanked Oku for the gifts, he asked them questions through his interpreter. Their answers hinted at their frustration at not having seen battle after having been delayed in the Japanese home islands for almost a half-year. Oku began by asking:

"How long have you been in Japan?"
"More than five months." He laughed and his teeth were not good.
"You must know Tokio [sic] well."
"I know every stone in Tokio," somebody said.
The General did not smile at this time. . . .
"Shall we see much fighting?"
"I think so—from a high place. You cannot see in the valleys—the kow-liang
 [millet] is too high to see over even on horseback. Yes, you will see the fight."[3]

But neither Fox nor Davis would ever get any closer than three miles from the Russian army. Their response was one of bitterness and regret for what they saw as wasted time and opportunity, and confusion and anger at the Japanese. Why would Japan welcome Western journalists to a war zone but prevent them from actually seeing battle? Fox found it a conundrum. For a better alternative, he wrote in the voice of an imaginary Japanese officer explaining a scenario in which all outside journalists were barred from the scene of battle:

"This is the business of Japan and Russia alone. Over here we don't recognize the Occidental European right of the newspaper to divulge the private purposes of anybody. We believe that war correspondents are harmful to the proper conduct of a war. Frankly, we don't want you out to the front, you can never go to it." That would have been a manly course. We could have had no just complaint.[4]

Unlike the other correspondents, after returning to the United States Fox received a detailed explanation and apology from a high-ranking Japanese diplomat. The apologist said that ignorant officers in the field failed to execute the accommodationist policies of the General Staff. And having learned from its mistakes, Japan would open up the war zone to those who followed Fox and Davis in the third and final wave of war correspondents, as well as correspondents such as Luigi Barzini who moved with the second wave, remained for many months despite the initial frustrations, and earned the trust of their Japanese hosts. So, too, did Frederick Palmer embed with the troops long enough at Liaoyang to win the confidence of Commander in Chief Oyama Gentarō and his staff officers; Oyama provided him at the end of the summer of 1904 with documents providing Palmer special privileges.[5]

Fox might have considered his war correspondence from the Russo-Japanese War—consisting of six dispatches published in *Scribner's Magazine*—to be a failure. His biographer thought otherwise, praising the quality of Fox's writing. An independent assessment would suggest Fox could take solace in three qualities of his correspondence: his keen observations about the face of war on the home front, the rollicking narrative of his travels through rough and broken country, and his impact on future reporting of the war. Fox, like Davis, was one of the most popular American writers of his day, acclaimed for his Appalachian novels *A Mountain Europa* and the *Little Shepherd of Kingdom Come*. His face and voice were recognized in cities throughout the nation via the years he spent on the lecture circuit, reading from his works and talking in hired halls to paying audiences. Japan apparently figured it had suffered a propaganda defeat through publication of the anger-filled dispatches of such famous war correspondents as Davis and Fox, and sought to rectify its error. However, as will be seen, the written apology failed in many ways to account for the treatment Fox received during his stay in East Asia.

John William Fox Jr. took a long and twisted road to being a war correspondent. He was born on December 16, 1862, in Bourbon County, Kentucky, not long after fierce fighting during the Civil War brought the border state under Union control. His father, John Fox Sr., was a once-widowed schoolteacher; his mother the former Minerva Worth Carr. John Junior was the first of seven children who supplemented three half brothers from the senior Fox's first marriage.[6] As one might expect, a family with ten children living on a teacher's pay had to make the family income stretch as far as it could. Still, John Senior cultivated ambition and curiosity in his children, and John Fox Jr. thrived in school. He passed Harvard University's entrance examinations in 1878, when he was fifteen years old, but lacked money to pay the tuition bills. Instead, he enrolled at the prestigious Kentucky University—now known as Transylvania University—in Lexington. The school pushed students to study Latin and Greek, and many took classes in theology. John excelled in his studies, retook the Harvard entrance test, and enrolled in the fall of 1880 at age seventeen. His classes put him on track to a legal career, but as graduation approached he had second thoughts about becoming a lawyer. He spent a summer earning money through hard labor, swinging a pick in the coalmines of Jellico, on the Kentucky-Tennessee border.[7] It was there he immersed himself in the culture of Kentucky mountain men and women, who would appear in various guises in his later novels. He then returned to Harvard and completed his studies, graduating *cum laude* in 1883 as the youngest of his class.[8] Not sure what to do but unwilling to return immediately to Kentucky, Fox decided to try his hand at being a newspaper reporter.

He started work at the *New York Sun*, a serious daily broadsheet known for being the first mass-circulation paper to sell for a penny starting with its first edition in 1833. By the time Fox arrived, the *Sun* was edited by the capable Charles Dana, who demanded clear, condensed news of all facets of New York life, including crime and court stories that the *Sun* had pioneered before the Civil War.[9] The work was difficult, often lasting sixteen hours per day with no days off, and paid $15 per week. Fox thought at first he would work only a short while before starting law school, but the thrill of finding and writing stories on deadline appealed to him and made him think of staying. "The excitement in it is very fascinating to me," he said, echoing generations of reporters who responded to the thrill of chasing down an exciting story on deadline. Fox learned how to craft prose that would appeal to readers, which was a necessity in the cutthroat journalistic competition of New York City. According to Bill York, Fox's biographer, Fox interviewed "murderers, robbers, prostitutes, pick-pockets, wife beaters, drunks, and policemen who were all too ready to use their clubs on criminals and reporters alike."[10] His night city editor applauded his style, saying, "Fox can write."[11] Publishing good stories excited Fox, but the daily grind and constant engagement with New York's dark underside began to wear him down. Fox left the *Sun* to try his hand at Columbia Law School, then gave that up in 1884 for a job at the *New York Times*, where his salary rose to $26 a week. Again, he grew tired of covering courts and crimes. He realized that working for the *Times* honed his narrative skills—he was particularly praised for his selection of details—and that he would be happiest as a serious writer. He left the *Times* and returned to Kentucky to write stories, poems, and, eventually, novels.[12]

For the next six years, Fox combined writing with a family mining business, real estate speculation, teaching school, and tutoring young students. His first big break as a writer came in 1890 when *Century* magazine agreed to serialize his novelette *A Mountain Europa* and to pay him $262—the equivalent of $7,000 in the early twenty-first century. Numerous short stories set in his native Appalachia followed in print, including "A Cumberland Vendetta," "The Last Stetson," "Through the Gap," and "Hell-fer-Sartin." Having made a name for himself in fiction, Fox took to the lecture circuit, reading and speaking to audiences about Appalachia and its people. Booked into mostly small-town venues by the Southern Lyceum Bureau, Fox finally secured a steady income with work that he enjoyed. *Harper's* published his first novel, *The Kentuckians*, to critical acclaim in 1897. Audiences' growing familiarity with his work no doubt helped push his novel *Little Shepherd of Kingdom Come*, which appeared in 1903, to become the first novel printed in the United States to sell one million copies. [13]

Before that, though, Fox traveled to Cuba in 1898 during the Spanish-American War to try his hand at war correspondence. His traveling companion was his best friend, Richard Harding Davis, whom Fox had met on the lecture circuit. Fox initially toyed with the idea of becoming a U.S. soldier and fighting against the Spanish army. His friend Theodore Roosevelt, who admired Fox's books and stories, offered him a place in the unit that would become the Rough Riders. But Fox turned down that offer in order to write under contract for *Harper's Weekly* magazine. He left Tampa, Florida, on June 14, 1898, on the *Iroquois* with *Harper's Weekly* illustrator Frederic Remington and landed eight days later at Daiquiri on the southern coast of Cuba. Davis accompanied a second landing to the west, at Siboney. The Spaniards had abandoned both landing sites, leading to an easy, almost festive, start to the invasion. Armed resistance began as the troops began marching inland and turning toward the Spanish stronghold of Santiago. Fox and Remington arrived at Las Guásimas, site of the first battle, after the shooting ended there. (Davis, who had beaten Fox to the jungle trail at Las Guásimas, not only reported on the exchange of gunfire but also fired a rifle in defense of American troops pinned down by snipers. The dense cover of the *guásimas*, or West Indian elm trees, hid the Spanish riflemen who had sprung the trap.) Fox initially despaired of seeing actual combat, but he need not have worried. On July 1, he took a position with American troops near San Juan and El Caney in the line of expected fire from Spanish defenses anchored at a blockhouse. Artillery exchanges preceded the charge of Roosevelt's Rough Riders to capture Kettle Hill during the Battle of San Juan Hill. Fox recorded the first boom of the American cannon with his trademark narrative detail:

> There was a cap explosion at the butt of the gun, a bulging white cloud from the muzzle, the trail bounced from its shallow trench, and the wheels whirled back twice on the rebound, and the shell was hissing through the air as iron hisses when a blacksmith thrusts it red-hot into cold water. You could hear the awful hiss so plainly that you seemed to be following the shell with your naked eye; you could hear it above the reverberating roar of the gun up and down the coast mountain; hear it until six seconds later a puff of smoke answered beyond the Spanish column where the shell burst. [14]

Davis won the reportorial laurels for his account of Roosevelt's charge for the *New York Herald*, which captured the public's imagination and helped launch Roosevelt's national political career. But Fox also acquitted himself well, particularly in his account of the casualties of combat. A procession of wounded filed to the rear as he watched, horror-stricken by the dismemberment and blood. "Men staggering along unaided," he wrote, "or between two comrades, or borne on litters, some white and quiet, some groaning and blood-stained, some conscious, some dying, some using a rifle for support, or a stick thrust through the side of a tomato-can, and not a crutch to be seen."[15] He wrote to his family that the sight deeply affected him. "I shall not wish, or need, to see it again."[16]

In addition to his visceral reaction to the death and destruction of war, Fox contracted typhoid fever and ran a high temperature. He returned to the United States after serving sixty-four days as a correspondent and earning $1,200 for his articles ($32,000 in the early twenty-first century) and a per-diem of $10. While he had vowed never to cover war again, he found himself missing the camaraderie with the officers and his fellow correspondents. And, like many who go to war, he found himself restless upon his return to his quiet home.[17] He came back to descriptions of war in his later novels, including *Crittenden* in 1900 and *Little Shepherd of Kingdom Come*. He set the former in the Spanish-American War and the latter during the Civil War. In *Crittenden*, he invented a war correspondent character named Grafton and had him react and speak as Fox had done in Cuba. Grafton, he wrote,

> was wondering how it would feel to be under fire, when just as they were crossing another road, with a whir and whistle and buzz, a cloud of swift insects buzzed over his head. Unconsciously imitating the soldiers near him, he bent low and walked rapidly. Right and left of him sounded two or three low, horrible crunching noises, and right and left of him two or three blue shapes sank limply down on their faces. A sudden sickness seized him, nauseating him like a fetid odor—the crunching noise was the sound of a bullet crashing into a living human skull as the men bent forward.

One man grunted, another cried out, and a third hopped out of the line of fire. A fourth, lying on the ground, told Grafton, "I've got it, partner . . . I reckon I've got it sure."[18] Grafton concluded he worked in a "ghastly business" and that he would not go to war again unless as a soldier.[19]

And yet when war came again four years later, Fox answered the call. *Scribner's Magazine* wanted one of its most popular writers at the front and asked Fox to go. According to York, Fox did not hesitate to agree despite his previous misgivings about witnessing carnage—he wanted to see Japan, he was in high spirits about his success as a writer, and he knew that Davis had already accepted an invitation from his publisher, *Collier's Weekly*, to be a war correspondent.[20] In his introduction to a book of his collected, edited dispatches, published after his return from East Asia, Fox explained his motivation:

> Not being a military expert, my purpose was simply to see under the flag the brown little "gun-man"—as he calls himself in his own tongue—in camp and on the march, in trench and in open field, in assault and in retreat; to tell tales of his heroism, chivalry, devotion, sacrifice, incomparable patriotism; to see him fighting, wounded—and, since such things in war must be—dying, dead.[21]

In this regard, he resembled Jack London, who had been called to war by the newspaper chain forged in the late nineteenth and early twentieth centuries by William Randolph Hearst Jr. London, who had never covered a war before going to Japan, had expected thrills.[22]

Fox left San Francisco, bound for Yokohama, Japan, on February 23, 1904, aboard the Pacific Mail Company steamer SS *China*. Also on board were Davis and his wife, Cecil. Davis and Fox found that time passed quickly and uneventfully (aside from Fox's seasickness) as they became even closer friends on the voyage. Davis would later describe Fox as "one of the best of men." After more than two weeks, including a layover in Hawaii, the *China* arrived at Yokohama on March 13.[23]

While waiting to go to the front, Fox traveled widely through the main Japanese island of Honshu. He wrote to his mother that he found Japan to be a "funny land" occupied by "funny people. Everything is miniature."[24] He considered Tokyo objectionably odorous, but otherwise expressed admiration in his initial impressions. "This is a wonderful little country. . . . My brain is still dizzy with the strange sights and impressions that I hardly know where to begin." He was enamored by the beautiful silk kimonos of the women and the low prices of merchandise—half of what similar goods would cost in the United States. A grove of cherry trees, in full bloom in April, looked like "one big flower" from a distance. One famous cherry tree was as "big as a poplar at the corner of our porch at home and its branches bend and droop like a willow."[25]

Fox wrote two dispatches to *Scribner's Magazine* describing the home front before he left for the Asian mainland. In the first, he described the muted impact of war on Japanese civilians. "It is not the Japanese custom" to shout or to march in parade, he was told.[26] Support for the war found quieter ways of expression that Fox detailed. Hundreds of thousands of Japanese skipped one meal each day in order to give more to the war effort, he said. Women gave up their hairdressing appointment once a month and donated the money they saved to the nation's defense. Servants of a particular nobleman donated a portion of their wages each month to national defense; when their employer found out and offered to raise their wages to make up the difference, they refused. A woman arrived late for a dinner party—a breach of etiquette—but offered as an excuse that she had to see her four sons ship out for the front. "How fortunate," a guest told her, "to be able to give four sons to Japan!" When the bodies of soldiers killed in action returned to the train stations of their home prefects, relatives displayed proud faces and no tears.[27]

In the second dispatch, Fox exchanged small talk with a Japanese woman who served him breakfast. Recognizing him as a foreigner, she asked him if he planned to go to Korea, site of the first combat. When he replied in the affirmative, she told him, "I want to go to Korea, but they won't let girls go." He asked why she wanted to travel to the front, and her eyes flashed defiantly in response: "To fight!"[28]

While seeing the sights on Honshu, Fox wrote home that he did not expect to witness much action. Already, delays imposed by the Japanese army on sending correspondents to Korea, as well as the army's announced reluctance to allow full access to the war zone, had turned him pessimistic. "The first batch of correspondents have gone—where nobody knows," he wrote his mother on April 3. "I am in the second batch and when we will go nobody knows. I think you can rest easy. I don't believe any correspondent will be allowed to [see] a single big fight. After it is over, we will probably be permitted to look at the field."[29] Over the next five weeks, he wrote his mother four more letters echoing his frustration. He said that the first wave of war correspondents "would just as well stayed in Tokio [sic]" because of the rules governing their movements.[30]

The return of the first wave of correspondents from the front confirmed Fox's concerns. He wrote, "They saw the Yalu fight from the top of a mountain three miles away and were not allowed to go on the battlefield even afterwards.... I don't believe any correspondent will even *hear* a bullet or shell in this campaign. *We are treated like children*, nuisances and possible spies."[31]

In late June, Davis sent a message to his and Fox's friend, President Roosevelt, complaining about the treatment they had received in Japan. Roosevelt contacted Secretary of State John Hay, who told Japan's ambassador to the United States, Takahira Kogorō, that Fox and Davis were the president's "special friends" and were unhappy. Hay also cabled Lloyd Griscom, the American consul in Japan, and asked him to speak with Foreign Affairs Minister Komura Jutarō in Tokyo. Meanwhile, Takahira also cabled Komura saying, "[P]rompt action to satisfy the President is very desirable." Komura demurred that the civilian government could not dictate to the armed forces. Takahira's reply emphasized the value of Western war correspondents to Japan, which looked to the United States as a possible peace broker and to Western banks for loans to offset the exhaustingly high cost of war. Takahira said American public opinion about the war hinged on swift and truthful accounts delivered by Western war correspondents—and, one would assume, that such opinion would be particularly bolstered if they portrayed Japanese courage, determination, and success on the battlefield. Takahira even urged the Japanese armies to allow correspondents to use their military telegraph lines.[32] Komura, after a meeting with Consul Griscom, agreed on June 29 to lay the matter before the military authorities, who evidently found the personal interest of the president of the United States sufficient to explore a change of policy.[33]

By July 7, Fox and Davis had sent an ultimatum to the Japanese government to demand that they be allowed to depart for the war zone—"we won't stay after the 17th of July." By then, Fox's recurring theme of disgust at his treatment had become such old news that he opened the letter to his mother which contained his ultimatum with other news—that he was sending her a present of fifty yards of white silk.[34] He apparently did not know that diplomatic discussions at the highest levels, coupled with negative press in the United States and on-the-ground complaints in Tokyo, were about to bear fruit. One of the sparks that broke the correspondents free from their virtual house arrest in Tokyo occurred after the Battle of Telissu on June 14–15. The battle took its name from a railway station about eighty miles north of Port Arthur. The Russian First Siberian Army Corps had attempted to break Japan's tightening grip on the Liaodong Peninsula and keep a land supply route open to the port. After the battle, according to Associated Press reporter William H. Brill, the commander of the Second Army, General Oku, reported that his Russian opponents had committed atrocities and "a number of violations of the rules of war" in their defeat. Accusations included killing of the wounded, mutilation of the dead, and artillery targeting of Japanese Red Cross hospitals. "Not one correspondent or one military attaché made use of these stories," Brill recalled. "They were to[o] serious to touch. No correspondent dared to state that these things were true. It was only the world of the Japanese against that of the Russians, who of course denied the stories as soon as they were officially published." No neutral observer had witnessed the deeds in question, nor had any observed what Brill called "unprecedented acts of valor." Brill said that the government of Japan realized it was missing an opportunity, particularly after the Ministry of Foreign Affairs "took up our battle for us."[35]

Unexpectedly, Tokyo newspapers took up the cause of the Western war correspondents. The *Jiji Shimpo* and *Hochi Shimbun*, among others, said the Japanese government was jeopardizing American and British amity by the treatment of military observers and accredited correspondents. The message played into the national allergy to rudeness and gained traction when combined with the Ministry of Foreign Affairs' own pleas.[36]

At last came the long-awaited order for war correspondents and military attachés. The General Staff summoned Brill and George Lynch as representatives of the U.S. and U.K. press corps, respectively. Brill said that upon entering the office to which he had been summoned many times without satisfaction, he was met by a smiling lieutenant.

"I have good news for you," he said.
We gasped. We had never expected to hear good news again.
"The correspondents attached to the second army
  will sail from Shimonoseki July 25."
"*Banzai*," yelled Lynch at the top of his voice, as he executed
  a few steps of an Irish reel in the corner.[37]

The Ministry of Foreign Affairs asked the correspondents to decide among themselves who would go with the Second Army. Brill, a Minnesota journalist who had covered the last Indian skirmish, the Battle of Leech Lake in 1898 between the U.S. Army and the Chippewa, was picked first as the representative of the Associated Press. Davis and Fox got the second and third slots at the recommendation of Hector Fuller, an admirer from the *Indianapolis News*.[38] Passes to the front were validated on the afternoon of July 15. Three days later, Fox, Davis, and sixteen other war correspondents—but not Fuller—boarded the *Empress of China* in the port of Yokohama, bound for Kobe and Moji. They did not know whether they would go to the siege of Port Arthur, to the encampment of General Oku's army, or some other destination.[39] The eighteen correspondents on board also included Melton Prior, Luigi Barzini, Bennet Burleigh, Lionel James, William H. Brill, and George Lynch, who had brought a bicycle to take him around the front. From Moji, a port at the northern tip of Kyushu, across the Shimonoseki Straits from Honshu, the correspondents steamed west and then north aboard the SS *Heijo Maru*. Fox had purchased a Japanese stallion named Fuji and secured the horse on board. Also he had procured the services of a Japanese servant, Takeuchi, to interpret for him and prepare his meals.[40] En route to the Asian mainland, the *Heijo Maru* encountered a Chinese sampan, giving Fox his first opportunity to observe ordinary Chinese civilians in their own territory. An old man and a child clambered onto the ship to sell some fish they had caught. The Japanese soldiers dropped a few coins, grabbed the fish, and shoved the sampan away from their ship. The sharp sendoff caused the sampan to collide with the *Heijo Maru*'s stern; the sampan overturned and sent the old man and child into the cold ocean water. Officers laughed during the ordeal as the fishmongers emerged from the water, righted their boat, and clambered aboard. The affair struck Fox as evidence of the "loftily superior, contemptuously patronizing" attitude of Japan toward China, which, after all, had provided Japan with "civilization, classical models, and a written speech."[41]

The correspondents sent up a cheer when they saw the rocky coast of Manchuria. They assumed they were headed to Port Arthur, and spirits rose when they heard an artillery report reach them across the water. They even got close enough to spot a signal station attached to the port. But the *Heijo Maru* kept going, and it became clear the transport was headed toward Dalny Bay, where the troops and correspondents would disembark in order to march toward General Oku's inland army. Upon landing, Davis noticed a coolie with a cart and beckoned to have him approach. The coolie loaded Davis's bags on the cart. A Japanese colonel, with no warning, tipped all of the cart's contents on the ground. Davis asked a liaison officer if he could have a different cart, and the answer came back, "Certainly." But when Davis had the coolie load the bags onto a second cart, the colonel dumped them out again. Davis had his interpreter explain that he was an accredited correspondent and guest of the army, but the colonel turned on him and swore. Fox considered this an ominous beginning to the land campaign in which correspondents lived as guests of the army.[42]

The caravan of soldiers and correspondents moved into Manchuria, stopping at three small towns. They traveled thirty-two miles on a day when the roads were good, but fell to fifteen miles as the terrain grew broken. North of Wafangdian (Wa-fang-tien), Fox received "a shock and a thrill." Sitting on a low stone wall at noon, he wrote, "a few carts filled with wounded Japanese passed slowly by. In one cart sat a man in a red shirt, with a white handkerchief tied over his head and under his chin. Facing him was a bearded Japanese with a musket between his knees. The man in the red shirt wearily turned his face. It was young, smooth-shaven, and *white*."[43]

The man was a Russian prisoner of war. He was the only Russian whom Fox would see during his travels in East Asia.

The caravan continued north through fields of millet twelve feet high, obscuring the view of surrounding countryside. The fields covered extensive ground, requiring two hours to traverse. "A richer land I never saw," Fox recalled. "It looks as though it would feed both armies, and yet there was no sign—no burned house or robbed field or even a cast-off bit of the soldier's equipment to show that an army had passed that way." The only sign of war, he noted, was the complete absence of women except for the very old and the very young.[44]

Finally the march reached the town of Haicheng, north of the base of the Liaodong Peninsula and only five miles from the Russian army. Military observers from other countries were taken on a reconnaissance tour, and Fox expected the journalists soon to have their own guide to take them to see soldiers preparing to fight. They billeted in Haicheng. In anticipation of being ordered swiftly to move out, the correspondents slept in their riding clothes. "With a sleeve-badge of identification on it—the Red Badge of Shame we call it—we can wander more or less freely within the city walls. We can even climb on them . . . but we cannot go outside without a written application from the entire company, and then only under guard," Fox wrote.[45] Three guards, all of them lawyers who advised the army on matters of international law, monitored the outsiders at all time. Brill said the guards kept the correspondents "practically prisoners" in Haicheng.[46] Acknowledging his lack of freedom, Fox titled his dispatch to *Scribner's Magazine*, half in jest and half in angry resignation, "The White Slaves of Haicheng." A guard explained that the Western correspondents had to be so closely restricted to avoid the possibility of a soldier mistaking them for Russians. However, later, when a few correspondents briefly escaped their guards' observation and went among the ordinary Japanese soldiers, they found a rousing welcome. General Oku and his staff also made a show of embracing the correspondents.[47]

Permission to move out arrived after the correspondents returned to Haicheng. The ubiquitous guards escorted the correspondents on a reconnaissance mission. It was far from satisfactory. The guides stopped several miles from units of the Russian army and used field glasses to pinpoint the enemy encampment atop a camel-backed mountain. "Holy Moses! But that was a terrifying experience," Fox wrote with obvious sarcasm. Davis ostentatiously sat in a trench and was ordered to move, as apparently he had crossed an invisible line intended as a boundary for his own protection. "We are getting pretty restless now," Fox said.[48]

The Japanese officers must have realized the risk of losing the correspondents' good will. Intending to provide something newsworthy and "while away the tedium," they arranged for a major to give a lecture on the recent Battle of Telissu. The major spoke like a college professor, drawing mountains, valleys, trenches, and groups of soldiers to illustrate his talk. "A certain division, he said, of a certain regiment, at a certain time had done a certain thing," Fox wrote. "It was a perfect lecture except that all the really essential facts were skillfully suppressed." The major then relayed details he had witnessed. Ammunition ran out on both sides, compelling the Russians and Japanese to fight hand to hand, he said. A Russian officer advanced, holding his sword, but his men refused to follow. Thereupon a Japanese officer came forward, and the two dueled with swords while their men observed. The major said the Japanese officer killed the Russian, whom the Japanese then buried with elaborate ceremony to honor him as a warrior. Fox wrote:

"How many men did the Japanese have in that fight," asked a correspondent?
"Just as many as they have now," was the illuminating answer.

> I wonder if anybody but the Japanese knows how many men they have really had in any fight, and whether in consequence their victories have been due to astonishing skill or overwhelming numbers.[49]

Finally, Fox, Davis, and some of their peers had had enough. They talked and decided that they would return home if they could not see a battle. They saw smoke and heard shells explode, ten miles away at Anshantien, halfway between Haicheng and Liaoyang, where the main body of the Russian army waited. Shell smoke dissipated around noon, and the guards moved the correspondents to a compound where they were told they would spend the night and see an engagement the next morning. The correspondents did not sleep, no doubt excited by their prospects. Before dawn the next day, the guards moved them single file, through darkness and pouring rain, toward the front. They waited for dawn to break at the foot of a hill. After the sun had risen, Fox climbed the hill but found no evidence of a battle. A guard rode ahead to reconnoiter and came back with news that the Russians had withdrawn. "We had a serious consultation that night," Fox wrote. "The artists couldn't very well draw what they couldn't see. Some of us, not being military experts, and therefore dependent on mental pictures and incident for material, were equally helpless." When Oku sent word the next day that there probably would be no decisive battle in the immediate future, correspondents Fox, Davis, Melton Prior, and George Lynch decided to go home.[50] Davis said that if they had stayed under the existing conditions, it would have been like "robbing your employers." In addition to the inability to view real action, Lynch blamed his departure on heavy censorship that left nothing of value to his stories.[51] Prior, the veteran correspondent whose coverage of twenty-seven wars beginning with the Third Anglo-Ashanti War of 1873–1874 had earned him the nickname Stormy Petrel, told a reporter upon leaving East Asia that "the Japanese system is censorship gone mad." Nine years later, he still bristled that the Japanese antipathy to correspondents should include those from the United Kingdom. He said he was "an Englishman and their ally."[52]

Before leaving, the departing journalists auctioned their belongings and gave away what they could not sell. Brill found the prices reasonable. "I got a camp chair, two disreputable looking note books which Fox had been unable to fill, a dozen lead pencils which Lynch never did have any use for, a few broken candles—the most precious acquisition of the lot—a few cans of sardines, a water bottle with a hole in it and Williams and Walker." Brill rechristened the doubly named Williams and Walker, Davis's black donkey, as "Van Bibber" in honor of a fictional character of Davis's. Brill said the remaining correspondents suffered a miserable evening after their four colleagues left the front to head back to Japan. "We had been a large happy family for some time and we didn't like to see the break come," he wrote. Other departures followed, and by late September the original eighteen correspondents accredited to the Second Army had been pared to six.[53]

Fox, Davis, Prior, and Lynch wound their way back to the coast and across the Yellow Sea to Yantai. There, to their extreme dismay, they learned that "real, continuous" fighting was under way at Liaoyang, and they had left three days before they might have witnessed it.[54] The battle, pitting roughly two hundred thousand soldiers on each side, was the first major engagement of the war.[55] It ended in a Japanese victory.

Fox left East Asia with scorn for the Japanese army but a great appreciation for the ordinary Japanese soldier. He had observed fierce determination both on the home front and in the war zone. The soldier "is concerned only with killing his opponent," Fox wrote, "and he doesn't seem to care whether or not he comes out dead or alive."[56] This made soldiers into formidable foes on the battlefield.

As for the attitude of the Japanese and the Western press toward each other, perhaps a sarcastic note to Fox from Jack London distilled the correspondents' opinion: "Gee! And don't we love the Japs!"[57] Fox's own thoughts on the matter appeared in dispatches to *Scribner's Magazine*. Instead of welcoming journalists and then having them sit idle for months before allowing them only a glimpse of war, Fox wrote that it would have been better if Japan had said up front that it did not welcome any Western war correspondents for fear they would damage operational security. Or, as an alternative, Japan could have been forthright about how long the correspondents would have to wait, rather than continually making promises it did not keep. Or Japan could have welcomed only English correspondents, given England's alliance with Japan, while announcing it would block all correspondents from the officially neutral (but Japanese-leaning) United States. "Nothing in all of this could have given offense," Fox wrote. Instead,

> The Japanese gave no open hint of unwillingness to have us go—no hint that we were not to go very soon. We were urged to get passes for ourselves, interpreters and servants at once. Most of the men obeyed at once, bought horses, outfits, provisions and wrote farewell letters—wrote them many times. This was the middle of March.[58]

After Fox and Davis's ship docked at Vancouver, British Columbia, in October, they used speeches and press articles to attack Japan's treatment of war correspondents. Their complaints caught the attention of Roosevelt, who called both to a meeting and urged them to halt their verbal assault. Fox took the opportunity to hand Roosevelt a memorandum detailing his experience at the hands of the Japanese—likely a version of what he would later print in the four final installments of his war correspondence in *Scribner's Magazine*. Roosevelt read it and forwarded it to Kaneko Kentarō, a classmate of the president's at Harvard University who served as Japan's special envoy to the U.S. government. Kaneko had been tasked to seek American help in securing a diplomatic ending to the war, and in 1905 that work would bear fruit in the peace negotiations Roosevelt brokered at Portsmouth, New Hampshire. Roosevelt found some merit in Fox and Davis's complaints, telling Kaneko that he hoped Japan would make clear to war correspondents what actions they could and could not take in order to avoid misunderstanding and frustration. Kaneko sent the memo and Roosevelt's comments to Minister of Foreign Affairs Komura in Tokyo. Komura agreed that press regulations could be relaxed as the war progressed favorably for Japan, but he told Roosevelt that complete secrecy had been necessary early in the war to cover troop landings in Korea and Manchuria. He denied Japan suffered from xenophobia, a point that had been raised by several correspondents. On that question,

Figure 4.1 John Fox Jr., photographed a decade after the war, left East Asia in disgust after never witnessing a battle.
Source: Library of Congress.

Roosevelt's attitude evolved during 1904. In the summer, he wrote to a friend that the Japanese were "different" than other peoples but nevertheless would be welcomed into the world's civilized powers. However, by December he had concluded that he did not doubt "that they include all white men as being people who, as a whole, they dislike, and whose past arrogance they resent; and doubtless they believe their own yellow civilization to be better."[59]

A personal response and explanation of Japan's initial treatment of Western war correspondents resides in Fox's papers at the University of Kentucky. There is no indication why it was sent, or on whose initiative. However, it is interesting to note the timing. At about the moment Fox, Davis, and the others left the front, the *Times* of London also announced to Japan that it would withdraw all of its correspondents except for one, Frank Brinkley. He had operated out of a base in Tokyo and since 1881 had owned and operated an English-language newspaper, *Japan Mail*. The *Mail* received financial support from the Japanese government and unsurprisingly maintained friendly relations with its cabinet ministers.[60] The *Times*'s financial investment in covering the war had reached £6,000, the equivalent of £720,000 just over a century later—at the time, £1 exchanged for about $5—and the editors decided to cut their losses. The enmity of the world's most prestigious newspaper struck a blow, which was compounded when the Western powers hinted at cutting Japan's financial lifelines. When the journalists leaving Liaoyang stopped in Yantai on the way back to Japan, the Japanese consul in that neutral Chinese city reported to Tokyo that the journalists' complaints had reached Russian ears, and Russian newspapers in East Asia had begun printing them. Another consul, Segawa Asanoshin in Yingkou (Newchwang), told his superiors that upon returning home, the disgruntled correspondents would "use every influence to prevent Japan from raising any loans either in the United States or in England."[61] Thus, the letter in Fox's archive would appear to have been written in response to pressure from Roosevelt and the angry ex-war correspondents, as well as Japan's desire to maintain the goodwill of officials who could influence public opinion and perhaps a favorable vote in Congress. The letter was written by Count Michimasa Soyeshima, a member of the House of Peers and authority on Japanese diplomacy, who had traveled with Fox across the Sea of Japan en route to the war zone. On October 30, 1904, he wrote to Fox to explain what Fox had called the military's "lack of faith" in Western journalists and to criticize the army's overenthusiastic censors.

"You must remember that we are fighting this struggle not for any territorial aggrandizement, not for the integrity of China, not even for the independence of Korea, but for our own national existence," Michimasa said. Japan had poured all of its energy into fighting the powerful Russian army and navy, and in its concentrated focus on victory it ignored "other matters which are perhaps equally important."

When foreign war correspondents came to Japan with the object of being allowed to go to the front, the military authorities, I hear, were very reluctant to give them permission, for the war meant a life and death struggle for us, and therefore they thought that they would not be able to give even a modicum of satisfaction to foreign visitors. The secret of success in war is, as everyone knows, to keep strict secrecy concerning the movements of armies and squadrons. The success of the press of the present day depends upon revealing the secrets of every corner of the globe. We knew very well from the first that it would be absolutely impossible for us to keep our military movements secret and at the same time give satisfaction to newspaper correspondents, both foreign and native. But I believe our authorities were afraid that in refusing to allow them to join one or two of the armies under Marshal Ōyama [Iwao] we would perhaps lose the sympathy of the Press of Europe and America which our extraordinary patience during the negotiations which preceded the commencement of hostilities had won for us. We issued "permits"; but then we hesitated and lingered.[62]

It was only when the correspondents' patience had ended that Japan decided to relent, Michimasa wrote. This change of attitude has been corroborated by documents in the National Archive of Japan. In March 1904, before Fox, Davis, and other correspondents left Manchuria, Japan's minister to Britain, Viscount Hayashi Todasu, argued that barring Western journalists from access to real war stories would come back to haunt the Ministry of Foreign Affairs. Allowing greater freedom would help maintain good will in Great Britain and the United States, to whom Japan looked for future economic partnerships. Excessive censorship of accredited correspondents in the field would "exasperate the press and . . . possibly cause revulsion against us," Hayashi noted, diplomatically avoiding the fact that such antipathy already existed. He urged the foreign affairs minister, Komura, to allow journalists to see combat but subject them to a "reasonable" level of field censorship to prevent the compromising of operational security.[63] Orders allowing greater freedom to war correspondents took effect about two weeks after Davis and Fox left Manchuria in frustration—perhaps hurried along by the unanimous letter of complaint filed by the second wave of war correspondents with General Oku's army. Those who came later to the war, or those who stayed despite suffering the early, extreme ways in which the army controlled correspondents, were able to see and report with more movement and less restraint.

The early press censorship had been too zealous, too punitive, Michimasa told Fox.

> Unfortunately . . . as officers in charge of the correspondents with the second army were approved two blockheads who know nothing of the outer world and who, as they would be no good in the fighting lines, were given this most

important task. This, I confess, was a great blunder on the part of our military authorities, a blunder which they have now found out. But it is too late, for those who had the greatest grievances, yourself, Richard Harding-Davis and George Lynch, have now gone back to their respective countries. Those who have remained have profited much by the blunder and grievances. Don't call it an injustice—the whole thing was a blunder, and it is human to err, especially when a man is fighting for his existence.[64]

In particular, Michimasa blamed two low-ranking officers on Oku's staff and a few correspondents who angered their overseers by violating the spirit if not the letter of their accreditation agreements. Jiro Okabé and Viscount Saté had acted cavalierly as guards, shepherds, and censors. But blame also rested on "two or three" correspondents, whom Michimasa did not name, who left the Japanese-controlled portion of the war zone to send uncensored telegrams to their newspapers, and on one correspondent, again unnamed, who attempted to report events from the Russian side after having lived among the Japanese. Michimasa concluded,

> Please remember that it was not through any lack of faith or through any anti-foreign feeling that we were not quite just in our dealings with you. It was, as I have said before, simply a blunder, and because we have blundered and because we have confessed that we have blundered, we hope we shall not lose the simpathy [*sic*] and support of so straightforward, so frank, so kind and so good a friend as yourself.
>
> My dear John Fox, we have now invariably cast our lot with the Western Civilization.[65]

Michimasa's explanation leaves out the fact that Fox, Davis, and their peers fell directly under the control of General Oku in Manchuria, and that Oku could have issued any order he choose to accommodate the correspondents. He could have ordered the "blockheads" to take the correspondents into the front lines, especially when considering that the army held complete censorship control over the dispatches of the press corps. If the journalists had seen something they were not supposed to have witnessed, or written or photographed anything secret, the army could have removed that information before sharing it via mail or telegraph. But that, however, would have required Oku to take initiative that countermanded his orders in word and spirit—an unlikely occurrence in a nation built upon the concept of unity.

Matters grew even more disturbing after Fox and his peers departed and Japan learned that its ability to borrow money from England and the United States was in jeopardy. Hayashi gauged public opinion in London and cabled the Ministry of Foreign Affairs in Tokyo with his findings. He quoted the

Daily Telegraph in one dispatch and noted that in general, the papers supported the Japanese troops but not their officers. The British newspapers had become "irritated by our treatment of their correspondents," no doubt a reference in part to the *Telegraph* as well as the *Times* pulling all reporters from the mainland. "Japan," Hayashi gravely observed, "must bear in mind that the unfriendly attitude of an organ of public opinion will be a source of great concern for us." In a follow-up cable, he added, "No doubt the unfavourable attitude of the war correspondents now made public is principally responsible for the present mood of the press which has hitherto endeavored to suppress its irritated feelings."[66]

Fox returned to the United States before most of his dispatches appeared in print. In 1905, *Scribner's* collected them in a book titled *Following the Sun Flag: A Vain Pursuit through Manchuria*. Fox's biographer, York, considers the collected dispatches to be among Fox's finest writing of a long and distinguished career, regardless of whether he had managed to actually observe battle.[67]

After war's end, Japan would attempt to mend fences with those who had served as war correspondents. The emperor of Japan mailed a medal to all Western correspondents who had covered the Russo-Japanese War, including the cantankerous Jack London, whom it had expelled.[68] Fox's medal arrived at *Scribner's Magazine* in the summer of 1907.[69]

Fox gave up war correspondence after his sour experience in East Asia. He returned to writing fiction. In 1908, his mountain romance *The Trail of the Lonesome Pine* became the first novel in the United States to sell two million copies. Both *Little Shepherd* and *Lonesome Pine* became grist for adaptation into Hollywood movies, the latter produced, written as a screenplay, and directed by Cecil B. DeMille in 1916. Fox married opera and movie star Fritzi Scheff in 1908, but the marriage ended in divorce five years later. He died of pneumonia on July 8, 1919, and was buried in Big Stone Gap near the Virginia-Kentucky line.[70]

His lasting legacy, in addition to his best-selling novels, includes the protest he launched with Richard Harding Davis that helped make Japan begin to change its mind in the middle of a war.

NOTES

1. "Notable Writers and Military Men Return from Japan," *Winnipeg* (MB) *Tribune*, October 15, 1904.

2. John Fox Jr., "The White Slaves of Haicheng," *Scribner's Magazine* 37, no. 2 (February 1905): 196–97.

3. Fox, "The White Slaves of Haicheng," 198–99.

4. John Fox Jr., "Notebooks," "Articles and Short Stories," box 8, Fox Family Papers, 1852–1962, 1852–1920 (bulk dates), Special Collections Research Center, Margaret I. King Library, University of Kentucky, Lexington, KY (hereafter FFP).

5. "Correspondent Returning: Frederick Palmer, Noted Descriptive Writer, Sailed on Empress," *The* (Vancouver, BC) *Province*, February 22, 1905.

6. Bill York, *John Fox, Jr., Appalachian Author* (Jefferson, NC: McFarland & Company, 2003), 13–14.

7. York, *Appalachian Author*, 18–25.

8. "John Fox, Jr., 1862–1919," http://carnegiecenterlex.org/wp-content/uploads/2018/01/John-Fox-Jr.-Biography.pdf.

9. Frank M. O'Brien, *The Story of the Sun, 1833–1918* (New York: G. H. Doran, 1918), 199.

10. York, *Appalachian Author*, 37–38.

11. Ibid., 40.

12. Ibid., 42–45.

13. Ibid., 103–7; and "John Fox, Jr., 1862–1919."

14. York, *Appalachian Author*, 132–45.

15. Ibid., 145–46.

16. Ibid., 150.

17. Ibid., 155–56.

18. John Fox Jr., *Crittenden: A Kentucky Story of Love and War* (New York: Charles Scribner's Sons, 1900), 165–66.

19. Fox, *Crittenden*, 167.

20. York, *Appalachian Author*, 181.

21. John Fox Jr., *Following the Sun-Flag: A Vain Pursuit through Manchuria* (New York: Charles Scribner's Sons, 1905), ix.

22. Jack London, "Japanese Officers Consider Everything a Military Secret," *San Francisco Examiner*, June 26, 1904.

23. York, *Appalachian Author*, 182–83; and John Fox to "Dear Mother" (Minerva Fox), March 18, 1904, box 4, 64m122, "Correspondence 1904–1920" folder: Letters, 1904–1910, FFP.

24. John Fox to Minerva Fox, March 18, 1904.

25. John Fox to Minerva Fox, April 3, 1904, FFP; and John Fox to Minerva Fox, April 6, 1904, FFP.

26. John Fox Jr., "The Trail of the Saxon," *Scribner's Magazine* 25, no. 6 (June 1904): 661.

27. Fox, "The Trail of the Saxon."

28. John Fox Jr., "Hardships of the Campaign," *Scribner's Magazine* 36, no. 1 (July 1904): 40.

29. John Fox to Minerva Fox, April 3, 1904.

30. John Fox to Minerva Fox, April 15, 1904, FFP.

31. John Fox to Minerva Fox, May 23, 1904, FFP. Underlines in original.

32. Takahira Kogorō to Komura Jutarō, June 24, 1904, file "3. the United State," in folder "Nichirosen eki no sai senkyo shisatu no tame gaikoku shimbun kisha jugun ikken," Nihon Gaimusho hozon kiroku, in Japan Center for Asian Historical Records,

Ref. B07091021400: Nihon Gaimusho hozon kiroku [Records of the Ministry of Foreign Affairs, The Diplomatic Record Office of the Ministry of Foreign Affairs], Japan Center for Asian Historical Records, National Archives of Japan, Tokyo.

33. Komura Jutarō to Takahira Kogorō, June 29, 1904, ibid.

34. John Fox to Minerva Fox, July 7, 1904, FFP.

35. William H. Brill, "Weary Weeks of Waiting," unpublished manuscript, box 11, "Manuscripts and Dispatches, 1898–1922," MS P813, Hascal Russell Brill and Family Papers, Minnesota Historical Society, Saint Paul (hereafter HRBP).

36. "A Letter from Japan: To the Front at Last," *Sydney* (Australia) *Morning Herald*, August 20, 1904.

37. Brill, "Weary Weeks of Waiting."

38. "Tributes to Richard Harding Davis," *Indianapolis Star*, April 13, 1916.

39. John Fox Jr., "Making for Manchuria," *Scribner's Magazine* 37, no. 1 (January 1905), 689.

40. Fox, "Making for Manchuria," 692.

41. Ibid., 693.

42. Ibid., 694–95.

43. John Fox Jr., "On the War-Dragon's Tail," *Scribner's Magazine* 37, no. 1 (January 1905): 55–57.

44. Fox, "On the War-Dragon's Tail," 58.

45. Fox, "The White Slaves of Haicheng," 197.

46. William H. Brill, "With the Army at Last," unpublished manuscript, box 11, "Manuscripts and Dispatches, 1898–1922," HRBP.

47. Fox, "The White Slaves of Haicheng," 197.

48. Ibid., 200.

49. Ibid., 202.

50. John Fox Jr., "The Backward Trail of the Saxon," *Scribner's Magazine* 37, no. 3 (March 1905): 275–76.

51. "Stories of the Tented Field: Opinions of War Correspondents," *The Province* (Vancouver, BC), October 12, 1904.

52. "Campaigns of a War Correspondent," *Victoria* (BC) *Daily Times*, November 20, 1913; and "The Eastern War May Spread Out," *Hawaii Herald* (Hilo), October 6, 1904.

53. Brill, "Liao-yang, Sept. 24," unpublished manuscript, box 11, "Manuscripts and Dispatches, 1898–1922," HRBP.

54. Fox, "The Backward Trail of the Saxon," 276, 279.

55. Edmund F. Mirriam, ed., *The Watchman* 86, no. 86 (September 8, 1904): 5.

56. Fox, "White Slaves of Haicheng," 203.

57. Jack London, n.d., box 8, "Undated and Fragmentary Letters" folder, FFP.

58. Fox, "Making for Manchuria," 689–90.

59. Robert B. Valliant, "The Selling of Japan: Japanese Manipulation of Western Opinion, 1900–1905," *Monumenta Nipponica* 29, no. 4 (Winter 1974): 435–36.

60. Hayashi Gonsuke to Komura Jutarō, July 1, 1904, file "2. United Kingdom No. 2," in folder "Nichirosen eki no sai senkyo shisatu no tame gaikoku shimbun kisha jugun ikken," Nihon Gaimusho hozon kiroku [Records of the Ministry of Foreign

Affairs, The Diplomatic Record Office of the Ministry of Foreign Affairs], Japan Center for Asian Historical Records, National Archives of Japan, Tokyo; and Dan Johnson, "Exporting Exoticism: Captain Brinkley's Japan Described and Illustrated," *Bridgewater Review* 34, no. 1 (May 2015): 27.

61. Valliant, "The Selling of Japan," 432–33.

62. Michimasa Soyeshima to John Fox, October 30, 1904, Scrapbook No. 7, box 11, FFP.

63. Hayashi Gonsuke to Komura Jutarō, March 31, 1904, file "2. United Kingdom No. 1" in folder "Nichirosen eki no sai senkyo shisatu no tame gaikoku shimbun kisha jugun ikken," Nihon Gaimusho hozon kiroku.

64. Michimasa to Fox.

65. Ibid. One of the Western reporters whom Michimasa described as changing sides likely was Edwin Emerson Jr. of *Collier's Weekly*, as detailed in chapter 9.

66. Valliant, "The Selling of Japan," 433.

67. John Fox Jr., *Following the Sun Flag: A Vain Pursuit through Manchuria* (London: Constable, 1905), 207.

68. Jack London, *The Letters of Jack London 1913–1916*, vol. 3, Earle Labor, Robert C. Leitz II, and I. Milo Shepard, eds. (Stanford, CA: Stanford University Press, 1988), 706, n.1. London did not care for his medal; he gave it away.

69. Alvey A. Adee to John Fox, June 28, 1907, box 8, "Undated and Fragmentary Letters" folder, FFP.

70. "John Fox, Jr., 1862–1919."

Chapter 5

Richard Harding Davis

Japan used the war correspondents little better than prisoners.

—Richard Harding Davis, 1904[1]

After fifteen days at sea, playwright, fiction writer, and war correspondent Richard Harding Davis and his wife, Cecil, arrived in Japan on March 13, 1904. The couple had left the United States on one of the last days of February, boarding a small yet comfortable boat in San Francisco and setting sail across the North Pacific Ocean.[2] Peter F. Collier of *Collier's Weekly*, one of the largest fiction and nonfiction magazines in the United States at the time, had hired Davis to follow the Japanese army in its impending war with the Russian Empire over the East Asian territories of Korea and Manchuria. Upon arrival, their boat lay still in the waters of Tokyo Bay as the crew and passengers were waiting to be escorted safely over the sunken mines resting on the seabed. As they took in the view of the Tanzawa Mountains framing the outskirts of Yokohama to the west, Davis noticed the crisp purple silhouettes leaning against the yellow afternoon sky. Taken aback by the tranquil yet alluring landscape of the Land of the Rising Sun, he wrote a letter to his mother to inform her of their safe arrival:

> It will be good to feel solid earth, and to see the kimonos and temples and geishas and cherry blossoms. I am almost hoping the Government won't let us go to the front and for a week at least Cecil and I can sit in the tea houses with our shoes off while the nesans [sisters] bring us tea and the geishas rub their knees and make bows to us.[3]

Soon he must have wondered if he had jinxed his own luck. Having covered numerous battles prior to his stay in Japan and being drawn to the exhilaration of war reporting, Davis had readily accepted the *Collier's* offer. However, this assignment had felt vastly different from his previous excursions. When traveling to San Francisco by train he sent a letter to his family in Philadelphia. The letter revealed that he knew little of the mounting conflict between the two empires and that he found it difficult to imagine battle scenes as grim as those he had seen when he covered the Second Boer War. In fact, he wrote, it was hard for him to take the assignment seriously at all. He foresaw that his time in Japan would be "[j]ust quaint and queer. A trip of cherry blossoms and Geisha girls."[4]

Having covered the Cuban revolt against Spain in 1896 and 1897, the Spanish-American War in Cuba and Puerto Rico in 1898, and the Second Boer War in South Africa in 1900, Davis was a seasoned war reporter. Yet, he arrived in Japan expecting little thrill from the prophesied battle between Russia and Japan. Five months later, a dispirited Davis left the East and sailed back to America. The closest he had come to a battle scene was the sound of distant gunfire.[5]

Some may say that no man is born a storyteller, but Davis might be the closest that one can get. He was never an avid student and seldom found joy in his studies as a young boy. Rather, he found excitement in leading expeditions up the Manasquan River from his family's cottage in Point Pleasant near the New Jersey coast. Trailing through forests and exploring unmarked eyots along the riverbank with his younger brother, Charles, Davis steered excursions fueled by a yearning for adventure. One small island gained particular favor with the two brothers and they named it, simply, The Island. According to Charles, the very same island would be christened Treasure Island by Scottish author Robert Louis Stevenson during one of his visits to America.[6] Stevenson's book of the same name, which told the tale of a daring coming-of-age voyage, would become a keepsake in homes across America. For the Davis brothers, the island was the center stage of their childhood.

Inspired by their excursions, Davis would write, direct, and, without failure, star in his own plays. As the elder of the two, Richard would always be the last-standing hero, while Charles would act as the spiteful villain whose death was inevitable, preferably by choking.[7] More often than not, the narrative arc would center on a cumbersome expedition through a rugged mountain pass—built with two tables and a chair.

While Davis's early life tells no tales of hardships, whether in finance or career advancement, he worked tirelessly for his fame; he was a relentless reporter and an unapologetic writer. Even though he had found little joy in his studies—first at the Episcopal Academy in Pennsylvania and later at Lehigh University in Bethlehem after a quick stint to Swarthmore College and, finally, a transfer to John Hopkins University in 1885[8]—Davis's talent for writing was evident among his peers and teachers. At his death in April 1916, a fellow Lehigh student and lifelong friend wrote of him:

> Prophets were as rare in the eighties as they have always been, before and since, and nobody could have foreseen that the name and work of Dick Davis would long before his untimely death . . . be better known throughout the world than those of any other Lehigh man. We who knew him in his college days could not feel the smallest surprise that he won himself quickly a brilliant name, and kept a firm hold upon it to the last.[9]

Davis's first published story, "The Hat and Its Inmate" appeared in *Judge*, a weekly satirical magazine, in 1882.[10] By 1884, he published a collection of short stories from his time at Lehigh in a book titled *The Adventures of My Freshman*. Even though his time at college had been shaped by his teachers' frustration with his lack of engagement, he would experience little failure in regard to his literary work as a young writer, seemingly exemplified by his first book selling out within a first year of its publication.

Despite the apparent fortune of his early work, Davis would come to discover that his first book had indeed been a complete failure. Years after the book had been published, and shortly after sold out, he discovered a box storing the entire collection in his parents' attic. In what can only be described as an act of care, his parents had secretly bought all of the copies upon realizing that no one else would do so, and quietly stowed them away. By the time he discovered the books in the attic, Davis had enjoyed years of success. And so, flustered, he wittily wrote in a copy of the book, "The reason the book did not sell is, I think, because some one must have read it."[11]

Unabashed by his first book's seeming failure, Davis embarked on a prosperous career as a journalist and a playwright. When he left John Hopkins University in Baltimore, he took on several short-term positions with local newspapers before landing a gig with the New York *Evening Sun*. At the *Sun*, he spiraled to fame for his take on controversial issues, such as abortion and suicide, and for his theatrical style. At the time he arrived in Japan, his farcical play *The Dictator* was receiving high praise in the United States.[12]

While writing fiction and urban journalism, Davis began perhaps the most brilliant of his careers. In late 1896, he embarked on his first efforts to be a war correspondent. Commissioned by William Randolph Hearst of the *New York Journal* to do a month of reporting on the Cuban rebels, he boarded the *Vamoose*, a small yacht owned by Hearst and docked in Key West, Florida, and sailed toward Cuba. At the time, Cubans had been at war with Spain for their independence for more than a year. Without notifying his family out of fear of his mother's disapproval, Davis, accompanied by artist Frederic Remington, was scheduled to journey to rebel-controlled territory in December of

1896.[13] The *Vamoose*, however, was caught in a tremendous storm that forced the crew to return to Key West. A distraught Davis found himself restlessly wandering Key West in search of a new vessel to transport them, desperate for the adventure he had been promised by Hearst. Nearly a week later, he and Remington boarded the SS *Olivette*, a standard passenger liner to Havana.[14]

Less than a week after arriving in Cuba, Remington threw in the towel and returned to the United States. The monthly gig they had been promised by Hearst was nearly over and they had yet to see Cuban rebels, let alone any battle. Rather, they had spent the days trailing through the countryside to get to a sugar plantation in Santa Clara province.[15] As Davis continued his trip southeast of Havana, he encountered the gruesome tactics employed by the Spanish army to force farmworkers out of their villages and into concentration camps. Smoke that stood as thick black columns against the blue sky revealed how the Spanish troops set houses and crops on fire, either killing the Cubans or forcing them to flee and be trapped.[16] These same methods would be used by American troops in the Vietnam War nearly eighty years later.

Davis struggled to not feel a sense of sympathy for both sides of the war that might color his journalism. While he reported on the horrid conditions of the Spanish camps that left the internees, primarily Cuban women and young children, ill and dying from fever, he also accounted for similar tactics employed by Cuban rebels. While his published accounts described the escalating tensions and their increasing callousness, his most famous story, "The Death of Rodríguez," centered on one valiant soldier's execution. The young man, Adolfo Rodríguez, had been sentenced to die by a military court and his execution was to be carried out by a firing squad. Davis narrated an emotional account of the young man's last breaths—from the detail of a cigarette dangling between his lips and a priest carefully placing his hand on the young man's shoulder, to the final roll of Rodríguez's neck as the bullets pierced his torso. Davis wrote of the young man's bravery in facing death with a steady composure, "not arrogantly nor with bravado but with the nonchalance of a man who meets his punishment fearlessly, and who will let his enemies see that they can kill but cannot frighten him."[17]

In February 1897, Davis returned to the United States on the *Olivette*. Despite one good story, he had seen none of the battle he had anticipated when accepting the job from Hearst.

Over the next year, American interest in the Cuban War surged because of economic interests haltered by the conflict and by sympathies arising from the war's blatant resemblance to the American Revolution, a fight against the colonial oppressor.[18] Despite the public's mounting interest in intervention, the White House sought to solve the conflict through peaceful negotiations. President William McKinley had long been reluctant to employ military force in Cuba, creating much frustration for Davis, who had hoped that his first trip to Cuba in 1896 would have been fueled by a war declaration.

However, on February 15, 1898, the explosion of the battleship the USS *Maine* in Havana's harbor startled the United States. Less than two months later, McKinley surrendered his quest for a negotiated solution and pleaded with Congress to declare war with Spain to end the conflict.

One year after first returning from Cuba, Davis once again headed south, this time as a correspondent for the *New York Herald*, the *Times* of London, and *Scribner's Magazine*.[19] Bolstered by a letter from Theodore Roosevelt who encouraged him to return to Cuba to cover the war, he impatiently waited for and boarded a train to Key West, hopeful that he could book passage on a ship to Havana in the nearest future. Davis and Roosevelt had first met in 1890, when Davis was a reporter for the New York *Evening Sun*, while Roosevelt, at the time a civil-service commissioner in Washington DC, visited his sister in the city.[20] By 1895, Roosevelt served as the president of the New York police board. Well aware that a close relationship with a reporter could prove fruitful, he invited Davis to accompany him on a night patrol along with another reporter, Jacob A. Riis.[21] However, it was not until the war in Cuba when Davis covered the fight of Roosevelt's volunteer Rough Riders—and eventually, aided in the battle against the Spanish himself—that the two grew closer. Nearly twenty years later, when Davis died in his home of an apparent heart attack, Roosevelt's admiration of his longtime companion was indisputable. Roosevelt wrote of Davis:

> He was indomitably cheerful under hardships and difficulties and entirely indifferent to his own personal safety or comfort. . . . He was as good an American as ever lived and his heart flamed against cruelty and injustice. His writings form a text-book of Americanism which all our people would do well to read at the present time.[22]

With the outbreak of the Spanish-American War, Roosevelt resigned as the assistant secretary of the Navy and joined the First U.S. Volunteer Cavalry in May of 1898. The unit would famously become known as the Rough Riders, or Teddy's Terrors, and was a diverse group ranging from rugged Western cowboys to young men from New York's finest families.[23] Their exploits were a story just waiting to be written, and Davis was eager to follow them.

By June 1898, Roosevelt and his unit had spent weeks training in San Antonio, Texas, and on June 15, they entered the sea off Tampa Bay and sailed for Daiquiri, Cuba. On foot, they marched to the Spanish-held Santiago de Cuba where they joined the U.S. Fifth Army Corps in the village of Siboney.[24] Davis arrived five days later, just in time to witness the most iconic fight of the Spanish-American War, the Battle of San Juan Hill.

Figure 5.1   Richard Harding Davis, America's foremost war correspondent, said the Japanese army treated him like a spy.
Source: Library of Congress.

On July 1, 1898, U.S. General William Shafter, commander of the Fifth Army Corps, ordered an attack on Spanish-held El Caney and San Juan Hill. As more than eight thousand Americans pressed forward, the Spanish defenders stood their ground and hundreds of American soldiers lost their lives in the confrontation. However, the Spanish were outnumbered and, inevitably, the U.S. Army captured the stronghold of Santiago and the Spanish surrendered.

Davis watched as the American soldiers charged up San Juan Hill and Kettle Hill, artillery shattering the mountainside as the soldiers trailed through tall grass in the sweltering heat.[25] Spanish guerrillas hid in the grass and in the trees, pouring bullets down on the cavalry division. The American soldiers eventually abandoned their horses at the foot of the hillside and continued on foot. As out of a Western movie, Roosevelt suddenly appeared on horseback. As he pushed forward among the soldiers fighting the bullet storm, Davis recounted:

> Roosevelt, mounted high on horseback, and charging the rifle-pits at a gallop and quite alone, made you feel that you would like to cheer. He wore on his

sombrero a blue polka-dot handkerchief, a la Havelock, which, as he advanced, floated out straight behind his head, like a guidon. Afterward, the men of his regiment who followed this flag, adopted a polka-dot handkerchief as the badge of the Rough Riders. These two officers [Roosevelt and General Hawkins] were notably conspicuous in the charge, but no one can claim that any two men, or anyone man, was more brave or more daring, or showed greater courage in that slow, stubborn advance than did any of the others.[26]

Having worked in public offices for nearly twenty years at the time, Roosevelt had learned that a positive relationship with the press could prove bountiful, and thus, it was no coincidence that Roosevelt had asked Davis to cover the battle of his Rough Riders. Davis's account of the bravery of Teddy's Terrors and the overthrow of the Spanish-held Santiago de Cuba propelled Roosevelt to the position of governor in New York the following year.[27] In March 1901, Roosevelt was installed as vice president under President McKinley, and when McKinley was assassinated that September, Roosevelt became the president of the United States.

After nearly ten days in Tokyo, Davis had seen no evidence of the war. Spending most of his time attending festivals with Cecil, writing stories on tea houses and dining out in the evenings, he found the trip more like a holiday retreat than the chaos of a war zone. Evident from his frequent correspondence with his mother, Davis found the days transforming from relaxing and sweet to drawn out and exasperating. The extravagance of having three private rooms, filled with flowerpots and fireplaces, soon lost its charm. As the days turned into weeks, still there was no war in sight.

Eventually, Davis was assigned to the second column of reporters, assigned to follow the Japanese Second Army at the front. On April 1, as the first batch of reporters left for the front line, he held little hope that they would get to see any action. It had become apparent that little information was arriving about actual combat in Korea and Manchuria, and only information that had been strictly censored was to leave the country. In a letter dated March 22, Davis wrote his mother that he knew less of the war than she did. He informed her that as reporters under Japanese supervision, he and his colleagues received none of the unauthorized news; "Were it not for our own squabbles we would not know not only that the country was at war but even that war existed anywhere in the world."

Davis's first article in *Collier's Weekly* appeared on May 7, 1904, under the headline "Making Time in Tokyo: The War Dogs Dine Out." However, the story had little to do with the war. Instead, it was an ode to Japanese hospitality, as Davis wrote of an extravagant dinner of traditional sweets and raw fish that he and his fellow reporters were served by silk-clad nesans in a wooden house that glowed from within; the nesans, the young female servers, would bow and clasp their hands to greet the reporters before serving them an elaborate meal in a room dimly lighted by paper lanterns. Davis marked the lack of furniture but noted the detailed paintings of landscapes and dragons carved into the walls around him. He told *Collier's* readers about the charm of the Japanese people, as he was taken aback not merely by the Japanese's hospitality but also their graciousness in adapting to European manners:

> The next night I dined after the European fashion, and when I saw how adroitly the Japanese officers at the dinner followed it, I was amazed at our [foreign reporters'] temerity of the night previous. For the first time I became conscious that the customs of our table are full of pitfalls. As some one has said, the Romans were able to conquer the world because they did not have to stay home and learn their own language.[28]

Stunned by the courtesy of the Japanese, Davis branded himself and his fellow reporters as "terrible dogs at war," whose thirst for havoc and battle stood in stark contrast with the floral garden parties and elaborate dinners arranged by the Japanese officers. He continued to explore Japanese cuisine and customs in astonishment, as the war appeared to come no closer in range as the days went by.

The following week, he wrote a review of a Japanese play.[29] As a famous playwright and the highest paid American reporter at the time, *Collier's* must have found it advantageous for Davis to distract himself with Japanese theater productions as he impatiently waited in line to embark to the front. Davis and Cecil had been in Japan for exactly two months with no war in sight, and Davis struggled to camouflage his frustrations in his writings: "When you have journeyed this far to send home news of battles, it is hard to find that the nearest you may come to being a war correspondent is to write criticisms of war plays."[30]

The Japanese theater, Davis noted, was strikingly similar to the American. The auditoriums resembled one another in layout and spacing despite slight Japanese architectural modifications, the storyline centered on love and heroism, and the actors paused to the audience's applause much as they did back home. One great difference, Davis wrote, was that love for country—so carefully cultivated during the proceeding decade by a public opinion campaign orchestrated by the government and the press—ranked higher than love for fellow humans. Touched by how patriotism overshadowed any other emotion or human relationship, the audience watched as a soldier in the play obediently farewelled his family as his wife wept and his son tugged at his feet. He showed no emotions and marched away. Another soldier tore apart a photo of his family before leaving for the front line. A stunned Davis found himself struggling not to weep in the audience. That night, he wrote, he drank to the Japanese army.

Around the same time, he wrote a letter to his mother in which he struggled to hide his growing frustration with his assignment in Japan. Despite the profuse cordiality, the excessive meals and the garden parties, his stay was clearly shaped by strict censorship and the growing resentment felt by any war correspondent yearning to see battle, close enough seemingly to smell the conflict yet too far away to see it for himself.

The love for country above all else was not merely a farce in the play, it was the utmost ideal of the Japanese people, Davis wrote. If a Japanese soldier expressed any hesitation or reluctance to risk his life for his country, it could prove fatal. Davis had heard several of such stories. He wrote about a young soldier who had publicly wept upon parting with his parents and, because no good use would come of a man who weeps when he is sent to war, the young soldier had immediately been executed by sword. Another officer had shot himself because he was taken prisoner by the enemy, while a third officer, a lieutenant, had shot his daughter because he had no one to care for her as he left for war.[31] Rather than being disturbed, Davis seemed astonished by the Japanese people's devotion to their nation. This seeming emotional brutality, Davis noted, was unlike any commitment he could imagine from American soldiers. The spirit of national identity was prevalent, both in the plays he witnessed and the war tales he was told.

New plays, written in response to specific events in the war, quickly drew huge audiences. Among the most popular was a fictionalized account of the failed attempt to scuttle a cargo vessel in the mouth of Port Arthur's harbor, which would have trapped the Russian fleet. Torpedo officer Hirose Takeo volunteered to lead the mission in late March. As the vessel neared its goal, Russian shells blew it apart. Hirose died attempting to save his crew. His selfless devotion to duty unto death ignited a whirlwind of adoration in Japan and packed thousands into the theaters. The play took some liberties: Hirose somehow has time for a love affair with a Russian admiral's daughter and outwrestles three giant Russians by using the Japanese martial art of *jiujitsu*.[32] The cult of Hirose worship spread to production and sales of his image on a range of souvenirs including buttons and porcelain wine cups bearing the Japanese words for "Gun God." Lafcadio Hearn, an expatriate Irish-Greek-American writer recognized as the greatest interpreter of Japan to the West, said schoolchildren received the lyrics to *The Song of Hirose Chūsa* in booklets adorned with Hirose's image. Hearn overheard the marching song "everywhere, at all hours of the day." Indicative of Japan's unity and devotion, the lyrics included:

> "Since I am a son of the Country of the Gods, the fire of the evil-hearted Russians cannot touch me!"—The sturdy Takeo who spoke thus: can he really be dead? . . .

> Nay! that glorious war-death meant undying fame ;—beyond a thousand years the valiant heart shall live;—as to a god of war shall reverence be paid to him. . . .[33]

On May 21, 1904, Davis published an article on the funeral of Commander Hirose.[34] A caisson draped in a Japanese uniform and followed by a brigade of soldiers carried the remains of Hirose to his burial site outside Tokyo. Though all that remained of him was a small piece of flesh, he was given a farewell with the honor of "half saint, half hero." Davis wrote an enthralling second-hand account of Hirose's final heroic act, in which he attempted to save a fellow Japanese soldier, a gunner, from a sinking ship that had been hit by a torpedo. Struck by a shell, Hirose had been torn into pieces. Davis must have wondered if this would be the closest he would come to the Russo-Japanese War, relaying tales of fallen heroes from his typewriter in Tokyo.

A disheartened Davis once again wrote his mother a letter. In it, he expressed his dismay with the censorship imposed by the Japanese commanders. Even though his articles in *Collier's Weekly* occasionally mentioned his bitterness about being far from the battle scene, the strict regulations were never part of the official stories. Each story he wrote and each letter he dispatched through Japanese hands were subject to strict censorship, he informed his mother. He did not know what words would be filtered out, and one can only wonder how much information was lost as the Japanese commanders blue-penciled his writings.

> My temper is vile to-day, as I cannot enjoy the gentle pleasures of this town any longer. . . . I am as cross as a sick bear. . . . while they [the Japanese officers] are conversationally perfect in politeness, the regulations they inflict are too insulting. However, you don't care about that, and neither do I. I am going to earn my money if I possibly can, and come home.[35]

Davis continued writing stories about the Japanese people and historical sites in and around Tokyo. Even though he did not hide the contempt he felt for his time in Japan in the letters to his family, his articles in *Collier's Weekly* rarely revealed this vexation. Upon visiting one of Japan's most famous tea establishments, the Tea House of the Hundred and One Steps, he wrote a compelling account of its owner, O Kin San. Davis was accompanied by a commander who had visited the same teahouse nearly half a decade earlier, and when O Kin San saw this same commander again she greeted him as a long-lost son. Baffled by the warmth of their reception, Davis wrote about O Kin San's kindness in disbelief. From the nesans dressed in dove-colored kimonos silently sliding across the floor in their one-toed socks to serve the guests tea and sweet cakes, to O Kin San's cooing welcomes of the commander. Davis was convinced that all was staged for the visiting foreigners' gratification. Nevertheless, he admitted, this apparent performance did not hurt anyone.[36] Davis wrote in awe about his encounter with O Kin San, applauded her wealth of wisdom and her generosity toward strangers. "To sit at the feet of O Kin San is to learn wisdom and courtesy, and to look out from her tea house is to bring yourself in touch with all the world," he declared.[37]

On June 13, Davis met Jack London, who had just returned from the front and was getting ready to board a ship and return home. London had grown increasingly bitter and, according to Davis, had little fondness left for the "wonderful little people."[38] Even though Davis himself struggled with the regulations imposed by the Japanese officers, he clearly still felt fondly about the Japanese people. Upon bidding farewell to London, Davis reminded him that soon the irritation would wear off and leave only pleasant memories about the time in Japan. London was not convinced. While envious that London got to return home, Davis, at the time, felt mostly gratitude toward the Japanese people. Nevertheless, two weeks later, a disgruntled Davis wrote his mother that "not even a siege of London could hold our thoughts from home."[39]

At the end of July, after being in Tokyo for more than four months, Davis and the second column of reporters were assigned to follow General Oku Yasukata's Second Army as it neared Liaoyang in Manchuria.[40] Landing north of Port Arthur, the batch of correspondents spent the first two weeks of August trailing behind the Japanese army along the Liaodong Peninsula. They stumbled upon several sites where battles had already taken place, before finally arriving in Haicheng, anticipating the great Battle of Liaoyang.[41] Despite the broken promises and delays that had shaped his first four months as a war correspondent under Japanese regulations, Davis found it hard to contain his excitement about the possibility of finally seeing a battle scene unfold in front of him. As he would later accentuate, he simply could not describe events he had not himself witnessed.[42]

In an article for *Collier's Weekly* written on August 25 and published on November 5, 1904, Davis accounted the anticipation of following in the footsteps of the Japanese soldiers and nearing the Russian army. Trekking through mud-covered paths and chin-high grass, the reporters were exhausted but excited. Yet, there was no battle in sight and the closest they came to live action was the smoke they could see above a mountain pass in the far distance. The two empires were fighting—nearly ten miles away. Davis's disappointment seeped through his writings. Once again, he found himself writing about the locals he met and not the war he had been promised.

Two encounters appeared to stand out to him. One was the sight of a Chinese woman whose clothes were modest and much less striking than those of the Japanese women he had spent months observing, but whose tiny, misshapen feet were tied up according to traditional Chinese foot-binding practices. The woman's apparent pain, evident from each step she took, struck Davis as abusive as he resonated with her suffering. Learning that women in China were being restricted and retained by their husbands and fathers, he saw them as crippled—physically, but likely also emotionally.

In the same article, Davis described his first encounter with a Russian soldier, who had been taken prisoner by the Japanese army:

> We had only to take one look at his fair skin and long yellow hair. To recognize the enemy we did not need to see his red shirt nor his trousers tucked in his boots. He was the first we had seen, and we eyed him as though he were a rare and savage animal. The little fierce corporal guarding him, rifle in hand, glared at us suspiciously, and the white man in the cart raised tired blue eyes and stared at the white men on the bank of the stream, and they back at him long and steady.[43]

It must have been a strange encounter for Davis and his fellow correspondents; the Russian's features were undeniably more similar to theirs than to those of the Japanese—whom Davis described as having identical, bronzed faces with buzzed short hair and bodies clad in white uniforms. For the first time, the reporters stood face to face with the enemy, who looked so very much like themselves.

The following day, Davis and the second column of reporters were led to Anshantien, where Oku's army was set to face the Russian forces. The encounter included the last promise to Davis that the Japanese officers would break. The battle unfolded on the other side of a mountain pass, out of the correspondents' view. Rather than feign interest, the reporters lolled on the grass and read two-month-old news of the Democratic National Convention in Saint Louis. Davis recorded in a memoir that this action "greatly disturbed" the Japanese officers tasked with supervising the movements of the Western correspondents.

> "You complain," they said, "because you are not allowed to see anything, and now, when we show you a battle, you will not look."
>
> [Willmott] Lewis, of the [New York] Herald, eagerly seized his glasses and followed the track of the Siberian railway as it disappeared into the pass.
>
> "I beg your pardon, but I didn't know it was a battle," he apologized politely.
> "I thought it was a locomotive at Anshantien Station blowing off steam."
>
> And, so, teacher gave him a bad mark for disrespect.[44]

When realizing that the battle was to unfold on the other side of a mountain pass and that the correspondents could not go any nearer than the four-mile limit where they had been held, Davis determined to leave the army once and for all. Alongside fellow reporters John Fox Jr. of *Scribner's Magazine*, Milton Prior of the *Illustrated London News*, and the London *Morning Chronicle*'s George Lynch, he decided to leave the East and finally return home. Struck with immense disappointment, he could no longer withhold his resentment for how the Japanese commanders had treated him. It was the end of August and he had spent nearly six months covering teahouses and theater plays in lieu of battle scenes.

The trek back through Manchuria proved a tasking one. As rain continued to pour, the trails back through the mountain pass as they steered for Haicheng and then Newchwang became increasingly difficult to navigate. While the group split over the course of the week, Davis finally made it to the harbor of Yantai (Chefoo) on September 1, after several days of riding through muddy trails in the endless rain. He immediately steered for the local cable station, where he intended to wire *Collier's Weekly* to notify his editors of his return. When Davis informed the operator of his name and position as a war correspondent, with the intention of sending his copy collect, the small Chinese clerk congratulated him and proceeded to bow and smile. Hesitant to meet the eyes of the Chinese man, Davis feared the worst—that he had missed out on a great story. "Why?" he reluctantly asked of the complimentary greeting. The clerk responded: "Because you are the first. You are the only correspondent to arrive who has seen the battle of Liao-Yang."[45] A sickening feeling settled in Davis's stomach as he learned that he had missed one of the largest battles in world history by three days.

Davis's fondness for the Japanese people had turned sour, and as he saw the American warship in the harbor of Yantai, he passionately described his delight to return to American territory:

> For six months we had tasted all the indignities of the suspected spy, we had been prisoners of war, we had been ticket-of-leave mean, and it is not difficult to imagine our glad surprise that same day when we saw in the harbor the white hull of the cruiser Cincinnati with our flag lifting at her stern.[46]

As he boarded the ship to return to the United States, a furious Davis was eager to part ways with the "dark-skinned keepers with the slanting, suspicious, unfriendly eyes, with tongues that spoke the one thing and meant the other."[47] But he also was distraught. His friend of twenty years, John Fox Jr., said, "[W]hen our ship left those shores each knew that the other went to his state-room and in bitter chagrin and disappointment wept quite childishly."[48]

In 1910, Davis published a book titled *Notes of a War Correspondent*, a compilation of his numerous excursions overseas. The chapter devoted to his assignment covering the Russo-Japanese War was rightfully titled "Battles I Did Not See." He wrote:

It was a noiseless, odorless, rubber-tired battle. . . . [T]he only thing about that battle of which you were certain as that it was a perfectly safe battle to watch. It was the first one I ever witnessed that did not require you to calmly smoke a pipe in order to conceal the fact that you were scared.[49]

While Davis never witnessed any battle scenes in covering the Russo-Japanese War, except when passing those where battles had ended long before, his published accounts for his time in Japan became tantamount to war correspondence in the early twentieth century. To a greater degree than his contemporaries Jack London and John Fox Jr., and far more than hardened war correspondents such as Frederick Palmer, Davis wrote stories that bore tribute to the people he encountered and steered away from the hard-news style to which other reporters adhered. The detailed accounts of his visit to the teahouses and his observations of local peasants and Japanese officers reflected the beginnings of a change in war reporting; rather than focusing on the war in sheer numbers and hard facts, he channeled his journalistic work into compelling narratives about the Japanese people. He drew comparisons between the people in the Far East and the Americans back home, the people whom he had come to know so well. His stories also revealed that the customs and traditions of the Japanese people far exceeded his expectations in terms of hospitality and generosity. The closest Davis would come to the combat of the Russo-Japanese War was the tales that were passed on by other reporters. Unlike his contemporaries, however, he paid little notice to the tales that had been passed on to him as he was of firm belief that a reporter can only truly report on what he has seen. Instead, he focused his writing on the people he encountered. He brought his subjects to life. While the spirit of national identity was a red thread throughout Davis's published accounts from his time in the East, his vivid descriptions of the land, the architecture and, above all, the people he observed, added emotional characteristics to the face of war.

Davis's last assignment as a war correspondent came with the outbreak of World War I. On August 13, 1914, Davis arrived in Liverpool, England. Unable to obtain credentials from the English authorities—as it was determined that only one American correspondent, Frederick Palmer, would be allowed to accompany the British army—Davis set out for Brussels to cover the arrival of German troops marching through the neutral country on their way to fight in France.[50] On August 20, he watched as thousands of German troops—or as he would refer to them, the "gray ghost"—marched down the cobblestone streets of Brussels: "For three days and three nights the column of gray, with hundreds of thousands of bayonets and hundreds of thousands of lances, with gray transport wagons, gray ammunition carts, gray ambulances, gray cannon, like a river of steel, cut Brussels in two."[51]

Even though it involved no vivid battle scenes or fighting, his report on the German overthrow of Brussels became his most famous dispatch. Davis compared the arrival of German troops to the haze of a gray fog rolling across the sea and their presence heavy as the plague enclosing the people in an invisible cloak.

Eager to follow the impending siege of France, Davis and a fellow correspondent, Gerald Morgan of *Metropolitan Magazine*, boarded a train to Paris. Taunted by poor luck, Davis was soon detained by German soldiers, and on suspicion of being an English spy he was held as a prisoner. Fearing for his life, Davis was kept locked up with no food and a hard floor to sleep on. His internment was short lived and he was released in Ligne on the condition that he return to Brussels.[52] A distressed Davis became increasingly anti-German after his arrest, which continued to color his coverage of the war. While his previous war coverage, especially of the Spanish-American War, had cemented modern warfare as relatively civilized in nature, a pained Davis described the Germans as dirty "mad dogs" who led a "hellish war."[53]

Distressed and forlorn, Davis returned to the United States and expressed strong beliefs that he judged the Germans guilty for the waste of human life. Upset with America's neutrality, Davis was not shy to call out President Woodrow Wilson and Congress for not taking a stance against Germany. Even though he never expressed it directly, it appeared his ego had been bruised when the German soldiers had arrested him, not recognized him as a famous author, and caused him to worry for his life.

Shortly before his fifty-third birthday, Davis suffered a heart attack and died in his home in Mount Kisco, New York. He left behind his second wife, Bessie McCoy, whom he had married in 1912, and their daughter, Hope. Ironically, Davis's last living hours, according to his brother Charles, had been spent writing an article on preparedness. He had stayed up late that evening and was discussing this very topic on the phone when he was stricken by a heart attack. With whom he spoke, no one knows.

NOTES

1. "Best Infantry in the World," *Minneapolis Journal*, October 13, 1904.
2. Charles B. Davis, *Adventures and Letters of Richard Harding Davis* (New York: Charles Scribner's Sons, 1917), 298.
3. Richard Harding Davis to his mother, quoted in ibid., 297.
4. Davis, *Adventures and Letters*, 298.
5. Richard Harding Davis, *Notes of a War Correspondent* (New York: Charles Scribner's Sons, 1911), 220–21.
6. Davis, *Adventures and Letters*, 6.

7. Ibid., 4.
8. Ibid., 15.
9. M. A. De W. Howe, *The Lehigh Burr*, April 1916, quoted in Davis, *Adventures and Letters*, 27.
10. Davis, *Adventures and Letters*, 47.
11. Ibid., 19.
12. Ibid., 301.
13. Arthur Lubow, *The Reporter Who Would Be King* (New York: Charles Scribner's Sons, 1992), 137.
14. Lubow, *The Reporter Who Would Be King*, 139.
15. Ibid.
16. Ibid., 141.
17. Richard Harding Davis, "The Death of Rodríguez," *New York Journal*, February 1897.
18. Lubow, *The Reporter Who Would Be King*, 156.
19. Davis, *Adventures and Letters*, 227.
20. Lubow, *The Reporter Who Would Be King*, 166.
21. Edmund Morris, *The Rise of Theodore Roosevelt* (New York: Random House, 2010), 509.
22. Theodore Roosevelt, "Davis and the Rough Riders," *Scribner's Magazine*, July 1916, 89.
23. "Rough Riders: The World of 1898; The Spanish-American War," Library of Congress, https://www.loc.gov/rr/hispanic/1898/roughriders.html.
24. "Rough Riders: The World of 1898; The Spanish-American War."
25. Lubow, *The Reporter Who Would Be King*, 183.
26. "The Rough Riders Storm San Juan Hill," Eyewitness to History, http://www.eyewitnesstohistory.com/pfroughriders.htm.
27. "The Rough Riders Storm San Juan Hill."
28. Richard Harding Davis, "Marking Time in Tokio: The War Dogs Dine Out," *Collier's Weekly*, May 7, 1904, 9.
29. Richard Harding Davis, "Marking Time in Tokio: A War Drama," *Collier's Weekly*, May 14, 1904, 11–12.
30. Davis, "Marking Time in Tokio: A War Drama."
31. Ibid.
32. "Songs of Russia and Japan," *Saint Louis Globe-Democrat*, September 11, 1904.
33. Lafcadio Hearn, "A Letter from Japan," *The Atlantic* 94 (November 1904): 632.
34. Richard Harding Davis, "Marking Time in Tokio: The Forty–Eighth Ronin," *Collier's Weekly*, May 21, 1904, 8–9.
35. Richard Harding Davis to his mother, May 22, 1904, quoted in Davis, *Adventures and Letters*, 304.
36. Richard Harding Davis, "Marking Time in Tokio: The Tea House of the Hundred and One Steps," *Collier's Weekly*, May 28, 1904, 10–11.
37. Davis, "Marking Time in Tokio."
38. Richard Harding Davis mother, June 13, 1904, quoted in Davis, *Adventures and Letters*, 305.

39. Richard Harding Davis to his mother, June 26, 1904, quoted in Davis, *Adventures and Letters*, 306.

40. Scott C. Osborn and Robert L. Phillips Jr., *Richard Harding Davis* (Boston: Twayne Publishers, 1978), 79.

41. Osborn and Phillips, *Richard Harding Davis*, 80.

42. Davis, *Notes of a War Correspondent*, 229.

43. Richard Harding Davis, "On the Track of the Army," *Collier's Weekly*, November 5, 1904, 22–30.

44. Davis, *Notes of a War Correspondent*, 215.

45. Ibid., 230.

46. Ibid.

47. Ibid., 233.

48. John Fox Jr., *R.H.D.: Appreciations of Richard Harding Davis* (New York: Charles Scribner's Sons, 1917), 65. This book is a collection of tributes to Davis after his death in 1916. Only 375 copies were printed as keepsakes; the citation is to a digitized version in the Richard Harding Davis archive at the University of Virginia Library, Charlottesville, VA.

49. Fox, *R.H.D.: Appreciations of Richard Harding Davis*, 229.

50. Davis, *Adventure and Letters*, 368.

51. "The German Army Marches through Brussels, 1914," EyeWitness to History, www.eyewitnesstohistory.com.

52. Osborn and Phillips, *Richard Harding Davis*, 83.

53. Richard Harding Davis, *With the Allies* (Toronto: The Copp Clark Company, 1915), 88–85.

Chapter 6
Luigi Barzini Sr.

La narrazione è un filo, e la verità è un tessuto.

—Luigi Barzini Sr., 1905[1]

War correspondent Luigi Barzini Sr. watched Japanese soldiers attack the Russian lines in Manchuria with frustration. "Anyone attempting to describe a battle at some point realizes that a battle is something indescribable," Barzini wrote in Italian in 1905 for *Corriere della Sera* (Evening Courier) of Milan, Italy's most prestigious newspaper. Whatever a war correspondent writes seems arbitrary and artificial, he said; war journalism is just a miserable bit of wandering. Barzini noted that describing a battle was like trying to show a great picture, such as the Sistine Chapel, by the light of a match that illuminates a small space but leaves the rest in darkness. What escapes the narrative is that everything happens at once. Telling the story implies order, but war is chaos, the opposite of order, he said. "How can one give an idea of the complexity of the facts?" Barzini asked. "Narrative is a thread, and truth is a fabric. (*La narrazione è un filo, e la verità è un tessuto.*)"[2]

Nevertheless, Barzini did his best to describe the slice of battle before his eyes. Describing the fighting in early March 1905 at Hanjapu,[3] Barzini noted that the Japanese Third Army under General Count Nodzu Michitsura threw itself at fortifications near a railway. The Russian defenders had set up four positions connected by tunnels and trenches, all screened by barbed wire.[4] Japanese troops deployed at night with plans to attack before dawn, but the battle did not begin until the sky brightened. Thus the Russians could see, and target, the enemy. Barzini recorded that as the Japanese advanced over 300 meters of open ground, the Russians responded with heavy artillery, field artillery, machine guns, and small arms. "The [Japanese] move is disastrous, but to retreat or stay under the shower of bullets would probably be even more deadly. . . . The first line is mowed. The second passes over the corpses, and continues."[5]

The attackers jumped into the Russian trenches. Sporadic gunfire continued, but most soldiers found rifles too slow in such close quarters and instead fell to using sabers, bayonets, rifle butts, and bare hands. Russian and Japanese troops rolled in the earth at the bottom of the trenches with bloody fingers grasping each other's throats and gouging at each other's eyes. The fighting moved Barzini to write, "He who has not seen the horrific wounds of the corpses in these pits, cannot imagine the monstrous melee that took place there."[6]

Barzini, representing neutral Italy, had sympathy for both the Russians and the Japanese. But he was most impressed by the character of ordinary Japanese soldiers, whom he repeatedly praised in *Corriere*. His writing focused on the impact of frightening new weapons, including machine guns and high-explosive shells, upon the citizen soldiers who filled modern armies and the natives whose lands formed the battlegrounds. He built war stories around human drama on a human scale. His writing also had a strong voice, including a wry sense of humor that emerged when he was not writing about death and destruction. Despite the strength and significance of Barzini's war correspondence, only fragments have been written in English about Barzini's wartime experiences. Interest in Barzini was rekindled in 2007 with the centennial reprinting, in English translation, of his account of traveling with Prince Scipione Borghese from Beijing to Paris in one of the first extreme-distance road races, and with the publication of an Italian-language biography a year later.[7] That biography, by Enzo Magri, has yet to be translated into English.

This chapter examines Barzini's war correspondence in East Asia with special attention to nineteen dispatches, each several thousand words long, about the war's decisive Battle of Mukden. Barzini lived among Japanese troops for many weeks at a time, longer than any other correspondent, allowing him to gain trust. The Russo-Japanese War of 1904–1905 was the first war that Barzini covered extensively and helped establish his reputation for excellence as a combat reporter. His writing style was superb; wartime journalism historian Phillip Knightley said Italian street vendors sold copies of *Corriere della Sera* by shouting Barzini's name instead of the headlines of his stories.[8] And the content matched the presentation—Barzini earned many exclusives and joined Frederick Palmer of *Collier's Weekly* and Bennet Burleigh of the London *Daily Telegraph* as perhaps the only three non-Japanese reporters to cover the war's climactic battle at Mukden, the largest land battle to that date. Barzini's Mukden articles were printed in *Corriere della Sera* and gathered in a book, *Guerra russo-giapponese: La battaglia di Mukden, narrata da Luigi Barzini.*

Barzini operated in the European tradition known as *grand reportage*, which emerged as a distinct genre in the late 1800s and early 1900s, epitomized by French war correspondent Albert Londres. Historian Jean Rabaut noted that *grand reportage* writers typically traveled far to immerse themselves in a big story.[9] They pioneered investigative journalism in Europe, marrying significant public affairs news stories with personal narrative, an eye for detail, and what Londres biographer Walter Redfern called "an exuberant and natural prose."[10] According to Redfern, Londres never forgot the "minutiae of war," adding, "Where he [Londres] excels is in passing on to readers something of the very feel of war: the noises, the smells, the catastrophic impact on the non-human world, the plausible attitudes and sentiments of the common soldier or citizen."[11] Like Barzini, Londres struggled with truthfully fixing war on paper. "Il ya deux guerres, celle qu'on fait and celle qu'on dit," Londres said. (Roughly, "There are two wars, one we fight and one we tell.")[12] *Grand reportage* war stories read like the serialized novels popular in late nineteenth-century Europe, based on eyewitness accounts and embellished with flourishes that imposed story frames on events.[13] Barzini's reporting from the Far East during the Russo-Japanese War fit within this broader tradition, as did journalist Adolfo Rossi's war correspondence for *Corriere della Sera*, first in 1895–1896 in Eritrea to cover Italy's war with Abyssinia, and in 1897 in the Greco-Turkish war.[14]

Barzini learned his journalistic skills from one of the most celebrated editors in the history of Italian journalism, Luigi Albertini of *Corriere della Sera*. Albertini analyzed newspaper work as if it were a science. As a young man, he covered events in London for the newspaper *La Stampa* in Turin, Italy, and took time to parse the operations of the *Times* of London. Albertini's biographer asserted that London and the *Times* "confirmed in him a faith in ideas and the possibility, in a free country, of promoting the elevation of minds through discussion and objective, unprejudiced criticism."[15] Albertini likely also absorbed the news style favored in Britain—a more literary narrative than the inverted pyramid emerging in the United States, although historian Hazel Dicken-Garcia has documented a growing emphasis in the 1890s among American newspapers on dramatic events and individual personalities, often organized around the "plot" of a news story, as a means of attracting readers.[16] Albertini would take his schooling in British journalism with him to Milan when he became editor of *Corriere della Sera* in 1900.

The existence of Italian foreign correspondents required Italian newspapers to have sufficient circulation and revenue to support sending reporters overseas for extended periods. Italian papers reached this age much later than their counterparts in England and the United States, in part because of the relatively late creation of the modern Italian nation, and in part because of low literacy rates. *Corriere della Sera*, founded by a family of textile magnates, began publishing in 1876. Its emergence as a prominent newspaper—considered today to be the most prestigious in Italy, somewhat equivalent to the *New York Times*—can be dated to the hiring of the brilliant Albertini as managing editor. Albertini invested the paper's profits in expansion. He hired more reporters and added newspaper supplements.[17] Albertini wanted to have *Corriere* follow a path similar to those of the best European and American papers. Wars and Italian emigration to the West provided big, important stories that Albertini believed could build circulation and prestige. Barzini was one of Albertini's discoveries as he looked for talent.[18]

Barzini was born on February 7, 1874, in Orvieto, Umbria. His father, Ettore, a tailor, created a means to gather quick and accurate measurements to fit a man for a suit of clothes, which brought him military business. When Ettore died, Luigi Barzini tried to run the family business but had no success. He left for Rome in 1898 and fell in with a friend and classmate, the journalist Ettore Marroni, who set him up to write and draw cartoons for small magazines. Barzini's flair for creating vignettes based upon observation caught the attention of Albertini. In the summer of 1898, shortly after he left *La Stampa* in Turin and joined *Corriere*, Albertini planned to install a rotary press to roll out a Sunday supplement in a push to create the largest circulation in Italy. Albertini was on the lookout for young talent to improve his newspaper and liked Barzini's writing. Albertini offered him the post of London correspondent. As Albertini wanted to inspect a press in London, he and Barzini agreed to travel to England together in July 1899. In London, Barzini bought a gray morning coat and striped trousers to blend in with the upper-class London crowd. He wanted to settle into a reporting routine, but Albertini cautioned him to learn about England first. For three months, Albertini said, Barzini should do nothing but read newspapers and books, and observe society, politics, and the arts. Albertini returned home, leaving Barzini on his own. The cub reporter could not help himself; after a month, he sent his first three dispatches: the frosty reception of dark-skinned South Africans in London; the return of an Arctic explorer; and the difficult lives of miners. His editor admonished him to tighten his writing to cut telegraph costs, an act that that shaped his prose just as he was beginning his journalism career. Magri wrote that maximum brevity led Barzini "to avoid literary embellishments and create a simple, direct, fast, naked style."[19] Barzini cultivated his characteristic agility with phrasing as well as a propensity to accurately portray character, such as the amused detachment he witnessed in ordinary British citizens. Barzini's stories began appearing regularly on *Corriere*'s front page.

Barzini's work must have impressed Albertini. In summer 1900, *Corriere* assigned Barzini to cover the uprising known in the West as the Boxer

Rebellion and in China as the Yihetuan Movement, in which peasants attempted to expel all foreigners. Barzini received a note from Milan asking whether he would be willing to travel to China to cover the siege of foreigners and Chinese Christians in the Legation Quarter in Beijing. He replied that he was "ready to go into the crater of a volcano."[20] He left on July 10 for the Far East, while the fifty-five day siege was still under way. Seven days later, the Chinese declared an armistice, and on August 14 soldiers of Western armies reached the legation district, ending the siege. Barzini arrived afterward, still looking for stories. He had a keen eye for detail, an empathy for ordinary soldiers, and a dry, even sarcastic, sense of humor. Wandering in and around Beijing on his horse Dispaccio (Dispatch), he gathered information for background, feature, and color stories. As he arrived at the archway to the legation, Barzini noted "a strange Japanese rose." It was the heads of a dozen Chinese rebels, tied together by their queues and hung upon a nail. He wrote, "This way, my readers, came civilization." He found that Westerners killed Chinese civilians regularly and for little reason. A German officer told him that he shot one Chinese a day to raise the morale of his troops.[21]

Most foreign correspondents left Beijing that autumn to cover the Boer War in South Africa, but Barzini stayed on, writing about religion, a primary cause of the rebellion, and ordinary life in China. Barzini's knack for travel and war correspondence made him the natural choice for an assignment when the souring of relations between Russia and Japan late in 1903 presaged another war. *Corriere* first assigned Barzini to go to Saint Petersburg, the Russian capital, to cover negotiations in late 1903 designed to avert war. Barzini left Europe on January 20, 1904, to head toward what he expected to be the war zone. "I decided to station myself on the Japanese side for an entirely professional reason," he wrote, having the unfounded fear that Russian censorship would be the worse of the two. He chose to travel by ship to Japan in order to avoid being detained if found aboard a trans-Siberian train when war broke out.[22] The attack on Port Arthur occurred with Barzini en route.

Barzini arrived in Tokyo and was accepted as a correspondent accredited by the Japanese Ministry of War. Barzini was initially assigned to the Second Army of General Oku Yasukata and expected to travel to the mainland to cover hostilities. However, Barzini did not get permission to sail until August 1904, six months after the start of the war. Meanwhile, the Japanese First Army—accompanied by several Western correspondents—landed in Korea and crossed the Yalu River into China. The Second Army landed on the mainland on May 20 and, ten days later, seized Dalny on the Liaodong Peninsula as a base for operations against Port Arthur. When the Japanese Third Army landed at Dalny, the Second Army marched northward to meet Russian troops moving to attempt to relieve Port Arthur, and the Third Army began a siege and assault on the Russian fortified port.[23] Concentrations of Japanese and Russian troops met northeast of the Liaodong Peninsula at Liaoyang and later at Mukden for control of land routes to Port Arthur. The fighting in late 1904 and early 1905 was bitter, figuratively and literally. Temperatures often plunged below zero degrees Fahrenheit.

Barzini waited in Tokyo for his chance to see the fighting. He finally was allowed to land on July 31 at Dalny, the previous site of the Second and Third armies' invasion of the Liaodong Peninsula. Barzini telegraphed Albertini about his arrival on the mainland. "16 correspondents yours included sailed on transport unknown landing believed Dalny," he wrote in English, the language approved for telegrams by Japanese censors. He continued:

> Authority issued very strict regulation for press telegraphic service from front. Correspondents not allowed send more 5 telegrams of 50 words in all daily so telegraphic correspondence very difficult. Afraid almost impossible but in compensation exciting moving magnificent and terrible spectacles expected to witness and describe.[24]

He rode hard for eleven days to reach the headquarters of General Oku of the Second Army six miles from the Russian outposts near Liaoyang. He arrived on horseback on August 10 at Haicheng, where he billeted with Richard Harding Davis, John Fox, and the other correspondents of the second wave. He waited there until the armies' commander in chief, Marshal Ōyama Iwao, arrived on August 23 to take charge of the combined force of Japan's armies. The Battle of Liaoyang began the next day.[25]

Military censorship made it impossible to report freely and in detail from the battle zones, he wrote in the introduction to his war memoir. If he wanted to telegraph a report, he had to leave the army and travel far to send his dispatches from the closest telegraph office not under military control, in Tianjin (Tientsin), across the Bohai Sea from Port Arthur. From there, on September 5, he sent telegrams of several dozen words about the Battle of Liaoyang, which had concluded the day before with a Russian withdrawal. He noted an "unspe[a]kable undefinable fe[e]ling of tragic reality in the air."[26]

By that time, most prominent Western correspondents had already left the war zone, upset by the severity of Japanese censorship and their inability to cover war as they had hoped. Writing after the war, Davis said the Japanese had destroyed the freedom of war reporters and predicted that future belligerents would copy their methods. If Davis and others had stayed for a few more weeks, they would have found the censorship loosened in the fall of 1904, a period coinciding with a series of Japanese victories in the battlefield that no doubt lessened anxieties about the potential impact of war news on national morale. It was during this easing of censorship that Barzini arrived at Liaoyang to witness what had eluded so many others: combat. He won that honor because he stayed patient, outlasted the strictest period of censorship, and eventually won the trust of Japanese soldiers and officers. "Was first correspondent entered Liaoyang," he telegraphed *Corriere*. "Russian town fired by shells was still c[h]urning thick smoke." His brief wire described Russian corpses, abandoned ammunition magazines, and low Russian morale. He then added a brief apology. "Misunderstandings" between field correspondents and the Japanese army had put him in a fix. The Japanese army required correspondents who left their area of control to return to Tokyo and be reapproved before returning to the war zone. This precaution, intended to reduce the risk of spying, meant Barzini lost valuable time getting his dispatches on the wire while fighting continued. He said he would return to the front at the end of September, "determined [to] do useful service after painful costly but involuntary failure."[27] Barzini filed his dispatches at Tianjin and went back to Tokyo to start over.

When he returned to the war zone, it would be to Mukden, site of the decisive land battle of the war. In mid-November, Barzini received a special permit from the Ministry of War to return. He left Osaka on a transport on December 1 and landed at Dalny on December 8. He sent a dispatch describing the siege of Port Arthur, predicting the garrison's fall into Japanese hands, and then headed north toward Shaho, site of a stiff Russian defense after the retreat from Liaoyang. In his memoir's introduction, he described his method to understand the Japanese army:

> The long stay in the same locations enabled me to get to know them, to gather information on the defenses and on the forces posted along the front. I was able with a map given to me by the Japanese General Staff to familiarize myself with local features and to understand the importance of military positions and later to be able to follow military movements with sufficient clarity. Great sources of information for me were battlefield hospitals and medication posts, because although a Japanese officer does not utter a word when he is in service, he's less reluctant to tell what has happened when he is out of the scene because of an injury.
>
> Correspondents of Japanese newspapers met in the battlefield always told me what they knew with the true courtesy of colleagues.[28]

Port Arthur fell on January 1, 1905, but the war continued. In February, the Battle of Mukden began. Nearly one hundred thousand troops released from duty at Port Arthur marched north to join the Japanese armies converging at the Manchurian capital. Barzini followed developments while traveling with Oku. He reported what he saw of the Second Army and gathered details on other Japanese forces after the battle's conclusion. He said he could not leave Oku's army while the battle was under way, nor did he want to leave it, as the Battle of Mukden was crucial to the war's outcome. To prevent his being mistaken for a Russian soldier, the army gave him a Japanese uniform. The army also gave him a wagon for his transportation and a daily ration of rice for himself and hay for his horse. The army guaranteed him a daily dispatch of one hundred words via the censored telegraph line, a final dispatch of five thousand words via censored telegraph, and access to the mail. His war letters, which became stories in *Corriere* and chapters in his memoir, took about three months to reach Milan.[29]

Barzini marveled at the miracle of communication afforded by a network of telegraph lines. It was a boon to correspondents, yes, but also the means to conduct modern warfare.

> It is the triumph of the telegraph. Without the railroad it would be impossible to feed such an army; but without the telegraph it would be impossible to make it act. A dispatcher riding on horseback would spend twelve hours in order to bring news to general command from the extreme flanks; the orders to the troops would arrive twenty-four hours late.
>
> The region was covered by a net of electrical wires running from fifty-six telegraph and telephone stations, distributed along the positions, ready to gather instantaneously news directed to the general staff of Marshal Oyama.[30]

He began his mailed dispatches about Mukden with a description of the Japanese military mind and the life of ordinary soldiers. He quoted a "secret memo" from Oku to his officers urging them to totally commit themselves to battle. The order made clear the importance of obedience and duty: "For us the war will end when the enemy is subjugated. . . . Until he is annihilated, our duty is not done. . . . Once positions are taken, they must not be abandoned. . . . Do not ever abandon weapons or ammunition to the enemy, under any circumstances."[31]

Barzini surveyed the land before him and hinted at the size of the coming battle: the Japanese armies were spread out across 160 kilometers.[32] Amid snow and temperatures that dipped far below zero, Japanese and Russian soldiers' bodies were torn by hand grenades, ripped by machine gun bullets, and crushed by boulders rolled from the heights. "[T]he frozen snow makes the terrain so slippery that it takes unprecedented efforts to proceed. The soldiers have to climb on their knees and cling with their hands. The wounded and dead roll down to the bottom of the valley," Barzini wrote. "The suffering of the soldiers, borne in silence, is indescribable. We have several cases of hypothermia. Most of the wounded die."[33] He said soldiers called the site of one encounter "Gigu-ku-dani," or "Valley of Hell."[34] Barzini noted that a Japanese colonel, given an order to assault a hill, replied that his men would take the hill or not come back. "The positions were not taken, and he did not come back," Barzini wrote. Before the assault, Barzini noted that the soldiers all drank sake, which he said was the "ritual libation" used before suicide.[35]

Barzini witnessed many such instances that revealed the Japanese mind. For example, he told readers that Japanese moral character was explained by small details, such as a dying lieutenant using his last moments of life to compose a poem. The lieutenant's poem contained the line *Kuni no tame*, or "For the nation." In such was revealed the strength of the country, Barzini wrote. The lieutenant struggled to continue, managing to add the word *sasageshi*, or "offered." He passed out and died in the night.[36]

Soldiers acted as if they were doing an ordinary job, Barzini said. He attributed that attitude to the composition of the ranks that made up both Japanese and Russian infantry. An army is composed of farmers, workers, students, and other men of every class, he wrote, but they endured war like veterans. "Human adaptability is amazing. The population of a bombed city gets used to living like this. At Port Arthur when no bombs fell, the quays were full of cars. They said, 'They have suspended the bombing, so we go for a walk!' It was as if you had said, 'It has stopped raining. We go out!'"[37]

Figure 6.1 Luigi Barzini of Milan, Italy, was one of the world's best war correspondents. He embedded with Japan's Second Army and witnessed the Battle of Mukden.

Figure 6.2 Correspondent Frederick Palmer witnessed Japan's censorship up close. In World War I, he served as the United States' chief military censor. *Source*: Library of Congress.

Such reportage aligned with the literary, E. L. Godkin school of combat journalism from the Crimean War—stories that depicted violence through a series of human-scale and human-interest pictures that, when combined like tiles in a mosaic or threads in a fabric, brought to the reader a deeper understanding of the war as a whole. Barzini's peers of this school included Richard Harding Davis, John Fox Jr., and Jack London. They told *stories* that had character, detail, and plot. For holding reader interest and illuminating the nature of war, their style far outshone the straight, William Howard Russell style of war correspondence practiced by just-the-facts journalists such as Frederick Palmer and William H. Brill. Here, for example, is how Palmer opened his account of events leading to what he called "the greatest battle since Gettysburg," the clash at Liaoyang, which Barzini also witnessed and reported:

For five months the First Army had not seen the sea, a plain, or a railroad train. When we fought, it was over hills and ridges; when we camped, it was in twisting valleys. On August 24, we were still at Tiensuitien, which is twenty miles from Liao-Yang. Before we might fight in the great battle we must fight two battles of our own. Before Kuroki could swing into line with Oku and Nodzu, and the three converging columns should form an intact force, we must take a chain of majestic heights on either side of the armpit-deep Tang River.

In that advance, the Second Division—the men of Sendai and northern Japan—formed the centre, the Imperial Guards our left, and the twelfth our right.[38]

Here is the lead paragraph of a similar bit of war correspondence from Associated Press reporter Brill on the same site and battle:

After 3 o'clock yesterday the Japanese succeeded in commanding Kaofengshik from Paoshankan, where their advance first began on August 23, and also from their position at Liang Chiksan on the east, in such a way as to force the Russian center and right flank, compelling the evacuation of Anshantien today. The Japanese south front, therefore, is several miles nearer Liao Yang.

At 3:30 o'clock yesterday Japanese shells from concealed batteries in the vicinity of Pao Shankan began falling on the road west of Kaofengshik, leading to Liao Yang.[39]

Undoubtedly a full picture of war demands that the reader absorb both styles of war reporting, the Godkin and the Russell. But when viewed side by side, comparing Barzini, Davis, London, and Fox against Palmer and Brill, it becomes clear which style more clearly captures the imagination. Reading Palmer and Brill is a labor for all but the most dedicated followers of war. Reading Barzini is both informing and entertaining. Small wonder news vendors in Italy sold *Corriere della Sera* by shouting his byline.

Barzini approved of the character of the ordinary Japanese soldier, but was less impressed by their enemies. Russians "lack in every virtue except those of resilience and bravery," he wrote. When Japanese forces entered a village abandoned by Russian troops, they found the stripped corpses of some of their comrades who had disappeared in the previous day's fighting. Some lacked obvious wounds, making it appear they had died of cold while naked. One had a bloody boot print on his face and broken teeth. This enraged the Japanese who found the body; they threw themselves at the next line of Russian defenses. The soldiers charged and captured twenty-seven Russians in a trench. Barzini witnessed what followed and considered it as evidence of the peculiar Japanese character:

Then a horrific scene took place. The furious Japanese pushed the unfortunate men out of the trench, and each one who emerged was shot. They fell one after the other amidst cries of revenge.

Who knows what would have been the frightening consequences, in such a vast battle, of the unleashing of all human ferocity latent in each man, if

General Asada, informed of the event, had not ordered immediate punishment of the main culprits of the massacre. And it was a very humiliating punishment for some Japanese soldiers; they were taken out of the front line of combat and sent to the rear.[40]

Particularly noteworthy of the account is that it depicted what military observers likely would describe as an atrocity: the slaughter of enemy combatants who were surrendering and offering no resistance. The article was published in June, three months after the battle, so it is almost certain that Barzini sent the dispatch via international mail so that it did not undergo Japanese censorship.

Barzini walked among wounded and dead Russians after a battle that left the Japanese controlling the field. Some corpses, their faces still expressing rage, clutched their rifles with dead hands. A few wounded soldiers crawled, dazed; others prayed before crosses and icons they removed from their jacket pockets. Recognizing Barzini as a fellow European, some made the sign of the cross and asked for relief in the name of Christ. "You cannot imagine anything more painful, more poignant, than having to pass close to so much pain and not being able to do anything—to close the eyes and ears, and go on with a broken heart," Barzini wrote.[41]

Barzini said his stories could give only his limited perspective of battle, especially in a modern war that stretched for miles. A war correspondent amid battle takes in little of the chaos, as he tramps all day across smoky plains, valleys, and rivers and then realizes he has crossed only a quarter of the battle zone. Only at night, he wrote, on a rooftop or up a tree to watch the flash of gunpowder as far as the eye can see, does the correspondent get a feel for the immensity of battle. At such times, "the whole universe is plagued by firestorm."[42] Nighttime attacks seemed surreal. Under cover of darkness, Japanese soldiers could not see the faces of their comrades or of the enemy. Their orders were "to kill the big ones" ("ammazzare i grossi")—a reference to the size of Russian soldiers compared with Japanese. Even so, Japanese soldiers in the dark continually shouted *Teki ka mikata ka?*—"friend or foe?"—and the Russians exchanged similar questions. In the midst of blackness and confusion, bayonets, rifle butts, and swords slashed through the air, and groans escaped from the dying. Blood flowed so freely that walking across the ground the next morning soaked one's shoes.[43]

The scope of battle tested the ideal of personal leadership. Barzini contrasted a modern war's general with the romantic ideal of Napoleon on horseback leading his troops. A painter depicting Napoleon's counterpart in 1905, General Ōyama, would capture him smoking a cigar in a Chinese room lighted by an iron stove, he said. Barzini set the rest of the scene for his readers: In the center of the room was a table covered with maps. Officers pointed at it from time to time and moved ivory pieces to mark the location of troops. On the wall was a large panel of electrical switches run by a group of operators and decoders. Above the switches were two clocks, one giving the time in Tokyo and the other by the stars. Ōyama signed documents as decoded messages became available, his orders were sent via telegraph, and ivory pieces moved about the map. "Farewell, paintings of Napoleon on horseback . . . fearless in the midst of bursting bombs," Barzini wrote.[44] "He [Ōyama] says a word, and afterward a few cannon destroy the countryside, or battalions disappear."[45]

Barzini stayed with the Japanese through the end of hostilities in northern China in 1905. His seven hundred pages of notes, often scribbled while the ink froze in his pen, give testimony to his apparent belief in the importance of his work. Barzini believed that a turning point in history was unfolding before him as war grew in size and complexity and a great nation arose from the slaughter. According to Knightley, "Alone among correspondents, Barzini understood the historical importance of what he had seen."[46] Barzini's collected dispatches about the Battle of Mukden still are often read in Japanese military schools.[47]

Barzini's time in the Far East solidified his reputation as a war correspondent. He went on to write dispatches to *Corriere* from France and Italy throughout World War I. Many were collected in a series of books, beginning in 1915 with publication of *Scene della grande guerra* (*Scenes of the Great War*).[48] In 1923, at the behest of Albertini, he started an Italian-language newspaper in New York City.[49] He stayed in the post of editor at *Corriere d'America* until 1931. After his return to Italy, he entered politics as a supporter of Benito Mussolini and won election to the Senate as a fascist. He died in Milan in 1947. His son, Luigi Barzini Jr., became a prominent journalist in his own right. The younger Barzini, working as a correspondent for *Corriere della Sera*, was aboard the USS *Panay* when it was sunk by the Japanese in the 1937 attack on Nanjing, China.[50]

Knightley described the period from the American Civil War through the beginning of World War I as a "golden age" of war correspondence. He based this assertion on the rise of the popular press, in part through the spread of literacy; the network of telegraph wires that put news from distant locations swiftly before readers far away; and the relative freedom to report without censorship from the battlefield. To this list, at least in Barzini's case, must be added the benefit of a patient and understanding editor in Albertini, who was willing to keep his star reporter on a yearlong assignment that encouraged high-quality reporting at the expense of a timely and steady supply of less-significant news dispatches.

There was a huge demand for press reports from war zones, Knightley wrote, unless they strayed from acceptably moral, romantic adventures into political commentary or too-realistic descriptions of violence and despair. Most reporting of the era cast war as "a thrilling adventure story," Knightley said.[51] But Barzini refused to romanticize war, choosing instead to describe in detail the kind of violence produced by modern weapons applied on a modern scale. Barzini also captured the reporter's dilemma of writing about modern warfare: battles occurred in such a huge arena that no single observer could reliably construct the narrative of conflict. Barzini reported small slices of life that he witnessed with his own eyes. He trusted that over time and through reading of multiple dispatches, his readers would assemble these images, like threads in a fabric, in a way that would allow larger impressions of warfare to emerge. To gather his threads, he lived for extended periods with Japanese soldiers near the front lines. While this method produces valuable eyewitness details, it carries the risk of the writer identifying too closely with the soldiers being observed. In this manner, Barzini's experience parallels the embedding program of the United States armed forces during the invasion of Iraq in 2003, when embedded reporters tended toward producing positive coverage of the troops around them.[52] Barzini appeared to empathize with the ordinary Japanese troops he covered and to marvel at their heroism, but he maintained enough detachment to avoid cheering the slaughter inflicted or suffered by either side.

As for Barzini's keenest virtues as a war correspondent, they start with patience. Japan's initially strict censorship and delays in allowing Western correspondents near the front drove off many veteran reporters, but Barzini stayed long enough to gain the confidence of the army, which rewarded him with the right to cable routine dispatches and a final account of five thousand words.[53] It also gave him time to feel confident in his assessment of the combatants—to write with authority as opposed to the snap judgments of reporters who, in modern parlance, "parachute" into the midst of conflict to establish a dateline, conduct a few interviews, and retreat to safety.

A second virtue, and related to the first, was the veracity of his reports. Barzini insisted on witnessing events he recorded. He did not make up stories like the billiard-playing colleagues he parodied while living in a Tokyo hotel. True, he knew that "witnessing a battle is not the same as knowing how the battle was fought,"[54] but he was honest about the strengths and weaknesses of his firsthand reporting style.

Third was Barzini's attention to detail—the kind of small detail in wartime that suggests larger conclusions. Barzini said that one could "measure the strength"[55] of the Japanese by such acts as their abhorrence of humiliation, their immediate response to orders that caused them to risk their lives, and their love of rituals including poetry and honorable suicide. No doubt readers in 1904 and 1905 learned not only much about war by reading Barzini, but also about the kind of people who fought it.

NOTES

1. Luigi Barzini, "La grande battaglia: La presa di Chantan: Si può descrivere una battaglia?" *Corriere della Sera*, Milan, Italy, June 19, 1905. A version of this chapter appeared in *American Journalism* 32, no. 1 (2015): 41–59. This revised and expanded version is printed with copyright permission of *American Journalism*.

2. Barzini, "La grande battaglia: La presa di Chantan: Si può descrivere una battaglia?".

3. Hanjapu was a tiny village south of Mukden (Pinyin: Shenyang or Hôten) and near the Sha River. Efforts to find Hanjapu's spelling in modern Pinyin were unsuccessful.

4. Luigi Barzini, "La grande battaglia: La presa di Hanjapu (Con l'esercito di Nodzu)," *Corriere della Sera*, June 23, 1905.

5. Barzini, "La grande battaglia: La presa di Hanjapu (Con l'esercito di Nodzu)."

6. Ibid.

7. Luigi Barzini, *Peking to Paris* (Lake Elmo, MN: Demontreville Press, 2007); and Enzo Magri, *Una vita da inviato* (Florence, Italy: Polistampa, 2008).

8. Knightley, *The First Casualty*, 44n.

9. Jean Rabaut, "Le grand reportage n'est plus ce qu'il était," *L'histoire* 41 (January 1982): 92–93. The headline of the article translates as "The big story isn't what it used to be."

10. Walter Redfern, *Writing on the Move: Albert Londres and Investigative Journalism* (Oxford, UK: Peter Lang, 2004), 213.

11. Ibid., 33.

12. Ibid., 39.

13. Jean Rabaut, "Albert Londres, Grand Reporter," *L'histoire* 70 (September 1984), 74.

14. Marcello Cimino, Presentazione di Adolfo Rossi, "L'agitazione in Sicilia: Inchiesta sui Fasci dei lavatori," http://www.spazioamico.it/Adolfo%20Rossi.htm.

15. Quoted in Frank Rosengarten, *The Italian Anti-Fascist Press: From the Legal Opposition Press to the Underground Newspapers of World War II* (Cleveland: Case Western Reserve Press, 1968), 34–35.

16. Giovanna Dell'Orto, *American Journalism and International Relations: Foreign Correspondence from the Early Days of the Republic to the Digital Age* (New York: Cambridge University Press, 2013); and Dicken-Garcia, *Journalistic Standards in Nineteenth-Century America*, 89.

17. Matthew Hibberd, *The Media in Italy: Press, Cinema and Broadcasting from Unification to Digital* (Maidenhead, UK: Open University Press, 2008), 26.

18. Magri, *Una vita da inviato*, 59.

19. Ibid., 8–17.

20. Ibid., 24.

21. Ibid., 31–32.

22. Luigi Barzini, *Guerra russo-giapponese: La battaglia di Mukden, narrata da Luigi Barzini* (Milan, Italy: Fratelli Treves, 1906), vii.

23. Ibid., x–xi.

24. Luigi Barzini, telegram, "Milano FR Tokio Press Corriere Milano, August 28 1904," Oggetto Barzini 363–99, Ministero per i Beni e le Attivita Culturali, l'Archivio Centrale dello Stato, Rome, Italy.
25. Ibid., xi–xii.
26. Luigi Barzini, telegram, "Milano Tokio Press (date obscured)," Oggetto Barzini 363–99, Ministero per i Beni e le Attivita Culturali, l'Archivio Centrale dello Stato.
27. Luigi Barzini, telegram, "Mylan Fr Fusan SR Sept-9-04," Oggetto Barzini 363–99, Ministero per i Beni e le Attivita Culturali, l'Archivio Centrale dello Stato.
28. Barzini, *Guerra russo-giapponese*, xiv–xv.
29. Ibid., xvi.
30. Luigi Barzini, "La grande battaglia: La battaglia comincia," *Correire della Sera*, n.d., Oggetto Barzini, l'Archivio Centrale dello Stato di Roma.
31. Barzini, "La grande battaglia: La battaglia comincia."
32. Ibid.
33. Ibid.
34. Luigi Barzini, "La grand battaglia: Contro alle Montagne (Con l'esercito di Kuroki)," *Corriere della Sera*, June 19, 1905.
35. Barzini, "La grand battaglia: Contro alle Montagne (Con l'esercito di Kuroki)."
36. Luigi Barzini, "La grande battaglia: Contro alla Putiloff (Con l'esercito di Nodzu)," *Corriere della Sera*, June 21, 1905.
37. Barzini, *Guerra russo-giapponese*, 55–56.
38. Frederick Palmer, "The Greatest Battle since Gettysburg," *Collier's Weekly*, November 5, 1904, 11.
39. [William Brill?] Associated Press, "Approaching Liao Yang," *Houston Post*, August 29, 1904.
40. Luigi Barzini, "La grand battaglia: Contro alle Montagne."
41. Barzini, *Guerra russo-giapponese*, 171.
42. Barzini, "La presa di Chantan."
43. Barzini, *Guerra russo-giapponese*, 130.
44. Barzini, "La presa di Chantan."
45. Ibid.
46. Knightley, *The First Casualty*, 65.
47. Ibid.
48. Luigi Barzini, *Scene della grande guerra* (Milan: Fratelli Treves, 1915).
49. "New Italian Newspaper," *New York Times*, December 28, 1922.
50. Nick T. Spark et al., "Suddenly and Deliberately Attacked: The Story of the Panay Incident," http://www.usspanay.org/attacked.shtml.
51. Knightley, *The First Casualty*, 43, 66.
52. Shahira Fahmy and Thomas J. Johnson, "Embedded versus Unilateral Perspectives on Iraq War," *Newspaper Research Journal* 28, no. 3 (Summer 2007): 98–114.
53. Barzini, *Guerra russo-giapponese*, xvi.
54. Ibid., v.
55. Barzini, "Contro alla Putiloff."

Chapter 7

Photographers and Illustrators

The Russo-Japanese War was notable for the fact that, although there were more men on the spot ready to transmit the news to the world than there have been in any other war in modern times, there never has been a war since the days of the telegraph and the professional correspondent [of] the daily news of which the world at large knew so little.

—James H. Hare, 1905[1]

Surrounded by ruined crops in a dense cornfield, five men lie on harvested tree trunks, barefoot and in tattered clothing. Their faces are strategically disguised by the photographer's vantage point, their bodies unresponsive. Four uniformed soldiers carry logs to the site. One of the men's caps is slightly tilted as with a crooked back he drags the end of a severed tree toward the lifeless bodies.[2] The black-and-white photograph captures a group of soldiers, busy yet tranquil, building a funeral pyre for their fallen comrades, preparing to part with their brothers in arms in a field of crops and smoke. The scene embodies the eerie yet common reality of warfare. However, the photograph captured by James H. "Jimmy" Hare on August 26, 1904, and reproduced in *Collier's Weekly* on November 5, came to signal a new era in the history of photography.

The conflict between the Japanese Empire and Tsarist Russia became monumental in its employment of modern weaponry, with the use of rapid-fire guns and high-explosive shells that would prefigure the violence of World War I.[3] The Russo-Japanese War also would be monumental in the implementation of advancing technology within photography; rapid-exposure cameras allowed correspondents to document the war through detailed imagery distributed to an international mass audience through the revolutionary halftone printing process. Before the battles in East Asia over Manchuria and Korea, combat scenes primarily had been depicted through illustrations sketched by war artists based on second-hand oral accounts or written reports. Some artists, such as Alfred Waud in the American Civil War, sketched what they witnessed on the battlefield, and such sketches would be fleshed out at the artist-correspondent's magazine or newspaper.[4] More often than not, illustrations were used as interpretive devices, emphasizing particular elements of the image or drawing on symbolism to create an emotional response, rather than serving as actual reporting tools.[5] When the Japanese attacked the Russian fleet in Port Arthur on February 8, 1904, the shelling not only catalyzed the outbreak of the war, it also prompted the first photographic account of warfare shared with a worldwide audience using modern photographic equipment and printing processes.

Thanks to technological advancements, including swift-exposure cameras allowing photographers to capture scenes of action in detailed shading, the images produced during the war cemented a new era for documenting combat and distributing visual information to the public.[6] Combining text and imagery, the theater of war was brought into the living rooms of homes thousands of miles from the actual battlefield through a fusion of dramatic visuals and written accounts.[7] At the start of the Russo-Japanese War, the modern news photographer was born, and as the war progressed he and his tribe proliferated.

At the outbreak of hostilities, several publications, including William Randolph Hearst's *New York Journal*, Peter F. Collier's eponymous *Collier's Weekly*, and Herbert Ingram's *The Illustrated London News*, were quick to send multiple correspondents to the Far East. Sparked by the Japanese government's censorship, the secrecy surrounding the war intensified, and with the rise of news photography foreign papers became increasingly eager to document the conflict. Competition grew fierce. Noted in a *Collier's* issue in May 1904, *Harper's Weekly*, a competing magazine, had run a photograph titled "A Skirmish between Japanese and Russian Outposts Near the Yalu."[8] While the photograph correctly depicted Japanese soldiers, the image was pure fraud. It was ten years old and from the Sino-Japanese War. Even though several publications stationed reporters, artists, and photographers in the East, desperation and the extreme measures papers were willing to go to have the latest—and most graphic—reports from the front became evident as the war progressed. In another example of competitive spirit, *Collier's Weekly* photographer Robert L. Dunn bought all of the photographic chemicals he could find in Korea in order to stymie any photographic rivals of his magazine. He wrote:

> I actually cornered the market in Korea. Realizing soon after my arrival there that I was the only correspondent actually "at the front," and that practically the

only other photographic apparatus in the country as in the hands of missionaries, I decided to make certain of a "scoop" . . . by making the other cameras useless. To this end I bought all the photographic supplies in sight, whether I could use them with my apparatus or not. Of course, I could make most of them of value in some way. . . . [I]t was not long before I controlled the photographic situation, and had thus doubled many times the value of the pictures I was taking, to say nothing of having added materially to the stock so necessary for my work.[9]

Among the correspondents stationed in the East were some of the most eminent war photographers and artists. American photographer James Ricalton, whose thirst for exploration would prompt him to trek many miles from Cape Town to Cairo,[10] was among the correspondents answering the call. So was English correspondent Ellis Ashmead-Bartlett, who would be the first to report on the disastrous landing and slaughter of troops from Australia and New Zealand on the Gallipoli Peninsula in Turkey in 1915 and thus instrumental to the Anzac legend.[11] James H. "Jimmy" Hare, a renowned British war photographer and world traveler, and Robert L. Dunn, a native of Memphis, Tennessee, who had stood within six feet of William McKinley when the president was assassinated in 1901, were assigned with a batch of reporters to cover the war for *Collier's Weekly*. Several illustrators also sailed to the Far East to document the conflict by putting pen or pencil to paper, including Frederic Villiers, a British artist who had covered nearly a dozen wars and who would embed with the Japanese troops alongside fellow *Illustrated London News* reporter Melton Prior.

News photography has its beginnings in war photography. Seven years after Louis-Jacques-Mandé Daguerre shared the first commercial photographic method with the world, American photographers created "daguerreotypes" of the Mexican-American War of 1846–1848. These images, primarily of soldiers and officers, had no negatives, instead being chemically developed into one-of-a-kind photographs. As there was no way to reproduce the photographs mechanically, the images made their way into public view via lithographs created by artists studying the original plates.[12] Photographic technology advanced during the next decade to replace the daguerreotype with a negative-based process using iodine and collodion, a sticky chemical based on gun cotton. British photographer Roger Fenton, working for the *Illustrated London News*, used the new process to document the Crimean War of 1853–1856, which had the Russian Empire on one side and the alliance of France, Britain, Sardinia, and the Ottoman Empire on the other.[13] It was the first time war, and thus the effect of war, was extensively documented and shared with a mass audience. The outmoded, unwieldy daguerreotype captured images on fume-treated, silver-coated copper plates using a solution of sodium chloride—common salt—to fix the image permanently onto the plate.[14] Yet, the daguerreotype elements were neither economically frugal nor easy to transport, as the equipment was heavy and fragile, and the exposure time too long to capture any moving subjects. When the collodion process—the use of glass-plate negatives—was invented in 1851, it revolutionized photography. It was twenty times faster than the daguerreotype, and unlike its predecessor, the collodion wet-plate was free from patent restrictions.[15] While this allowed for sharper and more detailed images through shorter exposure times, the process held its limitations. The collodion process necessitated that the photographer had to prepare and process the plate within a very brief window of time, exposing and developing the plate while it was wet. In addition, the weather had to be just right, not too wet and not too dry. This prevented taking several photos consecutively and made the process unreliable at times. Despite such difficulties, Fenton took more than 350 photographs during his time in Crimea.[16] Nevertheless, illustrations remained the most common approach to visually document the war to a mass audience; at the time, it was faster and more affordable to have an artist paint a scene than to capture a photograph and transfer it to a piece of paper via lithography or woodcut.[17]

At the beginning of the twentieth century, halftone printing had mostly replaced engraving, previously the primary method for transferring photographs to paper. The halftone process placed a screen over a light-sensitive plate and exposed it to a continuous-tone photograph comprised of many shades of blacks, whites, and grays. The screen and light transformed the spectrum of tones into a grid of pure-black dots of various sizes, mixed with small white spaces, which when viewed from a short distance gave the illusion of a full range of grays. Before halftones arrived, the printing process had been intricate; photographs could not be directly printed onto paper and, instead, illustrators had to trace and draw the image onto wood blocks before carving them and preparing them for print. The drawback of engraving had been twofold; it required skills and patience, but it also exposed each photograph to the individual engraver's interpretation, potentially having a significant impact on the translation of the photographed image.

Halftone printing sped up the process from camera to paper, and it allowed for greater details in terms of shadows and dimensions.[18] Moreover, the introduction of flash powder in the late 1890s allowed for candid indoor photography. This would be of paramount importance to one of the leading news photographers at the time, the Danish-born Jacob Riis, who documented the deplorable conditions of immigrant life inside New York tenements in the 1890s. Riis became a frontrunner for using the advancing technology to advocate for social reform in the United States at the turn of the century.[19]

The Russo-Japanese War not only trailblazed modern weaponry and technological advancements within photography, but it also gave rise to a challenge of the traditional use of illustrations in newspapers and magazines. When the conflict broke out in 1904, photography had been democratized; halftone printing allowed for fast reproduction, and film roll cameras made photography accessible to the public.[20] While some papers remained faithful to the use of illustrations—and many would eventually employ both drawings and photographs in their issues—several contemporary reporters, such as Gustave Babin of the French paper *L'Illustration*, argued that the authenticity and objectivity of photographs outweighed the value of illustrations as the latter were based on artists' translation of events, while photographs were a mirror of reality.[21]

MELTON PRIOR

Working for the *Illustrated London News*, the first illustrated weekly magazine in the world, British artist and war correspondent Melton Prior was among the foreign reporters sent to cover the war between Russia and Japan. By 1904, at nearly sixty years old, Prior was a seasoned illustrator with numerous other wars on his résumé, including the Zulu and Boer wars in South Africa during the last two decades of the nineteenth century.[22] On January 2, 1904, the *Illustrated London News* blared an announcement aimed at exciting its readers about upcoming war coverage by its premier war correspondent:

> Our distinguished War Artist, Mr. Melton Prior, this week sails . . . to Japan, on what may probably be his twenty-seventh war commission for this Journal. Mr. Melton Prior, who has seen fighting in every quarter of the globe, returned only a few months ago from active service in Somaliland.[23]

During his first few weeks in Tokyo, Prior's personal letters reveal his vexation with the war. Unlike many of his fellow reporters, both British and American, Prior seemed less eager to witness battle when he arrived in Yokohama, and more frustrated with the possibility of sleeping in scruffy tents and trailing through cold and muddy terrain. One can only imagine that his age and the outlook of spending months in the field with little to no comfort or luxury and with no promise of actually seeing combat would have hindered his excitement for his stay in the East. In a letter to his family, he wrote:

> We have sleeping-bags lined with fur, but our bedsteads are a failure. . . . [T]he cold wind is said to be awful ; and again, when the snow ceases, the country is a mass of greasy mud for two months on a stretch, so fancy what a place the campaign is to be in.[24]

One-and-a-half months after Prior's arrival, he wrote that it had been decided that he would be one of the fifteen reporters plus photographer Hare joining the Japanese First Army in the field. However, a week later, it became clear that the Japanese officers had changed their minds, allowing no artists to accompany the troops.[25] Growing increasingly impatient, Prior spent his days attempting to find inspiration for his work in Japan, but with little success. By the end of the war, however, nearly forty of his drawings appeared in the *Illustrated London News*.

In a letter dated March 20, 1904, Prior wrote about the difficulties of capturing a specific scene through drawings, unwittingly adding to the debate on the implications of using subjective illustrations as a news medium. The same evening, he and a group of fellow reporters had been invited with short notice to attend the opening of the Parliament, the National Diet Building, by Meiji, the 122nd emperor of Japan. Passing by the offices of foreign ministers, Prior described an empty hall bare of furniture except for one chair and a small table.[26] Quickly sketching the room, Prior wrote of the emperor's arrival at exactly 11 p.m.:

> The Prime Minister then handed him [Emperor Meiji] a roll on which the speech was written, and immediately the Emperor read it. Then just looking round the hall he picked up his *capie* (plumed headgear), and descending the steps walked straight out. The whole ceremony lasted about four minutes, and yet we are expected to give a faithful representation of the scene, with all the strange costumes worn by statesmen and officials. Of course it is absurd, but it will be done.[27]

Prior's words expose the difficulties of conveying a scene in Japan to a mass audience in Britain, or anywhere else in the world, through drawings. Oftentimes, the illustrators would find themselves responsible for drawing a scene to which they were only briefly exposed, or, in other scenarios, they were left to rely on second-hand accounts of events that their publications wanted them to illustrate. Inevitably, the drawings were greatly influenced by the artist's own interpretation and memory. Prior would sketch a picture in as much detail as possible before sending it to an artist, in London, who would draw the actual image to be engraved and then printed.

Prior's first sketch from Japan appeared on March 19, depicting Japanese citizens in the streets of Tokyo celebrating the defeat of the Russian fleet at Port Arthur.[28] In the drawing, a row of Japanese men dance down the street with paper lanterns in hand, as a Japanese woman with a child and a Western couple observe as passive spectators. Prior drew the Japanese clad in traditional garb, wearing draped kimonos neatly tugged around their waists with ornate *obis* (broad sashes). The men wear the traditional *jikatabi* boots, which distinctively separate the big toe from the rest of the toes, while the Japanese woman wear *tabi* socks resembling the jikatabi.

A few weeks later, another of Prior's sketches appeared in the *Illustrated London News*, under the headline "The 'Special War Edition' in Tokio: Japanese Journalistic Methods."[29] The sketch depicts vendors and newspaper boys outside the headquarters of *Jiji Shimpo*, a major newspaper in Japan, edgily waiting for news from the front as guards attempt to keep them in check. The sketch is full of movement and detail in both clothing and facial expressions.

According to his private correspondence, Prior thought warmly of the Japanese. Even when kept from going to the front, he did not let his frustration outweigh his admiration and candor toward the Japanese. In the letters, he wrote about the overbearing Japanese hospitality, and with fascination he described Japanese attire and culture to his family in Britain:

> They [Japanese military nurses] have such funny headdresses, and they march just like soldiers, with the same swing and all in step. Their caps are like bishops' mitres in calico, with a small red cross in front, and they had their rolled cloaks over the left shoulder, white gloves, short pleated black dresses, and boots. They looked very workwomanlike, very different from the ordinary Geisha.[30]

Despite Prior's fondness of the Japanese, not all illustrators portrayed the Japanese with the same kindness. A drawing that appeared in *Punch*, a British weekly satire magazine, on March 16, 1904, mocked the Japanese censorship of foreign correspondents. In the drawing by a *Punch* in-house artist, a Japanese soldier covers a reporter's eyes with a scarf imprinted with the word "censorship." The drawing is titled "The Wisdom of the East" and the Japanese officer tells the correspondent, "Abjectly we desire to distinguish honourable newspaper man by honourable badge."[31]

A sketch that appeared under the headline "Military Organisation and Enthusiasm at Tokio"[32] on April 9, 1904, exposed Prior's own impression of the Japanese people. As many other foreign reporters did, Prior expressed astonishment in his private correspondence about the ways of the Japanese troops. He admired their obedience and commitment to their nation, and in the sketch he had captured exactly that. The illustration depicts a train station full of Japanese soldiers getting ready to depart for the front line, but rather than chaos and emotional goodbyes, he presented the soldiers as "businesslike" and resolute warriors willing to die for their country.[33] He depicted the soldiers as stately and proper, their uniforms drawn with a great sense for detail and their postures stern and formal. It can be said that Prior drew his Japanese subjects with a sense of admiration, which would stand in stark contrast with the caricatures that had long played into the fear of the "yellow peril" and the racialized stereotype of the "weak, feminine, and semi-civilized" Japanese nation—the notion that had previously been cultivated in European publications.[34]

Prior died just five years after the war ended, and thus the Russo-Japanese conflict would be his last campaign. Two years after his death, the publishing house Edward Arnold in London printed and distributed his book *Campaigns of a War Correspondent*, which provided an extensive and personal overview of Prior's trials and tribulations throughout his career as an illustrator.

FREDERIC VILLIERS

> *Of the things that give war its glamour and its terror, of fighting and carnage, of endurance and bravery that seem superhuman, there is enough in these sketchy pages by the veteran war correspondent to furnish the thrill so cherished by those who know war only at second hand.*
>
> —New York Times *about artist Frederic Villiers, April 22, 1905.*[35]

British artist Frederic Villiers had also been sent to Japan to cover the advance of the Japanese troops through illustrations for the *London Evening Standard* while working alongside Melton Prior for the *Illustrated London News*. The two were among the most notable artists of the nineteenth century,[36] and the *Illustrated*'s decision to send both of its most valued artists suggests the importance of the war and the publication's interest in covering it firsthand. Villiers had studied art at the British Museum and the Royal Academy Schools in London before venturing off to document the Franco-Prussian War in 1871.[37] He would eventually document the 1877 Battle of Plevna in the Russo-Turkish War, where his artistic skills and bravery gained him fame in England. His popularity was further verified when he became the inspiration for the main character of Dick Heldar in Rudyard Kipling's 1890 novel *The Light That Failed*.[38]

Set in London, Kipling's book followed the journey of war correspondent and artist Heldar. His drawings of battle scenes in Sudan—where Villiers had been stationed in 1884, covering the so-called Nile Expedition in a failed effort to relieve the rebel-encircled Khartoum garrison under the command of Major General Charles George "Chinese" Gordon—became famous as he raced against time to finish his paintings, as he was slowly losing his eyesight due to wounds inflicted during war. Even though Villiers did not suffer from poor eyesight, the novel centered on his expeditions and talents, and Johnston Forbes-Robertson, one of Britain's finest actors, who would play Heldar when the book was adapted to a theater play, came to Villiers for advice on character immersion.[39]

While photography was forging the way for a new era of news documentation, artists were still in high demand during the Russo-Japanese conflict. Villiers was one of the few reporters present to cover the siege of Port Arthur. His sketches of Japanese soldiers reveal his sense for detailed shading, using pencils to create realistic dimensions and an almost smooth texture to each drawing. Unlike Prior's drawings, characterized by more vigorous and irregular pencil strokes, Villiers's sketches would be characterized by the layering of pencil strokes neatly blended to create a sense of photorealism. Prior and Villiers drew landscapes, seascapes, and figures, and although both artists steered away from stereotypical caricatures of the Japanese soldiers, their marks and textures were vastly different. Villiers's illustrations drew close resemblance to photography, and his sketches were oftentimes dramatic, occasionally somber.

One sketch, printed in the *Illustrated London News* on July 2, 1904, shows General Oku Yakusata's troops attacking Russian soldiers.[40] The drawing captures the chaos of war, as Japanese soldiers draw their bayonets and shoot their guns as they clash with the Russian entrenchment. One Japanese officer stands raised above the rest, sword in one hand while firing down at a Russian soldier, clearly executing him. Based on the perspective of the viewer, Villiers placed himself behind the Russian soldiers, providing a vantage point in which the Japanese officers in a fierce and heroic manner tumble the entrenchment, appearing to descend upon them from above. The caption below the drawing further underlines the remarkable achievement of the Japanese soldiers: "The capture of the strongly fortified Russian position at Kinchau and Nan-shan by General Oku's troops was a magnificent feat of arms that placed the Japanese among the foremost military peoples of the world."[41]

In the same issue of the *Illustrated London News*, another of Villiers's drawings was printed, titled "The Last Stand of the Russian Rearguard at the Battle of Yalu."[42] The drawing portrays a Russian officer waving a white handkerchief to indicate surrender. He is surrounded by the bodies of Russian soldiers, their wrenched mouths and glaring, empty eyes indicating excruciating pain as they died.

The scenes that Villiers captured were unlike those of many of his contemporaries. The drawings show that the artist repeatedly placed himself in danger as he was closely embedded with the Japanese troops. Why he was granted permission to closely follow the troops, unlike many of his contemporary artists and photographers, is not clear. Yet, it appears that the Japanese officers changed their minds in the fall of 1904, allowing Villiers to depict triumphs, such as Port Arthur. One reason may be that Villiers consistently portrayed the Japanese in a favorable light. He drew them as heroic and regal military figures who proved invincible time and time again—not much of a distortion of the imagination, as Japan never lost a battle in the war. His sketches were realistic and detailed, and resembled the quality of photography at the time. The *Illustrated London News* reproduced approximately thirty-five of his sketches during the war.

When the war ended in 1905, Villiers published a collection of his drawings and his own account of his stay in the East in the book *Port Arthur, Three Months with the Besiegers: A Diurnal of Occurrents*.[43] As with the majority of the foreign reporters, Villiers found himself astonished by the cordiality and etiquette of the Japanese. Soon after arrival in Tokyo, he acquired a young servant of whom he was extremely impressed:

> He was a clean, smart lad, and I noticed that he had a piece of paper for a pocket-handkerchief instead of the make-shift custom most Chinamen indulge in of using the floor. His pig-tail he had evidently great pride in. . . . His features were gentle and kind, and unlike the pronounced Mongol type.[44]

Contrasting with many of his colleagues, Villiers expressed little concern about the Japanese government's censorship. It appears that he had suffered less under the strict regulations and had been granted more artistic freedom than many of his peers. He had immersed himself among Japanese peasants and was fondly surprised by their demeanor and agility. He saw the Japanese army as calculated and heroic, leading military ventures that clearly outsmarted the Russian troops, an opinion that came to be mirrored in the drawings he sent to his editors. Villiers was particularly impressed by one Japanese officer overseeing his work, Major Yamaoka. He was the same officer who would later grant photographer James Ricalton freedom to photograph "whatever he pleased." Yamaoka allowed Villiers to fully immerse himself among the Japanese officers and appeared to grant him more freedom in what he communicated to his publications back home. The final words in Villiers's book were dedicated to Yamaoka:

> Yamaoka, with his ever-genial smile, wished me God-speed, and told me that, as I had seen three months of the hardest fighting before Port Arthur, the General had recommended me for the medal. I never left any army in the field with greater regret, nor have I been treated with more consideration and kindness by all ranks, from privates to generals, than with the Third Imperial Army of Japan.[45]

VIKTOR K. BULLA

Covering the war on the Russian front line was Viktor Karlovich Bulla. At only nineteen years of age, Bulla was one of the youngest war photographers to document the Russo-Japanese War. Son of famed German-Russian photographer Karl Bulla, the owner of a successful photography studio in Saint Petersburg, Viktor had grown up in an affluent family and was eager to pursue a career as a war photographer.[46] As Bulla had spent years training in his family's studio, his coverage of the war presented a sharp shift in his photographic compositions and subjects. While his studio portraits were idealized representation of esteemed Russian officials or soldiers, his images from the war captured a different reality and a different group of people. In the war, the subjects were not just noble officials, and their images were not always flattering. Rather, many of his photographs showed the other side of war, behind the scenes of combat; he documented wounded soldiers being transported on trains, intimate moments of surgery and pain, dueling armies in the vast and open fields, and soldiers patiently waiting next to the carts carrying the wireless transmission stations that provided radio communication between the troops.[47] He captured machine gunners at the front line, clad in tall, furry *kubanka* hats and thick uniforms made to resist the harsh weather, and he captured portraits of wounded generals and commanders. As Bulla captured the fighting peasants and the chaos of war, his work came to represent a new era of photography in Russia.[48]

Bulla accompanied the Russian army in its trek across windswept country and the frozen surface of Lake Baikal, which had yet to be spanned by railroad tracks, and he documented the homecoming of the survivors from the Battle of Chemulpo Bay in early February 1904.[49] Despite being faced with action-filled scenes of soldiers scaling rough terrain and priming for combat, Bulla implemented some of his studio techniques in the field. He occasionally staged his photographs, having Russian soldiers stand aligned with one another, harsh expressions on their faces.[50] In other photographs he captured the work of the medical detachment, such as Russian surgeons and nurses tending to the wounded. On other occasions, he set up the medical teams perfectly aligned in matching uniforms, such as one photograph that presents uniformed nurses and soldiers outside the medical train, which had been named "Her Imperial Highness."[51]

While photographs were used to show readers the realities of war, it can be argued that they also served as commemoration for the soldiers themselves; portraits of soldiers dressed in uniforms bedecked in military decorations would come to serve as a timeless ideal of the soldier's service and as a memento for the family if the soldier was to not return. Bulla's work appeared in the Russian journals *Niva* and *Irsky*, but as many other press correspondents would negotiate a deal with several publications, Bulla also made a deal with *Collier's Weekly* to ensure an extra paycheck while ensuring American readers had access to the war from the perspective of the Russian troops.[52]

After the war ended, Bulla returned to his family's studio in Saint Petersburg before eventually launching his own film company, *Apollo*, with his brother, Aleksandr Bulla. During a two-year period, the company released nearly forty documentary and feature films, and when World War I broke out, he continued employing his photographic skills to document the war both through still imagery and in film.[53] He fell afoul of the Stalin regime in the 1930s, was forced to make a confession, and then was executed.

JAMES H. HARE

On January 7, 1904, the SS *Siberia* departed the San Francisco Bay and sailed first to Honolulu, Hawaii, before setting out for Yokohama. On board, a batch of *Collier's Weekly's* finest correspondents found themselves yearning for battle stories on the Korean Peninsula. Among them was James H. "Jimmy" Hare, a British emigrant turned war photographer, who had spiraled to fame for his intimate portraits of Cuban soldiers during the Spanish-American War. Hare had worked as a press photographer for the *Illustrated American* until its destruction by fire in 1898. The publication had been the first weekly publication in the country to successfully reproduce photographs using the halftone process rather than the traditional engraving method, solidifying photo reportage as a mode of journalism.[54]

By the late 1890s, Hare drew the assignment to cover international armed conflicts for *Collier's*. His first major deployment happened when he captured life in Cuba in the aftermath of the attack on the USS *Maine* in Havana, before eventually covering the Spanish-American War. In 1901, he documented President McKinley's tour through southern and western states, photographing the president shortly before he was fatally shot during a two-day visit to the Pan-American Exposition in Buffalo, New York.[55] As soon as rumors broke out about the escalating tensions over disputed territory in East Asia, *Collier's Weekly* deployed Hare as one of its main photographers to cover the conflict between the Russian and Japanese empires.

Hare spent his first months in Japan bottled up in Tokyo as so many other reporters did, frustrated with the restrictions that kept foreign correspondents from crossing into Korea to follow the advance of the Japanese troops.[56] The reporters spent most of their days exploring conventional life in Japan. They dined according to Japanese tradition and entertained themselves with various events chosen by their Japanese hosts, from theater plays to afternoons at quaint teahouses.

It quickly became clear that any correspondent would have to be in great luck to escape the strict censorship by which the Japanese officers governed the foreign reporters. By late March, however, the Japanese government came under increasing foreign pressure and realized that limited coverage of their armies could prove favorable if their press campaign could be well administered. Thus, the government granted correspondents its first set of passes.[57] Among the five Americans was Hare.

Hare would follow the Japanese army until the end of the year and covered several battles during his time in the East. Two battles would be particularly memorable, those of Shaho and the Yalu River.[58] Following the Japanese First Army under General Kuroki Tamemoto, Hare trailed the soldiers as they crossed the Yalu River into Manchuria and confronted the Russian lines at the end of April.[59] It was the first major land battle between the two empires, and Hare, along with Jack London, was there to document the combat as it unfolded. *Collier's Weekly* ran his photographs on May 21 in a two-by-two layout with accompanying headlines and brief captions. The images depicted the troops on the move and gave the reader a sense of following the First Army's progress as it slowly but steadily occupied the rough terrain and approached the Russian lines.[60] Through dramatic imagery, combined with compelling narratives and detailed descriptions of the Japanese advancement over Russian troops, readers in the United States were brought directly to the riverbanks of the Yalu, watching as the mounted soldiers crossed the shallow waters approaching enemy lines.

In a profile sketch of Hare for *Collier's*, Frederick Palmer described how the photographer got his best shots.

> I wonder if those who saw the realistic pictures of the groups of wounded around the hospital tents at the Yalu realized at what they cost this little man, who is nearly in his fiftieth year He was the first of the correspondents' corps to cross the river. He trudged through miles of sand up to his knees. His pony was worn out; his weary servant promptly resigned. But Jimmy himself was up the next morning at daybreak, ill and pale, developing the first photographs of the army at the front to be published.[61]

Hare had to get close to the fighting because photography loses its impact from a great distance. Palmer said Hare sneaked away from his Japanese minders when they weren't looking in order to get close enough to capture action from a few feet away.

Hare also curried favor with Japanese officers, and it paid dividends. Palmer said that when Hare asked someone to pose for a portrait, his manner made the subject feel regally proud. That helped bring generals and other staff officers to his side, Palmer said.[62]

That photography such as Hare's was a new mode of news reporting was evident in the various publications that sent war photographers to cover the conflict. Each publication printed stories highlighting its photographers and their mission to its readers, accentuating the importance of photography in the new era of news reporting. A photographer would often have his photos printed in several publications—including Hare, whose photos appeared both in *Collier's* and in *L'Illustration*. In a June 1904 issue of the latter, the readers were introduced to Hare. The publication made sure to detail the conditions under which photographers worked and applauded their bravery in wandering the battlefield to capture imagery so that readers at home could get a firsthand view of the conditions in the East. Accompanying a photograph of Hare in front of a tent-laboratory, the publication informed its readers of the heroic photographer whose work was investigative, moving, and as objectively accurate as photography was deemed to be:

> Without mentioning the serious risks to which the war correspondent is exposed, photographer or journalist, when we understand the conditions in which these results were obtained, with the rudimentary tools he must use to perform the sensitive manipulations of the photographic arts, all done in the field, we remain a bit surprised and we do not want to question our respect, or, even more, our admiration of these bold and resourceful collaborators.[63]

On November 5, 1904, *Collier's* ran a photograph of a mounted Hare accompanying the Japanese army. Above the photo, a bold title stated, "The Greatest War Photographs Ever Taken," and a brief description highlighted the hazardous conditions under which Hare, and fellow photographers, worked.[64] The role of the war photographer was clearly defined and the fact that he courted danger legitimized the dedication to photographs in publications in the early twentieth century.[65]

As months progressed, Hare's photographs became increasingly graphic. By the end of the year, *Collier's Weekly* would run dozens of his photographs of the advance of the Japanese troops, scaling hillsides and getting raked by rapid-fire guns. One image showed troops solemnly searching the battlegrounds for dead soldiers, while another showed two Russian soldiers lying lifeless and covered in bloodstains at the bottom of a ditch while three Japanese soldiers, expressionless, stand aligned next to the scene.[66] The caption informed the reader that war was "brute butchery" but also "brute courage," clearly remarking that death is inevitable in war while underscoring the Japanese troops' bravery.

After the war ended with Russia's defeat in 1905, Hare returned home and continued to work as a war photographer, covering several wars including the First Balkan War of 1912–1913 and World War I. He died at eighty-nine in 1946, remembered as one of the pioneering photographers in photojournalism, instrumental in the coverage of the Russo-Japanese War, and a key component of the success of *Collier's Weekly*.

ROBERT L. DUNN

Jimmy Hare was not the only press photographer who had closely documented McKinley's campaign leading up to the president's assassination.

On the fatal day, September 14, 1901, fellow *Collier's* photographer and correspondent Robert L. Dunn, camera in hand, stood less than six feet from McKinley when he was shot.[67] Born in 1874, Dunn was both slim and short and with delicate features. His apparent qualities of being a common man allowed him to easily blend in with a crowd and capture his subject without much commotion. In January 1908, the *Sioux City* (Iowa) *Journal* wrote of the photographer's demeanor:

> Of less than average height, slight frame, with the finely chiseled features of an artist, a low, rich voice and modest, frank manners, Robert Lee Dunn, of New York and Everywhere, is not exactly the kind of a man the public mind would associate with the great game of making presidents.[68]

Yet, that was exactly what he did. Dunn captured McKinley and his running mate, Theodore Roosevelt, and carved their appearances into the memory of the American public. He captured the "Rooseveltian smile," which came to inspire caricatured portraits of the twenty-sixth president in historical accounts, and he traveled the world on international assignments, unobtrusively sliding into the background and documenting events as he saw them firsthand.[69]

By the time tensions eroded in the Far East, Dunn had made a name for himself both at home and in Europe. There was little doubt that *Collier's* had to send one of its most efficient and well-liked photographers to cover the territorial dispute, and on February 1, Dunn arrived in Korea. He spent his first week in Incheon (Chemulpo), a humming city west of Seoul and presiding as the capital's main port. He had managed to enter Korea without any press pass before the outbreak of the war and enjoyed unlimited access to the troops for more than four months before he was reluctantly returned to Tokyo by Japanese authorities.[70]

On February 9, the day after Japanese warships tumbled the Russian fleet at Port Arthur, they led another tremendous attack against the Russians at Chemulpo Bay. The evening before, thousands of Japanese soldiers had huddled in the bay area, and Dunn had been at the wharf, lighting up his flash bulbs and capturing their arrival as the night unfolded. On August 13, 1904, *Collier's* ran his account of the Battle of Chemulpo Bay and the subsequent days he spent photographing the war with his Kodak camera.[71]

In his own account, Dunn relayed that he nearly missed the attack on February 9, as he had left Incheon for Seoul. After hearing the sudden, distant *thumps* of torpedoes blasting Russian boats, he paid a *kurumaya*—rickshaw driver—handsomely to hastily take him back to the nearest train station. Yet, the battle had shut down all modes of public transportation at the station, so Dunn was forced to embark on the twenty-mile journey back, first by foot, then by horseback. When he finally returned to the wharf, he was met by the sight of shipwrecks and thick black smoke. Dunn captured images of the remnants of the Russian fleet, one photograph showing a dramatic explosion on a Russian gunboat while another showed the sinking of the boat, the top of the funnel and a broken mast barely surfacing the water.[72] He explored the wreck of the *Variag* at the risk of exploding its unfired, primed torpedoes, and attempted to shoot photographs of Japanese surgeons operating on wounded Russians but was refused permission.[73] The wreckage in the harbor testified to the efficiency of the attack. Dunn recounted:

> The onslaught of the Japanese upon the little Russian fleet was sudden, terrific, overwhelming. It could have but one result, and when the smoke of battle cleared away, and the great guns were once more silent, the smokestack of the sunken *Korietz* marked her burial spot, standing like a monument upon the field of battle to mark the first epoch in the struggle between Japanese and Russian for supremacy in the Far East.[74]

Dunn had arrived in Korea before other photographers and he guarded his equipment accordingly. His rolls of film were invaluable as no other photographer had been present to capture the attack at Chemulpo Bay and the progress of the Japanese troops in the aftermath. He had exclusive access to the soldiers on Korean soil and he knew that time was limited; despite the Japanese government's attempt to restrict the foreign press's access to Korean territory, the border would eventually be opened and other reporters would enter the field.[75] Dragging the Kodak camera on his shoulder, he photographed the soldiers and the peasants whom he encountered along his path. At night, he raced against changing weather and dropping temperatures to mix his developer with clean water brought on the heads of Korean bearers in order to successfully develop the films he had shot during the day. Any error, such as a change in the temperature of the water needed to mix with the developing powder, would mean that the film had been permanently damaged and the photographs lost. Almost every day for a month he dispatched his developed films via courier to one of the northernmost points on the west coast of Korea, and from there to Yantai, China, to be posted to *Collier's Weekly*.[76]

Dunn worked tirelessly and took full advantage of the four months he spent with the Japanese soldiers without any other war photographer in sight. His photographs gave *Collier's* readers a rare insight into the Japanese army, offering an up-close and personal portrayal of Japan's military progress in Korea. He spent the cold winter months closely following the army as the soldiers embarked on their quest for territorial supremacy, marching first to Pyongyang on the Taedong River in the West, then on to "Kwangstu" (possibly Gwangju) in the south, and, finally, to the Yalu River in the north.[77]

While Dunn's photographs were the Western world's only direct peephole into the Japanese troops' whereabouts for several months, his written descriptions of Asian culture and people would likely come to shape Western perception of the distant empires as well. In an article printed in the *San Francisco Chronicle* on July 3, 1904, Dunn offered an elaborate and defamatory account of the Korean peasants he encountered while stationed in the East. He presented Koreans as an inferior race, uncultured, and with feral mannerisms. With complete disregard for offending the people in whose country he had spent months as a visitor, he painted his experience in Korea as degrading and beneath any white man.[78] The ideals in the East, he argued, were as far from Western ideals as they could possibly be and so were the people. He mockingly wrote about the interpreter he had hired; the Korean had asked Dunn not to refer to him as "boy" but rather his name, to which Dunn replied "Mr. Yumata Du San [the interpreter's name], you're fired" and proceeded to kick the man "considerably above the level of his knees."[79] With the loss of the first interpreter, the next interpreter he hired appeared to be equally useless, if not worse, he noted.

Several of Dunn's written accounts of his time in the East would be printed in American papers, and there was no sugarcoating his views of the Korean people. One might wonder if it was karma that caused Dunn to experience unforeseen trouble when he asked his interpreter to exchange $150 into the local *won* currency. Unaware that one U.S. cent would equal thirty Korean won—today one U.S. dollar equals 1,154 South Korean won—Dunn ended with a "mountain of money three feet high, sixty feet around the base."[80] An article, clad with irony and humor, that ran in *Collier's* on June 4 told readers about the unfortunate event and was accompanied by a photograph of Dunn standing on top of the pile of coins as ogling locals walked past. As the writer noticed, it appeared that the acclaimed photographer was standing on "a huge heap of sausage, possibly procured as an addition to his field commissary."[81]

Dunn's time in Korea was painted by his dissatisfaction with the conditions under which he worked. It was incredibly cold, he relayed, Korean winters being some of the worst he had ever experienced, and there were no comfort and no food worthy of a white man, he said. However, his photographs would serve as a window into Japanese progress at a time where other foreign correspondents were stuck in Tokyo, impatiently waiting for the Japanese authorities to grant them a press pass. Nevertheless, Dunn's photographs were rarely battle scenes and more often than not, he documented the long marches of the Japanese troops, as they, perfectly aligned, passed through vast landscapes and small villages. The closest he would to document active combat would be the sinking ships after the attack at Chemulpo Bay. During his time in Korea he followed the Japanese army, but rarely witnessed direct battle. After being sent back to Tokyo in April, he was assigned to join the third column of reporters to be stationed at the front. He spent nearly two months peevishly awaiting his assignment, which never came.[82]

In the years after the Russo-Japanese War, Dunn continued to work as a press photographer in the United States. In 1907, he photographed the worldwide tour of Secretary of War William Howard Taft, and the following year he published a book, with a selection of his own photographs, about the soon to be twenty-seventh president of the United States.[83] He eventually turned from photography to finance and promotion of the San Francisco Bay District, including a role in the construction of the San Francisco-Oakland Bay Bridge, which opened in 1936. Dunn died at age seventy-eight near Columbia, California, in 1953.[84]

JAMES RICALTON

Working for pioneering photography company Underwood & Underwood, American photographer James Ricalton traveled to Japan and photographed the conflict, creating some of the war's most famous stereoviews, or double-image photo cards.[85] The nationwide stereography fad of the late 1800s and early 1900s saw hundreds of thousands of Americans collecting and viewing stereoview cards. The cards consisted of two images taken simultaneously by a special camera containing two lenses set apart by the distance between human eyes. When viewed through a special device, the two images on the card blended into one and gave the illusion of three dimensions. *Smithsonian Magazine* called the technology the "original virtual reality."[86]

Ricalton was a renowned world traveler, naturalist and big-game hunter, and in his lifetime he trekked to all corners of the world.[87] Born in the small village of Waddington in the most northern part of New York, Ricalton grew up just across the border from Canada. For years, he worked as a teacher before pursuing his passion for photography. By the late 1890s, he made a name for himself as a war correspondent covering the Spanish-American War and in early 1900 he traveled to China to cover the Yihetuan Movement, also known as in the West as the Boxer Rebellion.[88] Ricalton had a deep fascination with capturing moments using the stereograph technique. Underwood & Underwood published an account of his coverage of the Boxer Rebellion in 1901, in which he said:

> The stereograph tells no lies; it is binocular—it gives the impression that each eye would receive on the ground, affording essentially perfect vision and giving the most realistic ocular perception attainable in the photographic art. . . . [T]he stereograph virtually projects solid figures into space before us.[89]

Ricalton photographed subjects in the Far East and Underwood & Underwood sold the photographs, or stereoviews, in box sets to be viewed through stereoscopes. The boxes offered buyers a life-like experience of being at the very front line of the war, thereby transporting them in time and place.

Even though Underwood & Underwood rarely sold photographs with the photographer's name on them, a few of Ricalton's views from the war remained labeled. In a self-portrait from 1905, Ricalton sits with a group of Japanese officers of the Eleventh Division at Port Arthur. Surrounded by uniformed men with shaved heads and slick black mustaches, Ricalton, at the time sixty-one years old, stands out with his brittle mustache, ascot cap, and a white ribbon wrapped around his upper left arm to indicate that he is a correspondent.[90] While Ricalton documented the progress of both Japanese and Russian troops while in the East, it appears that he grew particularly close with the Japanese army. In the portrait, he sits arm in arm with a Japanese soldier.

Another of Ricalton's stereographs is taken at the front line in Tehling, Manchuria. The photograph shows the Japanese army neatly aligned in rows, watchfully expecting the advancement of Russian troops. Titled "Expecting an Attack from Russian Cavalry," the close vantage point illustrates how Ricalton had fully embedded himself with the Japanese soldiers, standing side by side with the troops as the enemy approached.[91]

While the Japanese government had gone to extreme lengths to limit the outreach of foreign correspondents, Ricalton was one of the handful of photographers who had been granted permission to fully embed with the army. At one point, when he had attempted to photograph Japanese soldiers huddled in shallow trenches, he was held up by Japanese officers who were ready to arrest him. When he insisted on his title as a correspondent accredited to the Third Army, the officers telephoned to headquarters to receive further instructions. According to the legend, Major Yamaoka of General Nogi Maresuke's staff said, "If it is the American photographer, Ricalton, let him take pictures wherever he likes."[92]

Ricalton's stereographs were taken close to the Japanese troops. His photographs reveal that unlike many of his contemporaries, he was granted virtually unlimited access. Yet his photographs were rarely graphic, more often portraying the soldiers undertaking smaller operations and trekking across windswept land and hills. He presented them as commendatory in his published works, which mirrored the tendency of his fellow foreign correspondents. In addition to his favorable portrayals of the Japanese, the War Office might have decided to grant him greater leeway than other photographers because of the nature of his medium. Stereographs took more time to make and distribute to retail stores than newspapers and magazines and thus would be less likely to compromise the shifting, time-sensitive battlefield operations.

The favorable portrayal of the Japanese army in the American and British press was greatly an outcome of the Japanese government's calculated public relations campaign set to promote a positive image of Japan by the turn of the century. The one-year Sino-Japanese War in 1894 had left the nation in an unfavorable light, leading the government to install a group of Ministry of Foreign Affairs officials to actively reshape the Western perception of Japan.[93]

By 1900, the ministry undertook an extensive investigation on the portrayal and subsequent public perception of Japan in the Western press. With the outbreak of the war, the majority of foreign reporters would follow the Japanese rather than the Russian troops. To the American and British public, Japan was primarily portrayed as a heroic, calculating, and admirable nation that had outwitted the Russians. The illustrations and photographs captured the nobility of the Japanese troops, their endurance, and love for their country. Images helped cement the perception of Japan as a stronghold on the world stage.

NOTES

1. Hare, ed., *A Photographic Record of the Russo-Japanese War*, 7.
2. Palmer, "The Greatest Battle Since Gettysburg,".
3. A. D. Harvey, "The Russo-Japanese War 1904–5: Curtain Raiser for the Twentieth Century World Wars," *RUSI Journal: Royal United Services Institute for Defense Studies* 148, no. 6 (October 2003): 58.
4. "The Eye of the Storm—How Alfred Waud's Sketches Captured the Carnage of the U.S. Civil War," *Military History Now*, April 21, 2017, https://militaryhistorynow.com/2017/04/21/the-eye-of-the-storm-how-alfred-wauds-sketches-captured-the-carnage-of-the-u-s-civil-war/.
5. Stephen L. Vaughn, *Encyclopedia of American Journalism* (Routledge, 2007), 386.
6. Christopher Stolarski, "Another Way of Telling the News: The Rise of Photojournalism in Russia, 1900–1914," *Kritika: Explorations in Russian and Eurasian History* 12, no. 3 (Summer 2011): 571.
7. Thierry Gervais, "'Le plus grand des photographes de guerre': Jimmy Hare, photoreporter au tournant du XIXe et du XXe siècle," *Études photographiques* 26 (November 2010), https://proxy.library.ohio.edu/login?url=https://search-proquest-com.proxy.library.ohio.edu/docview/864672684?accountid=12954.
8. "A Remarkable Photograph in Harper's Weekly," *Collier's Weekly*, May 21, 1904.
9. Robert L. Dunn, "In Korea With the Kodak," *Collier's Weekly*, August 13, 1904, 23.
10. Frank Emblen, "Intrepid Photographer: A Tribute," *The New York Times*, October 20, 1985.

11. "War Correspondent Ellis Ashmead-Bartlett," n.d., The Anzac Centenary Nation Program, https://anzacportal.dva.gov.au/history/conflicts/gallipoli-and-anzacs/events/battle-landing/war-correspondent-ellis-ashmead.

12. "Photo of the Week: Mexican-American War," Amon Carter Museum of American Art, https://www.cartermuseum.org/interact/notes-from-underground/photo-of-the-week-mexican-american-war.

13. Thierry Gervais, "Witness to War: The Uses of Photography in the Illustrated Press, 1855–1904." *Journal of Visual Culture* 9, no. 3 (December 2010): 372.

14. Vaughn, *Encyclopedia of American Journalism*, 386.

15. Ibid, 387.

16. Ibid.

17. Gervais, "Witness to War," 375.

18. Vaughn, *Encyclopedia of American Journalism*, 387.

19. Alexander Alland, *Jacob A. Riis: Photographer and Citizen* (N.p.: Aperture, 1975), 5.

20. Gervais, "Witness to War," 376.

21. Gustav Babin, "La guerre vue par les photographes: Jimmy Hare," *L'Illustration* 3238 (March 18, 1905), quoted in Gervais, "Witness to War," 376.

22. Melton Prior, *Campaigns of a War Correspondent*, ed. S. L. Bensusan (New York: Longman's Green & Co., 1912), 320.

23. *The Illustrated London News*, January 2, 1904.

24. Prior, *Campaigns of a War Correspondent*, 322.

25. Ibid., 324.

26. Ibid., 325.

27. Ibid.

28. "Rejoicing in Tokio over the Defeat of the Russian Fleet at Port Arthur," *Illustrated London News*, March 19, 1904.

29. "The 'Special War Edition' in Tokio: Japanese Journalistic Methods," *Illustrated London News*, April 2, 1904.

30. Prior, *Campaigns of a War Correspondent*, 323.

31. Bernard Partridge, "Wisdom of the East," *Punch, or the London Charivari*, March 16, 1904, 183.

32. "Military Organisation and Enthusiasm at Tokio," *The Illustrated London News*, April 9, 1904.

33. "Military Organisation and Enthusiasm at Tokio."

34. Rotem Kowner, "Becoming an Honorary Civilized Nation: Remaking Japan's Military Image during the Russo–Japanese War," *The Historian* 64, no. 1 (2001): 21.

35. "Villiers at Port Arthur," *New York Times*, April 22, 1905.

36. Steve Bottomore, "Frederic Villiers—War Correspondent," *Sights and Sounds: International Film Quarterly* 49, no. 4 (1980): 250.

37. Rotem Kowner, *Historical Dictionary of the Russo-Japanese War* (Lanham, MD: Scarecrow Press, 2006), 579.

38. Bottomore, "Frederic Villiers," 250.

39. Stephen Bottomore, "Frederic Villiers: War Correspondent," in *Re-Viewing British Cinema, 1900–1992: Essays and Interviews*, ed. Wheeler W. Dixon (Albany, NY: SUNY Press, 1994), 12.

40. Frederic Villiers, "'Scientific Fanatics': General Oku's Troops Storming the Russian Entrenchments at Kin-Chau," *Illustrated London News*, July 2, 1904.

41. Villiers, "'Scientific Fanatics': General Oku's Troops Storming the Russian Entrenchments at Kin-Chau."

42. Frederic Villiers, "The Last Stand of the Russian Rearguard at the Battle of Yalu." *Illustrated London News*, July 2, 1904.

43. Frederic Villiers, *Port Arthur: Three Months with the Besiegers: A Diurnal of Occurrents* (London: Longmans, Green, and Co., 1905).

44. Villiers, *Port Arthur*, 8.

45. Ibid., 176.

46. Stolarski, "Another Way of Telling the News: The Rise of Photojournalism in Russia, 1900–1914," 572.

47. "Russian-Japanese War 1904–1905 Photo Gallery Part I," All World Wars: Photographs by Viktor K. Bulla, https://www.allworldwars.com/Russian-Japanese-War-1904-1905-Photo-Gallery-by-Victor-Bulla-Part-I.html.

48. Stolarski, "Another Way of Telling the News," 575.

49. Richard Harding Davis and Alfred Thayer Mahan, *The Russo-Japanese War: A Photographic and Descriptive Review of the Great Conflict in the Far East, Gathered from the Reports, Records, Cable Despatches, Photographs, Etc., Etc., of* Collier's *War Correspondents* (New York: P. F. Collier, 1905), 90.

50. Davis and Mahan, *The Russo-Japanese War: A Photographic and Descriptive Review of the Great Conflict in the Far East, Gathered from the Reports, Records, Cable Despatches, Photographs, Etc., Etc., of* Collier's *War Correspondents*

51. "Russian-Japanese War 1904–1905 Photo Gallery Part I."

52. J. N. Westwood, *Russia against Japan, 1904–1905: A New Look at the Russo-Japanese War* (New York: SUNY Press, 1986), vii.

53. "Victor Bulla," Nailya Alexander Gallery, New York, http://www.nailyaalexandergallery.com/russian-photography/victor-bulla.

54. Christopher R. Harris, "The Illustrated American: 'A Revelation of the Heretofore Untried Possibilities of Pictorial Literature,'" *Visuals Communication Quarterly* 6, no. 4 (Fall 1999): 4.

55. Gervais, "The 'Greatest of War Photographers,'" 5.

56. Hare, *A Photographic Record*, 7.

57. Gervais, "The 'Greatest of War Photographers,'" 6.

58. Harvey, "The Russo-Japanese War 1904–5," 58–61.

59. Ibid., 59.

60. Gervais, "The 'Greatest of War Photographers,'" 6.

61. Frederick Palmer, "About Jimmy Hare: A Personal Sketch of the Collier's War Photographer with the Japanese First Army," *Collier's Weekly*, February 25, 1905, 18.

62. Palmer, "About Jimmy Hare: A Personal Sketch of the Collier's War Photographer with the Japanese First Army."

63. Babin, "La guerre vue par les photographes: Jimmy Hare," quoted in Gervais, "Witness to War," 377.

64. "The Greatest War Photographs Ever Taken," *Collier's Weekly*, November 5, 1904, 6.

65. "The Greatest War Photographs Ever Taken."

66. "A Russian Trench Captured by the Japanese in a Night Attack," *Collier's Weekly*, November 5, 1904, 10.
67. "Robert Lee Dunn: A Sketch," *Sioux City* (Iowa) *Journal*, January 19, 1908.
68. "Robert Lee Dunn: A Sketch."
69. Ibid.
70. Robert L. Dunn, "'Ways That Are Dark, and Tricks That Are Vain,'" *Collier's Weekly*, July 23, 1904, 9–10.
71. Dunn, "In Korea With the Kodak."
72. "Russo-Japanese War Extra," *Collier's Weekly*, March 26, 1904, 1–3.
73. F[rederick] A[rthur] McKenzie, "The Little Brown Man Laughs at Trouble," *The* (Chanute, KS) *Sun*, July 19, 1904.
74. Dunn, "In Korea With the Kodak," 20.
75. Ibid.
76. Ibid., 21.
77. Robert L. Dunn, "Miserable Corea!" *San Francisco Chronicle*, July 3, 1904.
78. Dunn, "Miserable Corea!".
79. Ibid.
80. "A 'Cash' Transaction in Korea," *Collier's Weekly*, June 4, 1904, 8.
81. "A 'Cash' Transaction in Korea."
82. "Little Rock Man With Jap Army," *The Arkansas Gazette* (Little Rock), July 31, 1904.
83. "Robert Lee Dunn: A Sketch."
84. "Robert Lee Dunn," Find a Grave, https://www.findagrave.com/memorial/103238587/robert-lee-dunn.
85. Gregory A. Waller, "Narrating the New Japan: Biograph's *The Hero of Liao-Yang* (1904)," *Oxford University Press* 47, no. 1 (2006): 46.
86. Clive Thompson, "Stereographs Were the Original Virtual Reality," *Smithsonian Magazine*, October 2017, https://www.smithsonianmag.com/innovation/sterographs-original-virtual-reality-180964771/. GAF View-Master updated the technology and its parent companies continued to sell stereographs into the twentieth-first century.
87. "Ricalton, James A.," Historical Photographs of China, University of Bristol, https://www.hpcbristol.net/photographer/james-ricalton.
88. James Ricalton, *China through the Stereoscope: A Journey through the Dragon Empire at the Time of the Boxer Uprising* (New York: Underwood & Underwood, 1901).
89. Ricalton, *China through the Stereoscope*, 11.
90. "Professor Ricalton, with Japanese officers of 11th Division, at foot of Takushan, Port Arthur" (New York: Underwood & Underwood, 1905), Library of Congress, https://www.loc.gov/item/2004665580/.
91. "Expecting an Attack from Russian Cavalry—Alert Japanese Near Tehling, Manchuria" (New York: Underwood & Underwood, 1906), Library of Congress, https://www.loc.gov/resource/cph.3b26198/.
92. "Outdoor Men and Women: Heroes of the Camera," *Outing Magazine*, April–September 1905, 733.
93. Robert B. Valliant, "The Selling of Japan: Japanese Manipulation of Western Opinion, 1900–1905," *Monumenta Nipponica* 29, no. 4 (Winter 1974): 415.

Chapter 8

Hector Fuller

> *I got him assigned to one of the Japanese armies, but this entailed a long wait, and he preferred to strike out on his own account. . . . He seems to be a very plucky fellow.*
>
> —Lloyd Griscom, 1904[1]

Hector Fuller did not represent a major newspaper or news organization, had no high-dollar contract as a war reporter, and was nearly totally unknown outside Indiana. Yet he grabbed one of the most significant journalistic prizes of the Russo-Japanese War. Representing the *Indianapolis News*, he hired a small sampan to take him without fanfare into the waters of the Russian stronghold of Port Arthur. The fortress city had been blockaded by the Japanese navy at the start of the war and cut off from reinforcement by land after the Japanese victory at the Battle of Nanshan on May 25–26, 1904, gave them the Russian port of Dalny and control of the neck of the Liaodong Peninsula. No news from independent observers reached the outside world from Port Arthur after its isolation. That made it an attraction for any Western reporter who could penetrate the Japanese and Russian perimeters for a scoop. Fuller is one of three candidates to be the anonymous reporter to whom Count Michimasa Soyeshima referred when complaining to John Fox Jr. about a reporter crossing into Russian territory after having been accredited by Japan. The others are Edwin Emerson Jr., discussed in chapter 9, and Scotsman Douglas E. Story of Britain's Newspaper Enterprise Association. Story was accredited to cover the Japanese First Army but left Tokyo a week after the attack on Port Arthur. He switched to the Russian side after inferring that Japan would be less accommodating to war correspondents than their adversaries.[2]

Defying death and serious injury, Fuller drifted under Japanese and Russian guns to land safely on the Liaodong Peninsula just one day's hike from Port Arthur. He was taken prisoner and brought before the highest military authorities of the Russian armed forces in control of the city. After extensive questioning, he was released and made his way back to neutral territory. His deal was most daring: In return for his risking his life, he became the only journalist to enter Port Arthur during the siege and to return with a description of conditions on the inside.

Fuller's background prepared him for covering war on land and sea. He was born in London, England, in 1864, but constantly was on the move. His father had served as medical inspector to the Turkish army during the Crimean War, took a commission in the British civil service,[3] and then was posted to the Madras Province of India. Fuller's younger brother served as an officer in the British army in India, assigned to act as bodyguard to a native prince. As a teenager, Hector served aboard the HMS *Worcester*, a training vessel for the sons of army and navy officers. He served aboard British ships for more than four years, sailing to India and the West Indies, and survived a mutiny attempt by the Lascar crew of a merchant ship loaded with rice, sugar, and spices. After leaving the sea, Hector joined the British army in India as a volunteer and rose to the rank of corporal before buying his way out of the service and returning to private life. As a young adult, he farmed in Nebraska while living in a sod house, managed a circus, and worked the diamond fields of South Africa. At century's end he settled into newspaper work. He briefly found work in New Orleans and New York before joining the *Richmond (Indiana) Item* and then at the *Indianapolis News*.[4]

Fuller left for Japan from the port of Vancouver, BC. His ship, the Royal Mail Steamer *Empress of China*, departed on February 23, 1904, with many ethnically Japanese passengers on board who were returning home to enlist and eighty-four Chinese being deported by Canada.[5] Fuller found the Japanese full of war spirit and kindly disposed toward Americans. Arriving in Tokyo on March 17, Fuller applied for credentials as a war correspondent and sought accreditation to cover the army during fighting on the Asian mainland.[6] He noted in his first dispatch from Japan that the people he met treated Americans with kindness. "The war spirit runs high, and the streets are filled with people, who cheer the Mikado's name and eagerly scan the latest bulletins," he wrote.[7]

Correspondents had attempted to write about mobilization before the surprise attack on Port Arthur, but Japanese officers opened the mail and censored "even the simplest notes," Fuller said.[8] And they struck all mention of troop or ship movements from outgoing telegrams. Such initial dispatches rested mostly on speculation, as officials refused to release any details. After the opening of the war, the accredited correspondents in Tokyo expected to accompany the First Army as it sailed for Korea, but the Ministry of War stalled on giving a definite date of departure. The correspondents' restlessness grew as more reporters, photographers, and artists arrived. Fuller wrote, "Meanwhile the correspondents possessed their souls in what peace they could. . . . [M]ore steamers arrived bringing more correspondents, and those who had come early to avoid the rush saw themselves overtaken by increasing numbers of their fellows, and all hope of 'early bird' advantage vanished."[9]

Like most correspondents, Fuller killed time by seeking feature stories and touring the country. In Yokohama, he remarked on displays of patriotism. "I have never seen a city so garlanded with national flags—not even London at [Queen Victoria's] royal jubilee, nor Indianapolis during convention times. The people are not rich. . . . but each house, each little shop, is made brilliant by a dozen or more flags."[10] He toured the Shinto temples in and around Tokyo and to his surprise found them converted into barracks crowded with soldiers.[11]

Frustrated by his waiting for nearly three months for permission to cover the action, Fuller took matters into his own hands. He told the *Indianapolis News* of his plans in a letter dated May 10—the last the paper would receive until after Fuller's return. Fuller wrote that he was "thoroughly disgusted by the whole show," and that he saw no prospect of any correspondents leaving for the mainland in the next month.

> In the meantime, bully good fighting is going on up north, and we are not intended by the Japanese government to see anything of it. The few correspondents who went with the first column are restricted to fifty telegraph words every three days, and they (the Japs) have issued an order that no correspondent is to approach nearer than three miles to the firing line. . . .
>
> I propose going by the Nippon-Yusen-Kisha line to Chemulpo and thence by native steamer to Chee-foo. . . . I am going alone . . . and shall try to get across in a Chinese junk. The Japanese expect the place to fall within the next three weeks, and I hope to be there when it happens. . . .
>
> I don't minimize the dangers of this sort of thing to myself. If I get caught by either side there will be the deuce to pay, but anything is better than this inaction and utter failure.[12]

On June 5, 1904, he left Yantai (Chefoo) on China's Shandong Peninsula. Drawing on his experience as a sailor in the British merchant fleet, he sailed seventy-seven miles north across the Yellow Sea in an open sampan to the Liaodong Peninsula. Two Chinese servants helped work the sails. He carried tins of corned beef, sausage, cocoa, sardines, and bottles of water.[13]

Off shore, near Port Arthur, Fuller's boat crossed paths with the *Fawan*, chartered by American reporter Stanley Washburn to gather news of the war by boat. Washburn noted in a dispatch dated June 8 that he had found Fuller and two Chinese oarsmen in an open boat, and that Fuller was attempting to sneak into Port Arthur without being stopped by the Japanese or the Russians. Fuller and Washburn spent an evening drinking Scotch and soda aboard *Fawan* and talking about the war. Fuller said he was off to interview General Anatolii Mikhailovich Stoessel, the commander of Port Arthur. In response to Washburn's fears that Fuller's mission would prove fatal, the Indianapolis reporter said he was willing to accept any losses "up to the right leg . . . below the knee." Washburn agreed to tow Fuller's boat closer to the shore before turning it loose to cover the final few miles on its own.[14]

And then . . . silence. Fuller's newspaper editors knew he had left Yantai for Port Arthur and had last been seen on June 10, but other than the news that Washburn had sent Fuller on his way, no word of his fate reached the United States. After four days, *The Indianapolis News*, fearing Fuller had been captured or executed, asked Indiana's two U.S. senators, Albert J. Beveridge and Charles W. Fairbanks, to take up the matter of Fuller's whereabouts with the State Department. The senators asked Secretary of State John Hay to plead with the Japanese Legation and Russian Embassy in Washington to investigate.[15] Three days later, the State Department got its answer. Lloyd Griscom, U.S. consul in Tokyo, received a visit by Stanley Washburn on June 17. Griscom cabled the State Department in Washington that Russian soldiers had arrested Fuller at Port Arthur.[16]

Fuller had landed on the shore of Louisa Bay, a few miles northwest of Port Arthur, at dawn of June 10. Despite the presence of at least eight Russian warships in the bay, Fuller managed "by the exercise of great vigilance in the gloom of night" to arrive undetected.[17] He bade goodbye to his two Chinese sailors and gave them his only gun, a revolver.[18]

As the sun rose, Fuller could see Russian soldiers working atop the hills near Port Arthur. By keeping to the valleys, he managed to work his way to a vantage point overlooking the city without being seen.[19] He made some observations of the port and the ships in the harbor, and then tried to retrace his steps to the point where his rowboat had landed, hoping to rendezvous with the Chinese sailors. It was then that he came face to face with a regiment of Russian soldiers digging entrenchments. Washburn must have waited offshore long enough to see this, as upon returning to Japan he shared the news with Griscom and sent a cable to the *Indianapolis News* saying that Fuller had been captured.[20]

Fuller recalled later that he did not know what he would say to the Slavic soldiers. Nevertheless, he thought the Russians would likely consider the binoculars he carried as the tool of a spy. He let the $35-glasses slip undetected to the ground as he walked toward the astonished, half-naked soldiers.

"Where is the officer commanding this regiment?" Fuller asked the nearest soldier. But the soldier spoke no English. Neither did the officer whom the soldier summoned to attempt a translation. After a few struggles with German, the officer and Fuller settled on basic French to communicate. Fuller showed the officer his papers and nodded when the officer asked if he were an "Americansky."[21] The officer dispatched an orderly to find someone who spoke English. A lieutenant, whom Fuller described as "cocky," read Fuller's papers, including a letter of introduction from Senator Beveridge that included the word "journalist." Fuller wrote, "The cocky one shook the letter in the face of the tall captain and said: 'Journal-eest. Americansky journali-eest!' and the little beast spat on the ground as if the words had a bad taste."[22]

Fuller was marched two miles at the point of bayonets to a hut in a Chinese village for interrogation. Along the way, Russian soldiers spoke to the troops accompanying Fuller, and the troops repeatedly replied, "Americansky spier." Fuller had forgotten that his American passport bore a stamp from Tokyo, which evidently made the Russians suspect he served the Japanese. At the hut, the Russians stripped Fuller naked and confiscated all of the contents of his pockets, including a copy of Charles Dickens's *Martin Chuzzlewit*. Eventually the regiment found an officer sufficiently fluent in English to question him. The inquisitor asked him many questions in a friendly manner and translated for a group of officers. Fuller recounted how he had sailed from Yantai in a sampan and landed a day's march from Port Arthur. He had come, he said, because having been constantly denied the opportunity to go to the front by the Japanese army despite his receiving accreditation, he had decided to try to see the war from the Russian side. The officers looked surprised but satisfied. They offered Fuller a cigarette from a silver box. All smoked and smiled.[23]

Fuller was then blindfolded and ordered to march. "A man with his eyes bandaged can always see a little, straight down his nose," Fuller recalled, and so he made mental notes of his surroundings as he walked along a road that rose and fell. These included "enormous guns" and barbed wire entanglements that protected the roadway. He sensed that the land was well protected and that soldiers surrounded him. He knew that the road was guarded because he heard the challenges of a series of sentries. A roving searchlight revealed a smooth, solid road and huge guns placed in embankments with finely trimmed grass. The escort took Fuller to a barracks and gave him black bread and water. Officers in evening dress entered, and Fuller repeated his story to a colonel who spoke no English. The interpreting officer told Fuller, "The colonel wants to know if you were not aware that Port Arthur is blockaded and that no one is allowed in?" "Yes, I knew it," Fuller replied, "but the blockade does not seem very effective. I came in here and there are Chinese vessels constantly coming in and going out." The colonel decided that Fuller, having no permission to enter Port Arthur, would have to leave. He ordered Fuller to be jailed until a junk would be available to take him away in two or three days' time. Fuller was led to a jail housing about fifty Japanese prisoners of war—soldiers and sailors seized during Japan's early attempts to block the mouth of the harbor. Some of them had gone insane during their captivity, he observed.[24]

Fuller saw enough of the city to characterize its morale as excellent and form an opinion that it would long withstand any Japanese siege. He wrote: "Port Arthur was full of life and gayety, quite of keeping with the stories of distress and short commons that had reached Chee-foo through Japanese sources." He found that the entrance had been freed of obstructions, battleships had been repainted, and the fortifications were being strengthened. "The garrison is larger than outside information has led me to suppose. The troops are in excellent condition, and the general health conditions of the city are good. It looked to me as though it were capable still of withstanding a prolonged siege." The night he entered the city, Russian officers hosted a gala ball, he added.[25] It was not something one would expect in a demoralized, encircled city.

During his two days in jail, he was questioned seven times in attempts to break his story.[26] One examiner grilled Fuller on the number and type of Japanese warships he had seen in the Yellow Sea, and where he thought the nearest Japanese coaling station might be. Fuller replied:

> I have been called an "Americansky spier." If I were to answer your questions, as to forces of the enemy, I might deserve the title. If I should tell you chaps what I know about the Japs, you may be quite sure that I am the sort of man who would tell the Japs what I know about you. I decline to answer any questions except those about myself.

Overall, he said he thought he had been treated well. He received bedclothes, soap, towels, black bread, water, vodka, cigarettes, and cabbage soup.[27]

Afterward, fearing that his interviewers might have found some inconsistencies in his repeated accounts of his entering Port Arthur, Fuller wrote a letter to General Stoessel requesting a personal interview. Stoessel agreed. Fuller likened the general to Ulysses S. Grant—same square jaw covered by a grizzled, cropped beard; steely, gray eyes; and a sense of power and determination. After the usual exchange of questions and answers about Fuller's arrival, Stoessel said he would let Fuller leave the garrison on the condition that he not try to return. Fuller agreed. Before he could depart, the Japanese army and navy shelled the city on the night of June 13. Fuller said he could see the explosions from the window of his cell. "When the affair was over, the Russian officers returned laughing to their quarters, reporting that the enemy had been easily repulsed," he wrote.[28]

Figure 8.1 Hector Fuller, seated in rickshaw at right, takes to the streets of Tokyo. He later sneaked into Port Arthur and won world acclaim.

Upon his release on June 21, Fuller was blindfolded. Given the choice of walking to his embarkation point or paying $20 to hire a Russian horse-drawn cab, Fuller chose the cab. He sat for three hours as the *droschka* took him to the edge of Louisa Bay. His blindfold removed, he and his Russian escort hiked over hills to the point where his sampan had landed, so he could identify the spot for his captors. "Immediately a sentry was placed at that point, and no one else will be able to repeat my success," Fuller wrote.[29]

> I was then sent away in a junk, along with a host of Chinese. These were the men of an entire village, who were being deported because the village had harbored some Japanese. The junk was escorted outside of the harbor by Russian torpedo-boats, and then was left to make its way alone, as best it could, across the gulf. The trip will not be forgotten. I was without food for sixty hours, but finally reached here [Yantai], little the worse for my ten days' experience.[30]

Fuller's Port Arthur venture caused a sensation in the Far East and in the United States. Washburn had reported Fuller's arrest as he attempted to enter the besieged fortress city, but nothing afterward. Absent any news from the Russians, the *Chefoo Daily News* and *Shanghai Mercury* had published reports that Fuller had been executed by the Russians.[31] When he emerged alive, "All the newspaper men . . . [became] sore about my success, but the papers have treated me very nicely, and I have received high praise, you will be glad to know, for my work," Fuller wrote his wife, Rose, after his release.

"I was the only man to risk my life in getting into Port Arthur, the only man in since the place was blockaded. In reality it was a big scoop and I ought to get some reward besides [the] story for it."[32]

His own newspaper hailed his courage. "The cable dispatches from him received yesterday and to-day . . . show that he has undergone remarkable adventures, this is what every one who knows Mr. Fuller expected," the *News* wrote. "Danger and the high tides of life are as meat and comfort to him."[33] Similar accolades appeared in many newspapers, but not the *Richmond Sun-Telegram*, rival paper to the *Item* that had previously employed Fuller as a reporter. If Fuller really had been imprisoned at Port Arthur, the *Sun-Telegram* wrote with the flavor of sour grapes, it was unlikely the Russians gave him much truthful information.[34] While that might have been true, there was no denying what Fuller saw with his own eyes and heard with his own ears. And there was no denying his courage.

Fuller told his son that he hoped to get a monetary reward from his newspaper and not just glory for his exploits,[35] but no mention of a salary increase or bonus could be found in Fuller's papers in Indianapolis.

The Associated Press carried the news of Fuller's release on its national wire. Stories appeared in the *New York Times* and *Washington Post*, among other papers. The accounts focused not only on Fuller's daring penetration of the blockade, but also on his observations as the only outsider to report directly on conditions in Port Arthur.[36] Fuller said the Japanese blockade had not been "effective," as the Russians had repaired their damaged warships, refortified the city, and found ways to obtain abundant food from Chinese sources that penetrated the lines. In addition, Fuller said the Japanese estimate of thirty-five thousand Russians in the city was too low—the actual number was at least fifty thousand, he believed.[37] He said he doubted that the town could be taken without the loss of 40 percent of an attacking force.[38]

Although no estimates of Japanese casualties were available for the long siege of Port Arthur, three separate frontal assaults failed in August, September, and October 1904. The Japanese tactics then turned to artillery barrages, tunneling, and entrenchments to weaken the Russian resistance and get soldiers close to the fort for a final assault. Stoessel decided to surrender at the beginning of January 1905 rather than fight a final pitched battle. When Japanese soldiers entered the city, they were astonished to find supplies of food, champagne, and ammunition, just as Fuller had reported. They also found more than forty thousand military survivors.[39]

Fuller paid a price for his scoop. As soon as he returned to Yantai, the Japanese government assigned spies to watch his every move. The Ministry of Foreign Affairs recalled his passport on the grounds that because he had been in Russian territory and within Russian lines, he could not remain on Japanese soil.[40] The Japanese army also refused to allow him to visit the front lines of the land war. Fuller asked Griscom for an official reason for his being denied access to the war zone as an accredited correspondent. Fuller wrote to Griscom:

> I shall have, of course, to give very full explanations to my newspaper on my return and I should be obliged to you if you would send me some official notification of the refusal of the Japanese Government to allow me to proceed to the front—even after my pass (which I still have) has been issued. I should also like to know, officially, the reasons for the withdrawal of my pass.
>
> You see, Sir, if I am unable to give full and satisfactory reasons for my return home I shall be of course in an exceedingly uncomfortable position.[41]

On August 3, nearly three weeks later, the State Department reported that the Japanese General Staff had decided that Fuller could not cross the lines to report war from both sides.[42] Getting his single scoop cost Fuller the opportunity to further report. Fuller need not have worried about the reaction of the *Indianapolis News*. Upon his capture, his editors said they appreciated the value of service he had rendered, and that he had "greatly distinguished himself and has scored a triumph over the world's greatest and most famous war correspondents."[43]

Fuller reflected in a letter to his wife on what he had gained and what he had risked to get his brief encounter with fame. "The trip I made was a good deal harder and more dangerous than I cared to let the papers know. It really was a wonder that I was allowed to get off as I did," he said.[44]

Fuller's account of his travels into and out of Port Arthur dwarfed his account of what he saw there: His front-page *Indianapolis News* summary of conditions in Port Arthur totaled six paragraphs, four of which dealt with the size of the garrison, the availability of food, repairs to Russian warships, and the repulse of a Japanese sortie.[45] His follow-up report, reprinted by the *New York Times* and *Washington Post*, devoted only three of nineteen paragraphs to conditions in the port, reserving sixteen for his personal narrative.[46]

Fuller was treated as a celebrity upon his return to the United States. He toured the country, lecturing on "Japan during War Time" to venues such as a Methodist Episcopal church in Noblesville, Indiana.[47] Newspapers sought and published his opinion. Fuller's prognostications proved off the mark, as he predicted in mid-August that Japan would lose the war through lack of resources, including enough capable soldiers to defeat the Russians.[48]

After returning home, Fuller worked a number of odd jobs. He was hired on as a private secretary to New York iron industry millionaire Gordon L. Mott and in 1912 set off around the world on the promise of $25,000 reward if he could fetch Mott's son, who had eloped without his parents' blessing. Fuller was unsuccessful.[49] By 1916, he served as the drama critic at the

Indianapolis Star.⁵⁰ For a while he owned a circus. In 1924, Fuller became publicity director for the National Cash Register Company in Dayton, Ohio—later to become the office machine giant NCR.⁵¹ Upon leaving Dayton after less than a year, he traveled to New York and struck up a friendship with Jimmy Walker, who served as mayor of New York City from 1926 to 1932. Fuller acted as a sort of official greeter for the city as well as orchestrator of welcome parades. He met incoming celebrities at the docks, whisked them downtown for a motorcade through police barricades, and delivered them to the mayor. Walker gave them a key to the city and Fuller presented them with a scroll of his own devising, often containing misspellings. He also was prone to getting names and titles wrong. He introduced the Romanian princess as "her imperial majesty," even though she had no empire, and named Great Britain's Ramsay MacDonald the "prime minister of the United States."⁵² Nevertheless, he remained a favorite of the mayor, traveling with him to Europe.⁵³ He apparently suffered from depression as he left public life. On December 3, 1934, he took his own life by asphyxiation from a gas stove. When police broke into his Queens apartment, they found his body beneath framed portraits of Walker and former New York Governor Al Smith.⁵⁴

"Poor old Fuller!" Walker said when told of the suicide. "It's a damn shame . . . he was always so philosophical and had such an excellent sense of humor—he probably needed it."⁵⁵

NOTES

1. "Lucky to Get Out Alive," *Indianapolis News*, November 17, 1904.
2. Story, *The Campaign with Kuropatkin*, 44.
3. "Career of an Indiana Journalist: Travels and Experiences of Hector Fuller of the Indianapolis News," *Evening Item* (Richmond, IN), February 20, 1904; and "The Turks in the Crimea," *Glasgow* (UK) *Herald*, July 30, 1855.
4. "Career of an Indiana Journalist"; "Fuller, Hector," *Who's Who in America*, (Chicago: A. N. Marquis & Co., 1908), 680; and "Hector Fuller, Out of Work, Ends Life," *New York Times*, December 4, 1934.
5. "News's Correspondent Sails for Seat of War," *Indianapolis News*, February 24, 1904; and "Sympathy of Korean Minister with Japan," *Indianapolis News*, March 1, 1904.
6. "News Correspondent Arrives at Tokio," *Indianapolis News*, March 18, 1904.
7. Ibid.
8. Hector Fuller to "My Dear Son John," July 3, 1904, John Louis Hilton Fuller Papers, Indiana Historical Society, Indianapolis.
9. "Trouble of Correspondents," *Indianapolis News*, March 18, 1904.
10. "Patriotic Fervor of the Japanese," *Indianapolis News*, April 4, 1904.

11. "Japanese Are Loyal: Observations Made by an Indianapolis War Correspondent," *The Richmond* (IN) *Item*, April 6, 1904.

12. "Fuller Captured by Russians: War Correspondent of the Indianapolis News Nabbed Near Port Arthur," *Indianapolis News*, June 17, 1904.

13. Hector Fuller, "Getting into Port Arthur—II," *The Reader Magazine*, December 1904–January 1905, 39.

14. Ibid., 44; and Barry, *Events Man*, 258.

15. "State Department Will Try to Find Hector Fuller," *Indianapolis News*, June 14, 1904.

16. "Thousand Japs Went to Death," *Fort Wayne* (IN) *Daily News*, June 17, 1904.

17. Hector Fuller, "Thrilling Experiences of the News War Correspondent," *Indianapolis News*, June 21, 1904.

18. Fuller, "Getting into Port Arthur II," 45.

19. Fuller, "Thrilling Experiences of the News War Correspondent."

20. "Hector Fuller in Port Arthur," *Indianapolis News*, June 17, 1904.

21. Hector Fuller, "Getting into Port Arthur II," *The Reader Magazine*, January 1905, 144–45.

22. Fuller, "Getting into Port Arthur II," 145–46.

23. Ibid., 147–51.

24. Ibid., 152–53.

25. Fuller, "Thrilling Experiences of the News War Correspondent."

26. Ibid.

27. Fuller, "Getting into Port Arthur II," 153–54.

28. Fuller, "Thrilling Experiences of the News War Correspondent"; and Fuller "Getting into Port Arthur II," 155.

29. Fuller, "Thrilling Experiences of the News War Correspondent"; and Fuller "Getting into Port Arthur II," 155.

30. Ibid.

31. Fuller, "Getting into Port Arthur II," 156.

32. Hector Fuller to "My Own Darling Wife," June 24 [1904], John Louis Hilton Fuller Papers.

33. "Mr. Fuller's Daring Exploit," *Indianapolis News*, June 21, 1904.

34. "Hector Fuller," *Indianapolis News*, June 24, 1904.

35. Hector Fuller to "My Dear Son John."

36. See, for example, [no title], *New York Times*, June 21, 1904; "Port Arthur Gay Despite War Measures," *New York Times*, June 22, 1904; "Set Free by Stoessel," *Washington Post*, June 22, 1904; "New Forts at Port Arthur," *San Francisco Call*, June 21, 1904; and "Fuller Says Japanese Are in for Beating," *Syracuse* (NY) *Journal*, August 15, 1904.

37. "Port Arthur Gay Despite War Measures"; and [no title], *New York Times*, June 21, 1904.

38. "Fuller Says Japanese Are in for Beating."

39. Richard Connaughton, *Rising Sun and Tumbling Bear: Russia's War with Japan* (London: Orion Books/Cassell Military Paperbacks, 2004), 256–57.

40. "A War Correspondent Banished," *Washington Post*, August 3, 1904; and "Not Allowed on Their Soil because He Entered Russian Lines," *Baltimore Sun*, August 2, 1904.

41. Hector Fuller to Lloyd C. Griscom, July 15, 1904, John Louis Hilton Fuller Papers. Underline in original.

42. Ibid.; and Alvey A. Adee to the editor of *Indianapolis News*, August 3, 1904, John Louis Hilton Fuller Papers.

43. "Fuller Says Japanese Are in for a Beating."

44. Fuller to "My Own Darling Wife."

45. Hector Fuller, "News Correspondent Is Released after Five Days at Port Arthur," *Indianapolis News*, June 20, 1904, 1.

46. See Fuller, "Thrilling Experiences," *Indianapolis News*; "Port Arthur Gay Despite War Measures," and "Set Free by Stoessel." A similar phenomenon continues in the twenty-first century, with advancements in reporting techniques capturing attention in the recent wars in Iraq and Afghanistan. See, for example, David Bloom's ability to report live video to NBC while traveling in a modified armor vehicle nicknamed the "Bloom mobile" in 2003 received much news coverage independent of what Bloom reported. See, for example, Ken Kerschbaumer, "Bloomobile: Iraq's Coolest Truck," *Broadcasting and Cable*, http://www.broadcastingcable.com/article/148693-Bloomobile_Iraq_s_Coolest_Truck.php; Mike McDaniel, "War Coverage on TV Enters New Territory," *Houston Chronicle*, March 30, 2003; and "TV Innovations Keep Pace in a Mobile War," *Pittsburgh Post-Gazette*, March 23, 2003.

47. "Correspondents [*sic*] Story: Hector Fuller Will Tell about His Daring Dash to Port Arthur," *Hamilton County Ledger* (Noblesville, IN), September 13, 1904.

48. "Japanese Are in for a Beating."

49. "Cupid Laughs at Stern Chase: Soldier of Fortune Loses Tilt and Gold," *San Francisco Call*, December 12, 1912.

50. "Realty Dealers Are Guests Here," *Indianapolis Star*, November 15, 1916.

51. "Former N.C.R. Publicity Man Ends His Life," *Dayton* (OH) *Daily News*, December 4, 1934.

52. Jim Bishop, "Who Recalls Hector Fuller?" *News Herald* (Port Clinton, OH), January 13, 1981.

53. "Former N.C.R. Publicity Man Ends His Life."

54. Ibid.

55. "Hector Fuller's Death Shocks Jimmy Walker," *Daily News* (New York), December 5, 1934.

Chapter 9

With the Russians

I could conclusively demonstrate, by citing many of the circumstances which surround the reporting of the present war between Russia and Japan, that the ONLY OBJECT OF THE RIGID CENSORSHIP MAINTAINED IS POLITICAL and, in my opinion, it is very bad politics, too.

—Thomas F. Millard, embedded
with the Russian army, 1904[1]

In January 1904 Melville E. Stone, the general manager of the Associated Press, a worldwide newsgathering organization, traveled to Saint Petersburg, the Russian capital, to arrange for favorable treatment of war news emanating in the Far East. He met with Count Vladimir Lamsdorf, minister of foreign affairs, and Viacheslav Konstantinovich Plehve, minister of the interior, seeking a lower per-word rate and priority for transmission of news by telegraph wire; guarantees that AP reporters would have access to top Russian officials; and an end to a byzantine censorship of news produced by foreign journalists in Russia for publication outside the nation's borders. Plehve agreed to favorable terms on rates and favorable placement of AP reporters' stories in the queue for wire transmission, and then arranged a further meeting with his minister of telegraphy. The bureaucratic shuffling produced more results. The telegraphic minister said he could guarantee that any news leaving Vladivostok or Port Arthur would arrive in Saint Petersburg within the hour via the trans-Siberian cable, which greatly pleased Stone. But there was even more good news to come. Without any solicitation by Stone or the American ambassador to Russia, Robert Sanderson McCormick, Stone was "commanded" to appear before Tsar Nicholas II, "By the Grace of God,

Emperor and Autocrat of All the Russias," at his private residence at the Winter Palace. In an interview with the *Chicago Evening Post*, Stone said the meeting lasted an hour. Stone told Nicholas that he had been well treated by the tsar's ministers and wanted only to explore the issues of censorship and reporters' access to Russian officials. Nicholas said he would order the army, navy, and all ministries to open their doors and welcome AP correspondents. That left the final matter of censorship. Stone described in detail the hassle of getting censorship approval for an American wire service reporter's story leaving the country:

> And as to the censorship, which after all, was the vital thing[,] under the then existing order a correspondent, after the most soul trying labor to secure a piece of news, was forced to drive two miles to the censor's house to have the stamp of authorization affixed and thence another two miles to the telegraph office. It frequently happened that the censor was not at his house, as he had other government duties to perform, and, in the event, he was in bed and asleep and could not be reached between midnight and 8 o'clock in the morning, the very hours that, owing to the seven hours difference in time, were the most important for the morning papers of the United States.[2]

Even if the reporter could find M. Lamscott, censor of foreign news, the bureaucrat habitually edited dispatches conservatively to avoid any release of information that might rile the tsar or his ministers, Stone said. That made him suppress more than was wise and hurt Russia in the eyes of the world, he added. To Tsar Nicholas II, Stone characterized Russian censorship as "ineffective" because a correspondent could take any objectionable message across the border into Germany and telegraph it from there. The most that Russian censorship could accomplish was to delay the release of news that eventually would reach the West. He concluded by saying, "Since these obstacles were put in the way of sending the truth out or Russia, there had grown up a regular traffic in the business of supplying the press of the world with false news from Russia." The emperor asked for a week to study the issue. Stone did not expect much to happen, especially after Plehve told him after the meeting with Nicholas that censorship could not be abolished. Disheartened, Stone traveled to Berlin, where he attended a dinner and ball with the American ambassador and chatted with Kaiser Wilhelm II. The war between Russia and Japan had begun by that time, and the kaiser promised to intercede on behalf of the Associated Press with his cousin Tsar Nicholas. Returning to Saint Petersburg, Stone learned from Count Lamsdorf that the tsar had approved the abolition of censorship of all outgoing foreign news dispatches, not just those of the Associated Press, minus matters directly pertaining to the security of Russian troops.[3]

Just as journalists had gathered in Tokyo before the start of the war, so too did correspondents visit Port Arthur in January and February 1904. The town itself presented a dour façade to visitors. Frederick McCormick of the Associated Press said Port Arthur's economy centered on the maintenance of the Russian fleet. That gave it a patina of industry and commerce, but if one looked closer, the hotels ranked among the "meanest" of the civilized world, and prostitution reigned as one of the city's most lucrative businesses.[4]

Visitors of any official standing were expected to pay a call at the offices of Port Arthur's only newspaper, the semiofficial, tri-weekly *Novi Krai* (New Region), or at the home of "Colonel" Artimeev, its editor. Artimeev acted on behalf of the commander in chief of all Russian forces in Port Arthur and Manchuria, Admiral Evgenii Ivanovich Alekseev. Artimeev, a civilian, announced his connection to the army and navy by always wearing a military uniform. When McCormick arrived at *Novi Krai*'s office, he told Artimeev that he would follow any regulations Alekseev thought necessary. The editor replied that the admiral would welcome an Associated Press reporter sharing news from Port Arthur with the world.[5]

Shortly after the Russian Christmas observance[6] on January 7, McCormick sought formal permission to accompany Russian troops in combat. He was dismissed by Alekseev's diplomatic secretary, Georges A. de Plançon de Rigny, on the grounds that there would be no war.[7] That remained the official line, but journalists in the Far East did not believe it. Many gathered in Port Arthur, and their presence became a daily reminder that not all shared the optimistic view of Alekseev and de Plançon. McCormick wrote:

> The presence of correspondents in Port Arthur had by the first of February begun to irritate some of the officials, and especially members of the fleet, where there were many who intelligently dreaded the future. Three war correspondents of foreign nationality had taken up residence in the fortress city, and Port Arthur was visited almost daily by correspondents from Chefoo [modern-day Yantai]. By those who dreaded the future, they were, as a class, regarded as harbingers of war and looked upon as vultures hovering over prospective carrion.[8]

The navy treated foreign correspondents as potential spies in the days leading up to the surprise attack. Foreign civilians suffered a series of arrests and often were tailed by Russian agents.[9] Nevertheless, they continued to publish news by wire of activities in the harbor and city.

McCormick was writing a dispatch just before midnight on February 8 when he heard shots and stepped outside. What sounded like gunfire continued for several minutes, but the townspeople had become inured to such noises by the Russian fleet's regular nightly exercises and did not react. Most residents stayed in bed and did not realize the significance of the gunfire until the next morning: Torpedo boats had crippled the battleships *Tsessarevich* and *Retvizan* and the cruiser *Pallada*. All three ships began sinking too quickly to be saved. Their crews ran them aground on the Tiger's Tail, a spit of land near the harbor entrance. McCormick printed Admiral Alekseev's one-word response to news of the severe damage to three of Russia's largest warships: "Impossible."[10]

Unlike the civilian population, the Russian garrison buzzed from the moment of the attack. E. K. Nojine, a Russian accredited to cover news from Port Arthur, wrote that the disorganziation of the fortified city after the attack was "ludicrous." Officers rushed to give and countermand orders, all to the background noise of telephones constantly ringing. "It was not a sight to inspire confidence," Nojine wrote. "It seemed as if the staff momentarily anticipated some fatal and sudden blow but did not know what to do to ward it off."[11]

McCormick hired a sampan to visit the three wrecked warships on the morning of February 9. While he was on the water, shells fired by arriving Japanese warships began falling around him. The spectacle reminded him of illustrations he had seen of naval engagements in the American Civil War. In the ensuing chaos, he witnessed the ship bearing *New York Herald* reporter Francis McCullagh, *Columbia*, disappearing behind the western headlands, bound for Yantai (Chefoo) where he would file his uncensored dispatch from neutral China. The firing lasted thirty-five minutes and then the Japanese warships withdrew.[12]

The Japanese and Russian fleets played cat-and-mouse throughout the spring, trying to lure each other into minefields, torpedo lanes, or artillery exchanges where one would have the advantage over the other. In the end, nothing dislodged the Russian fleet and Japan abandoned its hopes for a massive sea victory in favor of an army encirclement and siege.

On June 13, Admiral Alekseev ordered the Russian fleet to put to sea from Port Arthur in an effort to link up with warships at Vladivostok. The fleet, including the repaired battleship *Tsessarevich*, was ready to sail on June 20. Before it could get under way, however, the naval commanders discovered that a special edition of *Novi Krai* had announced the scheduled departure. All available copies of the paper were immediately recalled. Nevertheless, given the likelihood of Japanese spies in Port Arthur—"They . . . probably have a proof sheet," opined a Russian torpedo boat officer—the crews had no choice but to let their engine fires die.[13]

During the siege, *Novi Krai* published what news it could gather in the encircled city. Nojine wrote a column that regularly appeared during the fall of 1904. Titled "News of Novi Krai," it contained his personal observations. In a memoir, Nojine detailed his routine:

Every day, after going round the line of defences, I went to the Fortress Staff Office, where I was given all the telephone messages of the preceding twenty-four hours up to twelve noon that day. I busied myself with this budget in the office of the Chief of Staff, in his presence, and under the supervision of Lieutenants Kniazeff or Hammer.

When my account was ready I handed it to Colonel Khvostoff for him to see, and everything that I said relating to the operations of the fleet was given to Lieutenant Mackalinsky of the Navy, attached to the Fortress Staff, to look through. These two men deleted such parts of it as, in their opinion, ought not to be published, and at once returned it to me with permission to send to press.

He then sent the censored article to Artimeev in the *Novi Krai* editor's office. The editor also made deletions. "After he had done this—it always had to be done by him personally—the manuscript was sent to be set up [in type]. Two corrected proofs were sent, one to General Anatolii Mikhailovich Stoessel's office and one to the Naval Office, to be censored." If the censors gave final approval, they signed the manuscript and sent it to the printing house, where it was checked by the assistant editor, and sent by him to the type-room to be amended. From there a revised proof went to Artimeev to check against the censors' original remarks. Only then was it permitted it to be printed.[14]

Many military observers considered Port Arthur impregnable. Its harbor, site of an old Chinese city and a modern, dusty, Russian one, lay amid two concentric rings of hills punctuated by sharp peaks. Russian engineers had looked at the natural defense of the surrounding heights and decided to make them even stronger: they began building forts on the highest peaks and connected them with defensive lines including earthworks. Each fort had a supporting line of fire to its neighbors, meaning that any unit that captured one fort would be targeted with heavy fire from both sides. From the city limits to the first circle of defense was one mile. However, few of the forts had been completed by 1904, and they lacked ample artillery directed toward an attack from the landward side. The second defensive ring lay a half-mile beyond the inner ring. The land surrounding and between the rings had no trees or other cover, and the pitch sloped steeply. Any attacking army would have to negotiate the difficult terrain while facing shrapnel, machine gun fire, and rifle fire from multiple directions. Beyond the circling fortifications, defenses extended at least eighteen miles to the north. Trenches and camouflaged artillery cut across the Liaodong Peninsula from sea to sea, starting below the narrowest neck of land three miles across.[15] In the harbor itself, fourteen warships (not counting torpedo boats and the small, swift craft designed to destroy them) lay at anchor on the night of February 8. Seven of the warships were among Russia's largest battleships.[16]

British and American correspondents' demands for accreditation grew louder after the start of hostilities. Those wishing to cover war news from the Russian side needed connections. To be accredited, a war correspondent either had to be known personally by the Ministry of Foreign Affairs in Saint Petersburg, or had to be personally introduced to the minister of foreign affairs by the ambassador to Russia from the journalist's home country. Those requirements, along with the 8,000-mile train ride from Saint Petersburg to Mukden, which had sparse accommodations for civilians, kept the size of the press corps smaller on the Russian side than on that of the Japanese. In addition, the correspondent had to have a passport, a photograph verified by his consul, a letter of introduction from his newspaper or magazine, and also his signature on a brief accreditation agreement. Aside from the need for the personal connections to the Ministry of Foreign Affairs, the regulations closely paralleled those of earlier wars.

James F. J. Archibald, representing *Collier's Weekly* magazine, received accreditation in April. He expressed surprise when apprised of the relaxed state of Russian censorship, as he had been led to believe it would be "more radical" than that of the Japanese. Among the rules was one that said correspondents were "honor bound" to obey the regulations.[17]

Douglas Story, the first foreign war correspondent to gain accreditation, took it as a matter of pride months later when the chief censor, Colonel E. F. Pesteech, congratulated him because no British journalist ever attempted to evade the censorship rules. He did not say whether Americans or any other group had followed the same policy.[18] Story must not have found Russian censorship confining. He said the rules contained nothing "to create dismay,"[19] and he dedicated his war memoir to Pesteech and the other Russian censors, whom he called his friends.[20] Story did not complain about any redactions from his news articles when the newspapers in which they appeared eventually made their way into his hands after a journey from England.

Early censorship was lightly administered. At the start of the war, Russia had to invent a system controlling combat correspondence from scratch, as press censorship at the front had not been deemed necessary in any of its wars before 1904. Little mail left army encampments because most soldiers could not read or write; no marks of censors' pens have been found on printed matter from previous wars, indicating a relatively low interest in war-zone censorship among officialdom as compared with tsarist Russia's strong censorship of controversial domestic issues in its own press. During the Russo-Japanese War, letters written in the combat zones by Russian soldiers were exempt from censorship if the address indicated a delivery site within the Russian Empire. Leaks of sensitive information originating from the recipients caused the censors to close this loophole in World War I.[21]

Figure 9.1 Douglas Story, posing for a formal portrait, thought so highly of the chief Russian censor that Story dedicated his war memoir to the man.

The attack on Port Arthur surprised not only the Russian navy but also the officers in charge of security over information. Censorship of telegrams did not begin until three days later. Mail did not fall under military censorship until April 1904, when it primarily targeted war reporters, artists, and photographers. Even then, it remained irregular, varying by event and by officer's interpretation, until a unified censorship bureaucracy took hold in January 1905. Colonel Pesteech and two aides at the commander in chief's headquarters oversaw daily censorship of the press, while additional censors went through soldiers' mail.[22] If a correspondent wanted to wire a story to his newspaper or magazine from a site other than General Staff headquarters, the telegram had to be routed there, to Pesteech's office, to undergo any deletions or adjustments, and then sent back to the correspondent for transmission overseas.[23]

Early censorship involved a degree of self-restraint common to all correspondents not wishing to risk expulsion, as well as an admonition to follow simple instructions provided in accreditation documents. The accreditation agreement given to correspondents attached to the Russian army originally appeared in French. The translated version read:

> Each correspondent must undertake, in writing, not to spread any news containing criticisms, provisions or persons, to represent the facts in accordance with

the truth and to suppress any news that can't be managed/could be misinterpreted. The violation of these provisions, the indiscretions, the lack of suitable expression may result in some cases in being removed from the combat zone. For all reporters without exception, access to command, the docks and other marine installations, as well as the use of steamships on the roadsteads of Port Arthur and Vladivostock, are prohibited. Correspondents must undertake not to request exceptions to these provisions. When they arrive at the theater of operations, they must go to the headquarters and prove their identity by a photograph; the General Staff then directs them to the staff to whom they must report. They are responsible for their own staff. As a badge, they must wear an armband on their left arm. Encrypted messages are prohibited. Censorship of information takes place at headquarters, at the Manchurian army headquarters, and at the military administration of Khorbin, Nion-Chouang, Port Arthur and Vladivostok.[24]

While these conditions appear to be somewhat similar to those imposed by the Japanese army on foreign correspondents, the censorships differed in the field. As noted in chapters 3, 4, and 5, in late summer 1904 Japan kept reporters from seeing anything remotely resembling combat and added rules such as press pools and military liaisons ("minders") that further shaped the news to the army's liking. Japanese censors also displayed a willingness to cut seemingly innocuous lines from correspondents' dispatches.

Correspondents with the Russian army were issued a red silk brassard for identification.[25] Ordinary Russian troops did not seem to mind reporters in their midst and, for the most part, let them wander at will.

The Russian-controlled zone proved to be more dangerous than that of Japan. Two foreign correspondents died, although not in battle. The first, Lewis Leonard Etzel of the London *Daily Telegraph*, was shot on a junk at sea on June 6, 1904, by Chinese soldiers who mistook him for a bandit. Ironically, Story said, Etzel had been the first to sign his name to pledge donations to help Chinese citizens made destitute by the armies that rolled across their land.[26] Etzel was traveling with Ernest Brindle of the London *Daily Mail* along the coast of Manchuria, headed for the Liaodong Peninsula. Four sailboats manned by Chinese soldiers surrounded their junk and opened fire without warning. A bullet crashed into the back of Etzel's brain, and he died almost instantly. Brindle said the black-clad Chinese mistook the occupants of the junk for some pirates they had been seeking.[27] The crew hid the fact that the shooters had killed a Westerner for fear that they would slaughter all aboard to prevent that fact from becoming known to their superiors. Later, when safely away, Brindle demanded an official inquiry. The Chinese government found the soldiers at fault and placed some in prison. To Etzel's family the government gave £5,000 (nearly $700,000 just over a century later) as compensation for the loss.[28]

The other correspondent to die was Henry Middleton of the Associated Press. He and Story contracted dysentery, but while Story recovered, Middleton developed a high fever and knew he would not recover. He dispatched a note asking Story, in French, to return to Middleton's bedside and to see to his affairs. When Story made his way back to the hospital, he was greeted by a Russian surgeon who told him, "[V]otre ami, il est mort!" ("Your friend, he is dead!")[29] In addition to Etzel and Middleton, at least one Russian journalist died, shot through the chest while writing a dispatch about the Battle of Liaoyang.[30] And at least four Western correspondents, including Francis McCullagh, were made prisoners of war by the Japanese after the fall of Mukden.[31] (After his capture, McCullagh continued to act as a correspondent, even gaining an interview with General Kuroki Tamemoto of the First Army. When McCullagh asked what the general thought of his Russian counterparts, Kuroki said, "If they were as brave as their correspondents, they might be better."[32] In fact, the Russian soldiers typically fought ferociously.)

The most highly regarded among the other correspondents who traveled with Story was McCullagh of the *New York Herald*, an Irishman who had been the first to report the Japanese surprise attack on Port Arthur. On board the steamship *Columbia* just outside Port Arthur on the night of February 8, he was awakened by Japanese torpedoes exploding into the sides of Russian warships. As the sun rose the next day and he could see the damage done, he expressed shock. "I am not pro-Japanese, but I must confess that the audacity of this terrific first strike fairly took away my breath," he wrote. The sailors aboard the torpedoed vessels did not look like a fighting machine, he said, but rather "a mob—a silent, scared mob—looking with terror toward the abyss from which the monsters of the night had emerged."[33]

And that was before the Japanese navy returned after the sun rose. A squadron shelled the Russian ships, including the disabled capital vessels, and Port Arthur itself. The *Columbia* sneaked away to Yantai and McCullagh filed the first bulletin of the war's outbreak. Not long afterward he sought Russian accreditation. McCullagh spoke Japanese from having worked at a newspaper in Japan and Russian from moving to Port Arthur in September 1903 specifically to master the language.[34] That made him the rarity among the correspondents who did not require a translator. Story called him "one of the most fearless, if one of the ugliest" to ride to war among the corps of reporters traveling with the Russians. Other correspondents included Archibald; Richard Little of the *Chicago Daily News*; Frederick McKenzie of the London *Daily Mail* and Reuters news service; Thomas F. Millard of *Scribner's Magazine*; and George Denny of the Associated Press.[35] Joining them later from *Collier's Weekly* were Russian photographer Victor K. Bulla and reporters Henry J. Whigham (famous for twice winning the U.S. Amateur golf championship) and Edwin Emerson Jr.[36] Emerson, also representing

Joseph Pulitzer's *New York World*, previously had angered the Japanese government by switching sides. He had been accredited to join the Japanese army as it besieged Port Arthur but upon landing on the Liaodong Peninsula crossed the lines at Yingkou (Newchwang) to join the Russians. There was little the Japanese Ministry of Foreign Affairs could do, however, once Emerson received the somewhat reluctant backing of Consul Griscom and the U.S. State Department.[37]

Archibald filed one of the first uncensored dispatches from the Russian side. He left Mukden, the terminal of the trans-Siberian rail line, in late May 1904 and traveled on horse 200 miles through bandit-infested country to a Chinese town where he caught a train to Peking. Despite the difficulty he undertook to get out of the war zone, his dispatch to *Collier's Weekly* contained little significant news. He said six to ten trains arrived in Mukden every day, augmenting the Russian numbers of men, horses, and guns. Russian spirits remained high, he said, and enough food and crops under cultivation could sustain the army for a year.[38]

Japan kept spies in Mukden right under the Russians' noses, and so already had a clear picture of the conditions in the city. As Japanese could pass as Chinese or Koreans in the eyes of most Western observers, they could blend in among the local population. That gave them a distinct advantage over their Russian counterparts. Dugald Christie, a Scottish missionary who ran a clinic in Mukden, made the acquaintance of a Japanese spy after the Battle of Mukden. He had been posing as a Chinese businessman in the city for several years. He said he had made friends with many Russian soldiers and had close business relations with the occupying army. All the while, he and his staff gathered intelligence about the enemy and regularly sent intelligence to the Ministry of War.[39]

Spies and their operatives also had agreements with the telegraph offices. War correspondent Millard noted after the war that it would have been easy to send telegraphic messages from Mukden to anywhere in the world, including Japan, from terminals in Russian-controlled territory but without Russian knowledge. A few weeks after Millard arrived in Mukden, before the last major battle of the war, he was approached by a Chinese native who offered to send any messages to the Chinese capital without the Russians discovering the hole in their security. The man guaranteed they would arrive within three hours of Millard placing the text in his hands. The correspondent decided to put him to the test. "Knowing that the Russians had soldiers and operators in the office of the Chinese Telegraph Company, with orders to send no messages that were not stamped by the censor, I expressed doubt of his ability to deliver the goods. . . . I wrote a short private telegram and gave it to him. Within two hours he brought me a reply that carried on its face convincing proof of its authenticity." Millard realized that what he could do, Japanese spies could do and undoubtedly did. He decided not to take advantage of the opportunity as he had promised that he would show the censor all of his messages—and, if he had been caught, likely would have been shot as a spy.[40]

That decision undoubtedly came with some regret. Millard exhibited, among all correspondents with the Russians, the most distaste for the censor and his work. He complained to the *St. Louis Post-Dispatch*, the newspaper where he began his career, of the "severe treatment" of war correspondents by both the Japanese and the Russians. Opinions expressed in "high quarters" coalesced around the belief that the role of the independent correspondent would disappear in future wars, he said. He took issue with some of his comrades who defended the censors' work, which he found to be excessive and unjustified by military requirements. Examples of censorship that Millard singled out included a ban on the word "ambush" when describing a trap sprung by the Japanese, for the reason that it implied that Russian troops had been negligent to be caught by surprise, and the descent into insanity that caused one Russian officer to shoot another.[41] If censors lived by the rule of limiting deletions to those made necessary by a reasonable interpretation of military security, instead of enforcing regulations to avoid political embarrassment, there would be little just ground for complaint, he said. But individual censors exercised whims that sometimes eliminated legitimate news if they disliked a particular correspondent.[42]

Millard may have had a valid point about the Russian censor playing favorites among the correspondents—perhaps in an effort to curry favor with Britain, Japan's ally by treaty, by encouraging the work of British correspondents such as the Scottish-born Douglas Story. As noted, Story and the censor became friends; Anglophilia has long been common among some of the more liberal Russians. And the reporters at Port Arthur also seemed to have greater leeway than those with the army in the field. Even Hector Fuller, jailed by the Russians, was set free to write his observations. In a more draconian censorship, he would have been kept as a prisoner until the war ended or Port Arthur fell.

Millard told the *Post-Dispatch* that a few weeks before the publication of his interview on October 16, 1904, he and other correspondents dined with Russian officers including censor Pesteech. They said that the Russian government "was making a great mistake" by ordering the censor to remove some inoffensive details from news stories. According to Millard, Colonel Pesteech agreed but said he could not win that fight with his superiors.[43] A Russian war correspondent, Ieronim Pavlovich Taburno, who arrived at the front in December 1904 as a representative of the Saint Petersburg newspaper *Novoe Vremia*, also found Pesteech sympathetic but deferential to his superiors. The General Staff considered war correspondents to be no better than spies, Pesteech told Taburno, but Pesteech exhibited a more open mind. "I can say nothing but what is commendable about this officer, possessing tact to the highest degree and imbued with the sentiment of his duty," Taburno wrote. "Personally he considers the press from a much broader and more equitable point of view than his chiefs."[44]

Perhaps the timing of Millard's complaint is noteworthy. He left the Far East in late summer or early fall. By that time, the Russian army's string of battlefield losses had soured morale, and the officers might have been looking for excuses. It has always been fashionable to blame the messenger.

The many battles in Korea, Manchuria, and the Russian concession on the Liaodong Peninsula varied little in their outcome. Although human losses remained devastating and unsustainable, Japan never suffered an outright defeat although some battles would be considered a draw. This caused despair among the Russian troops, according to Whigham. They wondered why they could never win a great victory, which they expected against a nation they perceived as weaker.[45] The correspondents eventually came to blame Russian leadership, as the ordinary Russian soldier impressed them. Story stereotyped the Russian soldier as tough and obedient but not necessarily imaginative:

> Ivan Ivanovitch is . . . docile and respectful, long-suffering and slow to anger, simple of faith, and altogether lacking in the arrogance of the professional soldier. . . . The Russian private is never absolutely the soldier. He is the peasant in arms, dogged, loyal, and formidable, caring little for such elegancies of form as make the ornaments of the Green Park and of Greenwich Common.
>
> Ivan Ivanovitch marches to war loaded down with accoutrements, lugging great loaves of black bread and articles of personal adornment. He marches with the swing of a man accustomed to tramping, chanting his folk songs. He laughs at fatigue, he cares little for extremes of temperature.[46]

Yet when pushed too far, the simple peasant soldier could turn ugly. McCormick of the Associated Press witnessed the worst of human nature during the March 1905 retreat from Mukden, which halted Russian ambitions in Manchuria and effectively ended the land war. Russia had expended a great deal of blood but had nothing to show for it. In frustration at what they perceived as betrayal, soldiers looted hundreds of thousands of rubles from the caravan of the Russo-Chinese Bank as its officers fled before the advancing Japanese. Among the carts was a piano, the sight of which caused some to fly into a rage. Why, the soldiers asked, would officers take more care to evacuate a piano than wounded men still lying in the fields? They attacked the caravan, killing and robbing those traveling with it. McCormick wrote:

> The whole scene was rendered hideous by the braying of jackasses, which soldiers had all day been impressing into service.

Infantrymen attacked a battery, and were driven off by loyal Cossacks as they reached the money-chest. Soldiers, desperate and ferocious, seeking to wreck [sic] vengeance upon their officers for this last great calamity, or wanting a pretext for running away, inaugurated sympathetic panics by letting off their rifles and then plundered the officers' baggage, took the horses—even vehicles—and disappeared.[47]

By that time, Port Arthur had been in Japanese hands for three months. Japan brought Port Arthur to its knees by squeezing its food supply and wearing down its defenses and morale by pummeling the fortress city with tens of thousands of tons of artillery shells. But it was vicious, hand-to-hand combat that substantially reduced the Russian (and Japanese) manpower. Correspondent Ellis Ashmead-Bartlett of the *Times* of London, assigned to the besieging Japanese Third Army, observed the construction of tunnels and trenches to allow soldiers to get close to the defenders, but then stood in awe as wave after wave of Japanese troops, bayonets fixed in their rifles, rushed headlong into the Russian defenses. "The only mystery involved is the motive for the decision which caused the Japanese to make the immense sacrifice of life which was bound to result from frontal attacks on impregnable positions," he wrote.

Ashmead-Bartlett described the method of capturing the fortified city, so costly in human lives, as "obsolete." The scale of slaughter led him to write in 1906 that the world likely had witnessed old-fashioned assaults and close-order formations for the last time. Nine years later, he would see firsthand that such was not yet the case.[48] He covered the Battle of Gallipoli in World War I for the *Daily Telegraph* and witnessed Anzac troops rush across open ground into coordinated machine gunfire from the Turkish army. Only later in that war did battlefield tactics substantially change. Until then, in order to keep the public unaware of the scale of slaughter, the Allies-imposed press controls on the Western Front of that war exceeded even those of the Japanese.

NOTES

1. Thomas F. Millard, "Does the Conflict between Russia and Japan Mark the Doom of the War Correspondent?" *Saint Louis Post-Dispatch*, October 16, 1904. Emphasis in original.

2. "General Manager Stone Tells of His Work in Europe: Made Excellent Arrangements for the Associated Press to Get War News," *Buffalo Evening News*, March 29, 1904.

3. "General Manager Stone Tells of His Work in Europe: Made Excellent Arrangements for the Associated Press to Get War News" .

4. McCormick, *The Tragedy of Russia in Pacific Asia*, vol. I, 28.

5. Ibid., 44–45.

6. Russia follows the Julian calendar unlike the United States and most of the West, which follow the Gregorian calendar. The traditional Julian date for Christmas falls on January 7 according to the Gregorian version.

7. McCormick, *The Tragedy of Russia in Pacific Asia*, vol. I, 48.

8. Ibid., 62. The three foreign war correspondents apparently were McCormick, an unnamed Englishman, and "Neaudeau," evidently Ludovic Neaudeau, representing *Le Journal de Paris*, according to McCormick's memoir. He did not mention Francis McCullagh on board the *Columbia* in Port Arthur's roads.

9. Ibid., 64.

10. Ibid., 68–69.

11. Warner and Warner, *The Tide at Sunrise*, 196.

12. McCormick, *The Tragedy of Russia in Pacific Asia*, vol. I, 69–70.

13. Warner and Warner, *The Tide at Sunrise*, 305; and Connaughton, *Rising Sun and Tumbling Bear*, 132–33.

14. E. K. Nojine, *The Truth about Port Arthur*, ed. E. D. Swinton, trans. A. B. Lindsay (London: John Murray, 1908), 148–49.

15. Barry, *Port Arthur: A Monster Heroism*, 17–19; and Burleigh, *Empire of the East*, 48.

16. Burleigh, *Empire of the East*, 49–50.

17. Archibald, "Russia Makes Rules to Govern War Correspondents," 13.

18. Story, *The Campaign with Kuropatkin*, 176.

19. Ibid., 62, 64.

20. Ibid., n.p.

21. "Military Censorship in Imperial Russia, 1904–1917," The Rossica Society, http://www.rossica.org/RVG/_pdf/Imperial_Military_Censorship/Military%20Censorship%20in%20Imperial%20Russia%201904%20-%201917.pdf.

22. Ibid.

23. Ieronim Pavlovich Taburno, *The Truth about the War*, trans. Victoria von Kreuter (Kansas City, MO: Franklin Hudson Publishing, 1905), 88.

24. Takahashi, *International Law Applied to the Russo-Japanese War with the Decisions of the Japanese Prize Courts*, 395–96. The original French appeared as follows: "Les étrangères doivent produire une recommendation de leur gouvernement auprès du Ministère Russe des Affaires Étrangères. Chaque correspondant doit s'engager, par écrit, à ne propager aucune nouvelle contenant des critiques, des dispositions ou des personnes, à représenter les faits conformément à la vérité et à suppirmer les nouvelles qui ne peuvent se contrôler. La violation de ces dispositions, les indiscrétions, le manque de tact entrainent des observations, et, suigvant els cas, l'éloignement du théâtre de la guerre. Pour tous les correspondants sans exception, l'entrée de l'amirauté, les docks et autres installations de la marine, anisi que l'emploi de vapeurs sur les rades de Port Arthur et de Vladivostock, sont interdits. Les correspondants doivent s'engager à ne pas demander d'exceptions à ces dispositions. A leur arriveé sur le théâtre des opérations, ils doivent se render au quartier général et prouver leur identité par une photographie; l'état-major général les dirige alors sur l'état-major dont ils dépendent. Ils sont responsables de leurs domestiques. Comme insigne, ils doivent porter un brassard au bras gauche. Les dépêches chiffrées sont interdites. La censure des informations a lieu au quartier général, auprès de

l'état-major de l'armée de Mandchourie, et a l'administration militaire de Khorbin, Nion-Chouang, Port Arthur et Vladivostok."

25. Story, *The Campaign with Kuropatkin*, 62.

26. Douglas Story, "My American Comrades in the War the Best Man Could Have," The *Wilkes-Barre* (PA) *Leader*, April 3, 1905; and "Death of Lewis L. Etzel: Cut Down in the Beginning of a Life of Usefulness," *Wet Mountain Tribune* (Westcliffe, CO), June 11, 1904.

27. Brian Best, *Fighting for the News: The Adventures of the First War Correspondents from Bonaparte to the Boers* (South Yorkshire, UK: Frontline Press, 2016), n.p. This book does not have page numbers. The citation is to Chapter 14, "The Last Days of the Golden Age."

28. Ernest Brindle, *With Russian, Japanese and Chunchose: The Experiences of an Englishman during the Russo-Japanese War* (London: John Murray, 1905), 92.

29. Story, *The Campaign with Kuropatkin*, 135–37.

30. McCormick, *The Tragedy of Russia in Pacific Asia*, vol. I, 203.

31. McCullagh, *With the Cossacks*, 374–75.

32. Ibid., 339.

33. Francis McCullagh, "Heard Signal Guns That Proclaimed War On," *Saint Paul* (MN) *Globe*, April 24, 1904.

34. Francis McCullagh, "Fall of Port Arthur May Demoralize Russian Army," *Saint Louis Republic*, August 14, 1904.

35. Story, "My American Comrades in the War."

36. Ibid., and "Collier's Easter Number," *Collier's Weekly*, April 2, 1904, n.p.

37. Payson J. Treat, *Diplomatic Relations between the United States and Japan, 1895–1905* (Glouchester, MA: Peter Smith, 1963), 213; and "Killed as Spy by Russians," *San Francisco Chronicle*, June 21, 1904. An anonymous cable out of China erroneously announced Emerson had been mistaken for a spy and shot.

38. James F. J. Archibald, "With the Russians in Manchuria," *Collier's Weekly*, June 11, 1904, 11.

39. Dugald Christie, *Thirty Years in Moukden, 1883–1913: Being the Experiences and Recollections of Dugald Christie*, C.M.G., *Edited by His Wife* (London: Constable and Company, 1914), 183.

40. Thomas F. Millard, "The War Correspondent and His Future," *Scribner's Magazine* 37, no. 2 (February 1905): 247.

41. Millard, "Does the Conflict between Russia and Japan Mark the Doom of the War Correspondent?"

42. Ibid.

43. Ibid.

44. Taburno, *The Truth about the War*, 88.

45. H. J. Whigham, "Kuropatkin's 'Old Man of the Sea,'" *Collier's Weekly*, August 6, 1904, 8.

46. Story, *The Campaign with Kuropatkin*, 194–95.

47. Frederick McCormick, *The Tragedy of Russia in Pacific Asia*, vol. II (New York: The Outing Publishing Company, 1907), 28–29.

48. Ellis Ashmead-Bartlett, *Port Arthur: The Siege and Capitulation* (Edinburgh, UK: William Blackwood and Sons, 1906), vi–vii.

Chapter 10

Conclusion

It is too much to say that the war correspondent has been abolished, but his sphere has certainly been narrowed to the smallest possible dimensions.

—*Brooklyn* (NY) *Daily Eagle*, 1904[1]

H. L. Mencken delighted in creating hoaxes. When he was a young journalist in Baltimore, he sometimes sat in a bar with two other reporters and made up plausible stories for publication. He believed deception revealed more about the deceived than it did about the deceivers. Those who could not see through the manipulation were "boobs" and "yokels." In one of his most enduring hoaxes, Mencken claimed President Millard Fillmore popularized the bathtub. However, his favorite hoax—his "masterpiece of all time"—involved fabricating a news story about the naval battle between Japan and Russia at the Tsushima Strait that ended the shooting phase of their war. Historian Edward A. Martin said, "In the absence of on-site reports he invented a story, which he made plausible by using real names and realistic details as well as an authoritative journalist's voice." Mencken was pleased later to discover that he had guessed the victor correctly, as well as "every particular of the slightest importance."[2]

Mencken set out to tell a clever lie but told the truth.

But what is "truth?"

That was the crux of the arguments debated by journalists, cabinet ministers, and army and navy officers during the Russo-Japanese War. For the Japanese Ministry of War and its censors in 1904–1905, truth was not unlike the Truth with a capital "t" as described in the Gospel of John. It could not be seen, heard, intuited, or scientifically tested, but when shared as the foundation of one's faith—or in this case, its analog in Japanese nationalism—it demanded utter acceptance by the faithful. As Mencken discovered, reality and fiction can be manipulated in ways so they are not easy to distinguish. According to Martin, Mencken found that "truth exists in the telling, somewhere beyond verisimilitude."[3]

As children (again, it is tempting to say, "Once upon a time"), we determine truth through direct experience. *That* flower smells sweet, *that* ball bounces, *that* icicle is cold. Later, we discern truth through induction and deduction; we draw conclusions about all flowers, balls, and icicles. Over time, experience builds a model of the world in our heads. But we experience only a tiny fraction of the world firsthand. "Each of us lives and works on a small part of the earth's surface, moves in a small circle, and of these acquaintances knows only a few intimately," wrote media philosopher Walter Lippmann in 1922 in his monumental book *Public Opinion*. He continued:

> Of any public event that has wide effects we see at best only a phase and an aspect.... Inevitably our opinions cover a bigger space, a longer reach of time, a greater number of things, than we can directly observe. They have, therefore, to be pieced together out of what others have reported and what we can imagine.[4]

This layer of truth, which we synthesize from "what others have reported and what we can imagine," runs a distant second to our own experience in its potential for verification. Much of it comes through others speaking to us, whether they are family, friends, teachers, preachers, or politicians. An even greater portion comes to us through the media: newspapers, web pages, television programs, books, Twitter, Instagram, and so on. These new truths from outside our immediate senses help create generalizations that Lippmann called "stereotypes," borrowing a term first applied to the duplication of printing-press cylinders that allowed the inking of newspapers on more than one press at the same time. Stereotypes have developed some strongly negative connotations, but when Lippmann wrote about them in 1922, he considered them shortcuts for people navigating through each unique day. Unfortunately, shortcuts sometimes—often?—lead to false conclusions. Not all flowers are sweet.

Lippmann said, "The only feeling that anyone can have about an event he does not experience is the feeling aroused by the mental image of that event."[5] That mental image is subject to alteration, reinforcement, and repudiation. And all *those* processes are prone to distortion. Wars are fought not only on the battlefield but also in the hearts and minds of the combatants and the observers on the home front. This was true during the Peloponnesian War and the Crusades, and remains true today. What Japan did in

1904 was to integrate news, propaganda, and censorship into a campaign to create favorable pictures in the heads of its soldiers and civilians, as well as readers of newspapers and magazines abroad. In so doing, it anticipated the twentieth-century phenomenon of postmodernism, which says there is no "Truth." Instead, truth—with a lower-case "t"—is what we make it out to be. The Russo-Japanese War may have been the first truly modern war not only in its huge, conscripted armies of civilians and weapons of mass slaughter, but also in its creation of "truths" intended to mobilize public opinion, both through promotion of positive narratives about the war and censorship erasing conflicting accounts. As Russo-Japanese War correspondent Thomas F. Millard observed,

> Governments cling to censorships not to prevent information from reaching an enemy, but because they afford an opportunity to conceal things which civilization has a right to know and an interest in knowing, and because they may be used to cover up incompetence and the inhumanity which invariably attends even the most humane war.[6]

Elimination of press censorship might make modern war impossible, he speculated.[7] But it was already too late to test that theory.

And so the sun set on the golden age of war correspondence, during which journalists, governments, and armed forces placed more emphasis on facts than fictions, and rose on a new age where truth is clay to be tossed, shaped, smashed, and remade.

Admittedly, that is an imperfect generalization about war correspondence. A few journalists in 1904–1905 invented news in the absence of the real thing. Ten-year-old photographs of the Sino-Japanese War found their way into print in the United States as images of Japan at war with Russia. Mencken invented a sea battle. And, as Luigi Barzini pointed out, reporters at Tokyo's Imperial Hotel, hounded by their editors but helpless to get real war news, sometimes made things up. But the vast majority of journalists remained true to their calling and tried to be accurate. War correspondent Richard Barry recorded a telling episode in his memoir of the Russo-Japanese War, *Port Arthur: A Monster Heroism*. He watched a sixty-year-old news photographer from upstate New York, James Ricalton, carry thirty pounds of camera and tripod into the perfect position to capture the image of a Japanese siege gun as it fired a 500-pound shell at a Russian warship outside Port Arthur. Barry wrote:

> Four of the shells were dropped yesterday into the *Retvizan* and *Pallada*. To-day the gunners will try to put in another. Ricalton plans to have his camera all set and tilted at the proper angle behind. Then as the gunner pulls the lanyard he

presses the bulb. He has stuffed his ears with cotton so the shock will not break the drums, for a gunner yesterday was deafened for life. He will probably be hurled to the ground and his camera may be smashed, but he wants [to photograph] the shell hurtling through the air, no bigger than a bee, while the dust of the recoil curls up over the emplacement and all the grand tensity of power and motion is about the place.

"Why take the risk?" say I, "when you can so easily take the gun at rest and then paint in a little dust and that wee dot up in the air."

"But it wouldn't be the real thing," said he, and he started off.[8]

Japan perfected two major ways to shape the story. One part focused on suppression: elaborate contracts for correspondent accreditation; battleground access rules that shut out pesky witnesses and their inquiries about potentially bad news; military liaisons or "minders," who, when a journalist *was* allowed in the war zone, severely restricted where he (and it was always a "he" in 1904) could go, what he could see, and whom he could interview; and press pools, also known as the "Great System" in which one reporter received the day's "truth" from a press officer and then was required to share it with all other correspondents. The other part concerned promotion: a systematic assessment of public opinion followed by public relations campaigns to strengthen it or change it. The promotion campaign, which we likely would call propaganda today, targeted two audiences. One was Japan's own people. The other was the West, which was expected to provide needed loans and, Japan hoped, welcome the empire into the circle of civilized nations at war's end. To the first group it gave only war news that had been tinged, in Melton Prior's words, *couleur de rose*. It saturated the home islands with military dispatches scrubbed of unpleasant details (such as hundreds of deaths aboard the battleship *Yashima*, as detailed in chapter 1), followed by the release of heavily censored dispatches from Western correspondents. Their "independent" confirmation of the previous official accounts promoted Japanese citizens' continued confidence in their government and armed forces. Even before the war, as the "religion" of national unity in addition to the adoration of duty, honor, and the emperor solidified their grip on Japan, the nation's newspapers had raised a nearly unanimous voice calling for all-out war.

Western journalists watching assaults on Port Arthur were astounded when masses of Japanese troops charged headlong at machine gun pits and heavy artillery. They did not yet realize the power of propaganda to make people act against such basic drives as the instinct to survive. Lippmann, speaking of the French in a later conflict, said, "We have learned to call this propaganda. A group of men, who can prevent independent access to the event, arrange the news to suit their purpose. That the purpose was in this case patriotic does not affect the argument."[9]

Some war correspondents, such as Jack London, associated the seemingly ubiquitous forces reshaping the news with something fundamentally Asian in color and character. London could not imagine such pressures and constraints occurring in what he called a "white man's war." He was wrong—not only did such censorship occur in later wars, yet also in the lesser but nonetheless real, contemporary constraints imposed on war correspondents by the Russians. Europeans first tightened the screws in 1914. Peyton C. March, who had predicted a sea change in military censorship in 1905 after watching the Japanese army at work, personally saw his vision come true in World War I—primarily a "white man's" war. Promoted to major general, March became U.S. Army chief of staff in March 1918. Upon taking office, he bemoaned the "muzzling censorship" on the Western Front that he said was preventing the home front from getting the news it deserved, and vowed to ease the restrictions on American correspondents.[10] Fortunately, he had the ear of President Woodrow Wilson and two influential army officers who had observed the Russo-Japanese War and shaped U.S. press policy in World War I: censor and former correspondent Frederick Palmer, and John J. "Black Jack" Pershing, who commanded the American Expeditionary Forces in France. Pershing had witnessed the end of the war in Manchuria in 1905 alongside fellow accredited attaché Major General Arthur MacArthur. In late 1905, the elder MacArthur toured military bases in Japan with his twenty-five-year-old son and aide-de-camp, Douglas, further absorbing the methods of the victors.[11] March announced the lifting of some World War I censorship restrictions in mid-June 1918, such as the reversal of Pershing's rule censoring the addresses of American casualties, and began weekly press conferences.[12] Regardless of the late changes, however, rigorous censorship remains one of the hallmarks of the war.

Restraints on Western-style wartime journalism reached new dimensions in the Nazi propaganda machine of World War II. Far less restrictive policies, yet still reminiscent of Japanese-style press restraints, emerged in the U.S. Army in the Southwest Pacific during World War II, when Douglas MacArthur, who had risen to the rank of five-star general by 1944, imposed some the strictest American censorship rules of the war. He had learned about the press not only in Japan in 1905 but also while serving as both information officer and censor while heading Secretary of War Newton Baker's Bureau of Information in 1916.[13] In World War II, MacArthur demanded, among other things, that reporters downplay casualties under his command and tout his role in victories.[14]

Powerful press controls dominated coverage of the British invasion of the Falklands in 1982, as well as the U.S. invasions of Grenada in 1983, Panama in 1989, and Iraq in 1991. During Operation Desert Storm, the 1991 ouster of Iraqi forces from Kuwait, American armed forces mirrored the Japanese

Ministry of War in 1904 by instituting severe limits on reporters' access. The United States established press pools and created military liaisons, known to the press as "minders," who shadowed accredited journalists' movements. Censorship sometimes delayed release of sensitive information for days.[15]

Japan had acted in 1904 in response to the spirit of the time and place. As a small nation facing a large and powerful enemy, it needed to marshal *all* the forces at its command to have even a chance at victory. These included not only the traditional powers of men and machines, but also public opinion at home and abroad. Unique circumstances favored its quest. Japan, an island nation, carried out its fight on the mainland. Western war correspondents could not pass as East Asians, and so had slim chance to sneak into Korea and Manchuria by sea on Japanese ships. On the battlefields, not only did they fail to blend in among the Japanese soldiers, but nearly all of them also had to rely on interpreters to understand events around them. Those interpreters teamed up with military liaisons to limit access to news that did not meet official approval. Correspondents might be lucky to glimpse a portion of battle early in the war, but what that portion meant in the grand strategy they likely would know only if generals on site shared that knowledge. When army officials did choose to give press briefings through English interpreters, their announcements often were terse and shared through the pool system, ensuring all correspondents got the same brief, approved message. "All is going according to plan" was the entirety of one such statement to the press in the war zone, according to correspondent Frederick Palmer.[16]

In addition to restricting information, Japan controlled the technology of communication. Dispatches from Japanese-controlled territory in East Asia had to be sent by one of three methods: painfully slow postal service, military-controlled telegraph wires, or boat trip across the sea to access uncensored telegraph lines. Hiring a boat carried its own risks, as warships on the lookout for spies patrolled the sea-lanes. Unlike their counterparts in the Civil War and Spanish-American War, correspondents had no opportunity to enjoy an easy ride to an uncensored telegraph station outside the Japanese war zone.

In short, unless they accepted high levels of risk, Western war correspondents were only as independent as Japan allowed them to be.

Kept from getting the usual stories about strategy and tactics, ground that was gained and lost, and descriptions of battle—the commonplace arithmetic of death—many of the reporters covering the early months of the war turned to other subjects. These included people caught up in the machinery of war, typically ordinary soldiers and civilians. This was the style of E. L. Godkin in the Crimean War—a style initially denigrated as too soft to be a substantial or significant account of violence. Journalists such as Richard Harding Davis, John Fox Jr., and Jack London considered human-interest war reporting to be inferior and went home when they could not follow the standard template of guns and glory. It is therefore very strange that a war that had zero accredited female correspondents should be associated with male journalists who unknowingly foreshadowed a sea change in war reporting that began with women correspondents in the 1930s and 1940s. Martha Gellhorn of *Collier's* is often credited with significantly changing the focus of war reporting during her coverage of the Spanish Civil War in the late 1930s and in World War II. For example, in Madrid, in July 1937, Gellhorn wrote only of what she saw in the streets and cafes and inns: a twisted piece of shrapnel that killed a little boy while he held an old woman's hand; a janitor whose house took a direct hit from a bomb dropped by an airplane; and bloody stretchers lined up in the hallway of the Palace Hotel. This style of reporting focused on civilians in harm's way, crystallizing the war on a personal scale. It became even more strongly associated with American women war correspondents during World War II although some male correspondents, such as columnist Ernie Pyle, also practiced it. The United States accredited 127 women to be war correspondents in World War II but forbade them from covering combat, fearing, among other reasons, that they would crack under war's intensity (men did too!) and that their presence might induce soldiers to take unnecessary risks to protect them. These restrictions prodded the women to look for new angles in war stories—personal and moving accounts of doctors, nurses, the wounded, and most of all the indigenous people whose lives the wars destroyed.[17] To call Richard Harding Davis, John Fox Jr., Luigi Barzini, or Jack London "feminine" in their non-combat stories likely would have made them bristle, but that is the heart of the matter.

The fact that Japan won the war burned itself into the brains of Western military observers. Tiny Japan, mustering all its resources in a total war, gained control of the Western Pacific, erased Russia's eastern line of defense, captured the capital of the eastern Russian Empire, grabbed land and bases from which Russia had hoped to dominate the Far East, and destroyed the army of a much larger nation. It also expanded the Japanese empire and contributed to the Russian Revolution of 1905, forerunner to the one in 1917 that split the world into communist and noncommunist camps. McCormick wrote of Japan turning the planet upside-down:

> In nineteen months the world was altered. Not only was it changed politically, geographically, and militarily, but scientifically, for the East has taught us unrevealed uses of our implements of war, of our principles of diplomacy, and it will teach us to abandon our science of ethnology and to modify our ethics, our politics, and our religion.[18]

It is a military cliché that at the outbreak of a new war, generals begin by re-fighting the previous one. Military attachés from Western nations walked the ground in Korea and Manchuria and saw the future of warfare. As noted in the introduction to this book, Captain March came away from the war convinced all future combatants would find similar methods of censorship a "necessity."[19] He added, "Although the Japanese have not completely solved the problem, it cannot be doubted that their censorship has been of distinct advantage to them."[20] Germany, which itched to flex its muscles on the world stage after the unification of its diverse states in the nineteenth century, reached the same conclusion as March. "In 1905, by wintertime, the lessons of Manchuria were pretty well digested in Germany," wrote war correspondent Frederick McCormick. "And Germany had but one provision unsettled; it was the question of war correspondents. Germany's war correspondents in Manchuria—all of them army men, naturally—when consulted by the General Staff at Berlin, deprecated war correspondence in Germany when 'the war' came."[21] Germany allowed American journalists into war zones under its control during World War I but censored their accounts carefully.

When war shook France and Britain in August 1914, both came to the same conclusion as Germany: keep the press far from observing the fighting, or if that was not possible, keep it under authoritarian censorship. France accepted applications for accreditation to the war zone under its control, but set up barriers to actual accreditation. For example, it required that accounts of battle be written in letter-perfect French. Naturally, the test given to prospective correspondents read like a ninth-grader's nightmare, with grammar questions so difficult no American applicant could pass it. Reporters who managed to make the minimum grade found themselves with constant military escorts and stories primarily limited to press statements by officers.[22]

At least France had a nominal system of press access. Britain did not during the early months of the war. Ian MacPherson, member of Parliament and under-secretary of state for war, said the United Kingdom modeled its press bureau specifically on what military observers had seen in Japan a decade earlier.[23] Field Marshal Lord Herbert Kitchener, secretary of state for war until his death in 1916, despised the press, and when the German army broke through Belgium on its way toward Paris, he ordered the arrest and expulsion of any journalists found wandering the battlefields behind British lines. Kitchener announced in August 1914 that any newspaper in the United Kingdom found to have published war news other than the official releases of the government's press bureau would be "suspended." This led newspapers in the United States to remark on the oddity of such an order in a nation that had grown accustomed to press freedom.[24] A day's worth of official bulletins released for publication in the United Kingdom early in the war totaled about a half-column's worth of a typical newspaper. Most news from across the English Channel came from a British officer, Colonel Earnest Swinton, whose accounts managed to paint rosy pictures of an army that, in reality, faced muddy trenches, barbed wire, machine gun fire, and toxic gas attacks—not to mention slaughter on a scale even greater than that of Liaoyang and Mukden.[25] It took an intervention by Theodore Roosevelt, as in 1904, to bring change. The former president urged the British foreign secretary in January 1915 to allow independent American journalists into the British war zone in order to counter the propaganda Americans were reading from German sources. "The only real war news written by Americans who are known to and trusted by the American public comes from the German side; as a result of this, the sympathizers with the cause of the Allies can hear nothing whatsoever about the trials and achievements of the British and French armies," Roosevelt wrote. The British Expeditionary Force agreed to begin accrediting Americans, but initially the only one to win approval was Russo-Japanese War news veteran Frederick Palmer. In 1915 he filed jointly to the three main press associations of the United States: Associated Press, United Press, and International News Service. This three-pronged approach guaranteed that most Americans would read his stories, as virtually all newspapers larger than village weeklies subscribed to one or more of the syndicates.[26] But all got the *same* story.

The Western journalists of the Russo-Japanese War had foreseen what might happen in future conflicts in the absence of independent, non-military observers. Bennet Burleigh of the London *Daily Telegraph* said in his memoir of the war that the ministers in the Japanese Ministry of War had "crude ideas" about war correspondents.

> First, to do without them; second, to trick them; third, if possible, to burke or crib them. "Other times, other manners." No general can eliminate education or the printing-press from the world's affairs. As he cannot, if wise, he will have these agencies, or such of them as he can muster, fighting for his side. If not, he and his cause will suffer in some degree. For if he won't have war correspondents, then all he issues for publication is properly received as a mere ex parte statement, of little value compared with independent testimony.[27]

In Manchuria, the absence of independent observers resulted in the Western media's refusal to give credence to Japanese-supplied stories of Russian atrocities, which led to adjustments in Japan's information campaign. The flip side of true stories not being accepted is that without the Fourth Estate acting as a check on the military and the government, false stories can proliferate unabated and be taken as gospel. Burleigh wrote, "And your modern general, moreover, will find that his soldiers, his officers, his camp followers, and 'rumour' with its huge ears and many tongues, does more hurt than any number of reputable correspondents."[28]

Absent the eyes and ears of war correspondents on the Western Front in the opening months of World War I, rumors of atrocity took on the clothing of truth. Distortions deemed to be useful helped shape pictures in civilians' heads, and the home nations acted on those images of war as if they were real. As the German army marched through neutral Belgium to get at its adversary France, stories surfaced of inhumane treatment of Belgian civilians. These included bayonetting of babies, amputation of civilians' hands, and widespread rape and torture. More extreme atrocity rumors told of civilians seeing a soldier crucified and a German bucket filled with eyeballs.[29] After the war, when tempers had cooled and historians who had gained renewed access to the prior war zones could ask questions, the atrocity rumors that had helped swell anti-German fever in the United States could not be verified.

Even true events got twisted. The American press framed the 1915 torpedoing of the steamship *Lusitania* as a German atrocity, even though Germany had warned that its U-boats would consider any ships, regardless of flag, to be fair game for sinking in combatant waters near Britain.[30]

Upon entering the war in 1917, the United States joined its World War I Allies in a campaign of publicity, propaganda, and censorship, all under the direction of the federal Committee on Public Information and headed by newspaperman George Creel of Colorado. The CPI left accreditation to the armed forces, which made reporters pledge to follow censorship regulations and post a bond that would be forfeited if they did not. The reporters enjoyed more freedom than those who had covered the Russo-Japanese War, including the right to move about the battlefield.

Domestically, the CPI went into overdrive. It distributed hundreds of news releases as well as propagandistic pamphlets and posters. It also set up a small army of so-called "Four-Minute Men" to give brief pro-war talks in movie theaters and other venues. Newspapers and magazines at home received a CPI card listing censorship recommendations instead of regulations—reflecting the lack of domestic censorship laws due to the strength of the First Amendment of the U.S. Constitution. President Wilson had edited the card himself, indicating his level of interest in shaping public opinion on the home front. Although domestic censorship was voluntary, the Espionage Act and Sedition Act, both passed during American participation in the war, threatened prison time and fines on anyone making spoken or written statements that disrupted the work of the army or navy, or in the case of the latter act, that expressed contempt of the U.S. government, its president, and other symbols of national unity and purpose. The United States might not have an emperor as its national father, but it had its own figureheads and objects of veneration.[31]

The CPI, driven by the monomaniacal Creel, did not consider it a journalistic sin to exaggerate facts for the sake of propaganda, nor to lie on occasion for the sake of short-term gain. These ethical lapses eventually caught up with the organization, earning it the epithet "Committee on Public Misinformation."[32] They also contributed to a backlash against government propaganda after the war that only became stronger once the worst of the German atrocity stories were debunked in the 1920s. "Propaganda," which had begun as a neutral term for a mass publicity campaign, became a dirty word by the 1930s, particularly after the Nazi campaigns of Propaganda Minister Joseph Goebbels perfected the techniques of the CPI and coupled them to monstrous lies and terrors. American advertising mogul Edward Bernays, nephew of Sigmund Freud, came up with the term "public relations" as a neutral term for mass persuasion and described it in a book he rushed into print after Lippmann's *Public Opinion*. Whereas Lippmann hated the "manufacture of consent" through mass media campaigns, Bernays believed modern, complex society required some methods to define and mobilize opinion. His 1923 book *Crystallizing Public Opinion* "performed PR for PR," wrote historian Sue Curry Jansen.[33] Bernays truly believed mass persuasion techniques to be at the heart of a large, modern democracy, and his status as nephew to Freud gave him insights into the best ways to use political and advertising messages to make media consumers act on their conscious and unconscious desires. In his 1928 book *Propaganda*, Bernays made the bold statement that the invisible manipulators of public opinion were the "true ruling power" in the United States.[34]

Linguist Noam Chomsky, author of an influential 1988 book titled *Manufacturing Consent* and frequent critic of the press, examined the legacy of World War I, which owed much to the Japanese inventions of 1904. In a 1997 speech, Chomsky said:

[The] American business community was also very impressed with the propaganda effort. They had a problem at that time. The country was becoming formally more democratic. A lot more people were able to vote and that sort of thing. The country was becoming wealthier and more people could participate and a lot of new immigrants were coming in, and so on.

So what do you do? It's going to be harder to run things as a private club. Therefore, obviously, you have to control what people think. There had been public relation specialists but there was never a public relations industry. There was a guy hired to make [billionaire John D.] Rockefeller's image look prettier and that sort of thing. But this huge public relations industry, which is a U.S. invention and a monstrous industry, came out of the First World War. The leading figures were people in the Creel Commission. In fact, the main one, Edward Bernays, comes right out of the Creel Commission. . . . He wrote a book called *Propaganda* . . . and it starts off by saying he is applying the lessons of the First World War. The propaganda system of the First World War and this commission that he was part of showed, he says, it is possible to "regiment the public mind every bit as much as an army regiments their bodies." These new techniques of regimentation of minds, he said, had to be used by the intelligent minorities in order to make sure that the slobs stay on the right course. We can do it now because we have these new techniques.[35]

The Russo-Japanese War, and especially the Japanese information campaign that aimed to manipulate war correspondents for political and military gain, helped create the complex and often scary world of modern mass media. The pictures in our heads are now fair game for manipulation not only by governments and armed forces, but also by anyone with access to the World Wide Web. Journalists are not exempt from this criticism. Like medicine and law, the professions of broadcasting and print journalism—and public relations and advertising, for that matter—have codes of ethics.[36] But unlike law and medicine, there is no test that one must pass to be certified as a mass communicator, nor any legal enforcement of penalties for those who deliberately ignore the ethics codes in order to distort and mislead. As Douglas Story noted in his memoir of the Russo-Japanese War, journalists followed the censorship rules. In later wars, particularly the invasion of Iraq in 2003 that embedded journalists within military units, almost all journalists also followed the rules. Had they violated censorship rules and published news that compromised operational security, they might have found themselves on the receiving end of enemy artillery shells, or worse. Bennet Burleigh captured these ideas in his memoir, *Empire of the East*:

> What a creature that correspondent would be who would betray the host with whom he remained an honored guest! And what a contemptible enemy that must be who trusts to the newspapers as its intelligence department in time of war, and not to their own and well-organized and costly system of spies, scouts, and special service men![37]

And so we return to, and conclude with, the central question deeded to us by the Russo-Japanese War: What is truth? The answer has become even more difficult to discover in the twenty-first century, as social media have made it possible for anyone on the Web to claim the mantle of "journalist," post a story to cyberspace, and call it true. Many governments and military offices around the world attempt to put the most positive spin on bad news, if they report it at all. The United States and United Kingdom spend huge amounts on public relations but call it public diplomacy. The U.S. State Department spends more than $1 billion each year in an attempt to influence foreign opinion; likewise, the Pentagon invests in propaganda aimed at foreign governments and foreign citizens. British journalism professor Florian Zollman identifies these expenditures as occurring in a campaign of "news propaganda strategy" and "perception management" that becomes more intense during wartime.[38]

Yet at a time when accurate and significant press coverage should demand skepticism and scrutiny of such government "spin," many journalists have abandoned the credo of objectivity that has dominated the American news model for a century. One need look only at the results of a survey of television news viewers about their beliefs about the U.S.-led invasion of Iraq in 2001 in order to find evidence that journalists can spin, too, intentionally or unintentionally. The survey, conducted in discrete polls in June, July, and August-September 2001 by the Program on International Policy Attitudes, presented 3,334 Americans with three patently false statements about the war: that the United States had found weapons of mass destruction in Iraq, that world public opinion favored the invasion, and that the Iraqi government had links to the Al Qaeda terrorist group that had launched the attacks of September 11, 2001. Sixty percent said at least one of the three false statements was true. The percentage was highest among viewers of the conservative Fox Broadcasting Company; 80 percent of its viewers agreed that at least one of these false statements was true. The numbers dropped, but remained unsettlingly high, for the other major networks—CBS, 71 percent; ABC, 61 percent; NBC, 55 percent; CNN, 55 percent; PBS and National Public Radio, 23 percent. Print media collectively registered at 47 percent.[39] And all this occurred *before* the ubiquity and potential distortion of social media arrived with the advent of Facebook in 2004 and Twitter in 2006.

The only way to navigate toward the truth, it appears, is for consumers of news to assume the responsibility of vetting information in ways that previously had fallen to journalists and their editors. We must ask ourselves of any story, whether about war or any other topic: Who created it? What are their credentials? What is their track record regarding accuracy? What would they have to gain or lose if we accepted their version of events? What do other voices say?

Japan in 1904–1905 gave the world a model that mobilized public opinion to win a war—but at a cost of widespread gullibility for news stories of which we approve and cynicism for news of which we do not.

We still live in that world.

NOTES

1. "Restricting the War Correspondent," *Brooklyn* (NY) *Daily Eagle*, August 14, 1904.
2. Martin, "On Reading Mencken," 248–49.
3. Ibid., 249.
4. Walter Lippmann, *Public Opinion* (New York: Harcourt, Brace, 1922), 79.
5. Lippmann, *Public Opinion*, 13.
6. Millard, "Does the Conflict between Russia and Japan Mark the Doom of the War Correspondent?"
7. Ibid.

8. Richard Barry, *Port Arthur: A Monster Heroism* (New York: Moffat, Yard & Company, 1905), 111–12.

9. Lippmann, *Public Opinion*, 42.

10. "March Back, Urges Less Censorship," *New York Herald*, March 2, 1918.

11. John T. Greenwood, "The U.S. Army Military Observers with the Japanese Army during the Russo-Japanese War (1904–1905)," *Army History* 36 (Winter 1996): 2, 13.

12. C.C. Brainerd, "Wilson Lifts Censorship; Public to Get Weekly News of Troop Movements Abroad," *Brooklyn* (NY) *Daily Eagle*, June 16, 1918.

13. "Maj. Douglas M'Arthur Aid [*sic*] to War Secretary," *Washington Evening Star*, June 30, 1916.

14. Frederick S. Voss, *The Journalistic Coverage of World War II* (Washington, DC: Smithsonian Institution Press, 1994), 26.

15. For an overview of press controls in Operation Desert Storm, see John R. MacArthur, *Second Front: Censorship and Propaganda in the Gulf War* (Berkeley: University of California Press, 1993). The U.S. armed forces in World War II, the Korean War, and the Vietnam War generally enjoyed much warmer and more open relations with the press, due largely to widespread negative reaction to excessive press controls in the previous wars. The 2001 assault on the Taliban in Afghanistan was an anomaly because Special Forces, which operate under a cloak of anonymity, carried out the assignment, typically in conjunction with Afghan rebels fighting in extremely rough mountain terrain. Peter Baker of the *Washington Post* spent six months in Afghanistan and never had the opportunity to interview an American soldier. Reaction to the secrecy surrounding the Afghan operation encouraged the popular embedding program during the invasion of Iraq in 2003. In that war, the Pentagon told its public affairs officers in the field, "We need to tell the factual story—good and bad—before others seed the media with disinformation and distortions." See Michael S. Sweeney, *The Military and the Press: An Uneasy Truce* (Evanston, Illinois: Northwestern University Press, 2006), 185–89.

16. Frederick Palmer, *With My Own Eyes, A Personal Story of Battle Years* (Indianapolis: Bobbs–Merrill Company, 1933), 239.

17. For a study of how women changed war correspondence, see *No Job for a Woman: The Women Who Fought to Report World War II*, directed by Michèle Midori Fillion (New York: Hurry Up Sister Productions, 2011), DVD. Fillion profiles reporters Martha Gellhorn and Ruth Cowan, as well as reporter/photographer Dickey Chapelle. For a more detailed examination of Gellhorn, see Caroline Moorehead, *Gellhorn: A Twentieth-Century Life* (New York: H. Holt, 2003); and "Reporting America at War: Martha Gellhorn—High Explosives for Everyone," Public Broadcasting Service, https://www.pbs.org/weta/reportingamericaatwar/reporters/gellhorn/madrid.html. Richard Harding Davis wrote an even earlier example of Gellhorn-style reporting in 1897 during the Cuban insurrection against Spain. His story "The Death of Rodriguez" featured a tightly focused description of the firing-squad execution of a young Cuban rebel. It likely was the origin of the cinematic cliché of the condemned man being blindfolded and given a last cigarette. See Davis, *Notes of a War Correspondent*, 3–14.

18. McCormick, *The Tragedy of Russia in Pacific Asia*, vol. I, 4.

19. Peyton C. March, "Report No. 6, War Department, Office of the Chief of Staff, Washington, January 3, 1905," Reports of Military Observers Attached to the Armies in Manchuria During the Russo-Japanese War, Part I (Washington, DC: Government Printing Office, 1906), 55.

20. W. S. Schuyler, J. F. Morrison, Carl Reichmann, and Peyton C. March, *Reports of the Military Observers Attached to the Armies in Manchuria during the Russo–Japanese War*, pt. I. (Washington, DC: Government Printing Office, 1906), 55.

21. Frederick McCormick, *The Menace of Japan* (Boston: Little, Brown and Company, 1917), 18.

22. Sweeney, *The Military and the Press*, 39.

23. Arthur S. Draper, "Inside Workings of Censorship Explained by British Secretary," *Saint Louis Post-Dispatch*, July 8, 1917.

24. See, for example, "Strict Censorship of News Is Being Enforced by Big Nations at War," *Saint Louis Post-Dispatch*, August 14, 1914; and "Only Brief Reports from War Zone Permitted to Pass Rigid Censorship Imposed by Belligerents," *Albuquerque* (NM) *Journal*, August 19, 1914.

25. Knightley, *The First Casualty*, 86–88; and Emmet Crozier, *American Reporters on the Western Front, 1914–1918* (New York: Oxford University Press, 1959), 57.

26. Haverstock, *Fifty Years at the Front*, 164, 174.

27. Burleigh, *Empire of the East*, 448.

28. Ibid., 446.

29. Sweeney, *The Military and the Press*, 40–42.

30. James Morgan Read, *Atrocity Propaganda 1914–1919* (New Haven, CT: Yale University Press, 1941), 199–214; and Harold D. Lasswell, *Propaganda Technique in the World War* (New York: Peter Smith, 1938), 208.

31. Sweeney, *The Military and the Press*, 43–54.

32. Thomas Howell, *Soldiers of the Pen: The Writer's War Board of World War II* (Amherst: University of Massachusetts Press, 2019), 6.

33. Sue Curry Jansen, "Semantic Tyranny: How Edward L. Bernays Stole Walter Lippmann's Mojo and Got Away with It and Why It Still Matters," *International Journal of Communication* 7 (2013): 1094.

34. Edward Bernays, *Propaganda* (New York: H. Liveright, 1928), 9–10.

35. Noam Chomsky, "What Makes Mainstream Media Mainstream," lecture at Z Media Institute, June 1997, Information Clearing House, https://web.archive.org/web/20190119121556/http://www.informationclearinghouse.info/article26193.htm. The man hired to improve the public image of ruthless Standard Oil magnate John D. Rockefeller was Ivy Lee, often considered one of the founders of modern public relations. Rockefeller retained Lee in 1914 after the National Guard opened fire with machine guns, killing striking miners, wives, and children at a coal mine Rockefeller owned at Ludlow, Colorado. See Kirk Hallahan, "Ivy Lee and the Rockefellers' Response to the 1913–1914 Colorado Coal Strike," *Journal of Public Relations Research* 14, no. 4 (2002): 265–315.

36. Among the many codes of ethics for professional communicators are the following: Society of Professional Journalists, https://www.spj.org/ethicscode.asp; Associated Press Media Editors, https://www.apme.com/page/EthicsStatement; Associated Press Statement of News Values and Principles, https://www.asne.org/content.asp?pl=236&sl=351&contentid=351; Radio Television Digital News Association, https://www.rtdna.org/content/rtdna_code_of_ethics; Society of American Business Editors and Writers, https://www.asne.org/resources-ethics-sabew; Public Relations Society of America, https://www.prsa.org/ethics/code-of-ethics/; and Standards of Practice of the American Association of Advertising Agencies, https://ams.aaaa.org/eweb/upload/inside/standards.pdf.

37. Burleigh, *Empire of the East*, 446.

38. Florian Zollmann, "Is it Either Or? Professional Ideology vs. Corporate-media Constraints," *Westminster Papers in Communication and Culture* 6, no 2 (2009): 106.

39. Steven Kull, "Misperceptions, the Media and the Iraq War," The PIPA/Knowledge Networks Poll, Program on International Policy Attitudes and Knowledge Networks, October 2, 2003, https://web.archive.org/web/20031202082736/http://www.pipa.org/OnlineReports/Iraq/Media_10_02_03_Report.pdf, 7, 13.

Bibliography

ARCHIVES

Barzini, Luigi Sr. Ministero per i Beni e le Attivita Culturali, l'Archivio Centrale dello Stato. Rome, Italy.
Brill, Hascal Russell, and Family Papers. Minnesota Historical Society, Saint Paul.
Davis, Richard Harding. University of Virginia, Charlottesville.
Dokuritsu Gyosei Hojin Kokuritsu Kōbunshokan. Tokyo, Japan.
Fox Family Papers. University of Kentucky, Lexington.
Fuller, John Louis Hilton. Indiana Historical Society, Indianapolis.
Library of Congress Digital Images Collection. Washington, DC.
London, Jack and Charmian. Utah State University, Logan.
The Reminiscences of Stanley Washburn, 1950. The Oral History Collection, Columbia University, New York.
Straight, Willard. Cornell University, Ithaca, NY.
Washburn, Stanley. Minnesota Historical Society, Saint Paul.

BOOKS

Alland, Alexander. *Jacob A. Riis: Photographer and Citizen*. N.p.: Aperture, 1975.
Andrews, J. Cutler. *The North Reports the Civil War*. Pittsburgh: University of Pittsburgh, 1955.
———. *The South Reports the Civil War*. Princeton, NJ: Princeton University Press, 2015.
Ashmead-Bartlett. *Port Arthur: The Siege and Capitulation*. Edinburgh, Scotland: William Blackwood and Sons, 1906.
Barry, Richard. *Events Man: Being an Account of the Adventures of Stanley Washburn, American War Correspondent*. New York: Moffat, Yard & Company, 1907.

———. *Port Arthur: A Monster Heroism.* New York: Moffat, Yard and Company, 1905.

Barshay, Andrew E. *State and Intellectual in Imperial Japan: The Public Man in Crisis.* Berkeley: University of California Press, 1988.

Barzini, Luigi. *Guerra russo-giapponese: La battaglia di Mukden, narrata da Luigi Barzini.* Milan, Italy: Fratelli Treves, 1906.

———. *Peking to Paris.* Lake Elmo, MN: Demontreville Press, 2007.

———. *Scene della grande guerra.* Milan: Fratelli Treves, 1915.

Bernays, Edward L. *Crystallizing Public Opinion.* New York: Boni and Liveright, 1923.

———. *Propaganda.* New York: H. Liveright, 1928.

Best, Brian. *Fighting for the News: The Adventures of the First War Correspondents from Bonaparte to the Boers.* South Yorkshire, England: Frontline Press, 2016.

Boyd, James. *Japanese-Mongolian Relations, 1873–1945: Faith, Race and Strategy.* Leiden, Netherlands: Global Oriental/Brill, 2010.

Brindle, Ernest. *With Russian, Japanese and Chunchose: The Experiences of an Englishman during the Russo-Japanese War.* London: John Murray, 1905.

Brown, Charles H. *The Correspondents' War: Journalists in the Spanish-American War.* New York: Charles Scribner's Sons, 1967.

Bullard, F. Lauriston. *Famous War Correspondents.* Boston: Little, Brown and Co., 1914.

Burleigh, Bennet. *Empire of the East: Or Japan and Russia at War 1904–5.* London: Chapman and Hall, 1905.

Campbell, W. Joseph. *The Year that Defined American Journalism: 1897 and the Clash of Paradigms.* New York: Routledge, 2006.

Christie, Dugald. *Thirty Years in Moukden, 1883–1913: Being the Experiences and Recollections of Dugald Christie, C.M.G.* Edited by His Wife. London: Constable and Company, 1914.

Connaughton, Richard. *Rising Sun and Tumbling Bear: Russia's War with Japan.* London: Cassell, 1988.

Creelman, James. *On the Great Highway.* Boston: Lothrop, Lee & Shepard Co., 1901.

Croly, Herbert. *Willard Straight.* New York: The Macmillan Company, 1924.

Crozier, Emmet. *American Reporters on the Western Front, 1914–1918.* New York: Oxford University Press, 1959.

Davis, Charles Belmont. *Adventures and Letters of Richard Harding Davis.* New York: Charles Scribner's Sons, 1917.

Davis, Richard Harding. *Notes of a War Correspondent.* New York: Charles Scribner's Sons, 1911.

———. *With the Allies.* Toronto: The Copp Clark Co., 1915.

Davis, Richard Harding, and Alfred Thayer Mahan, *The Russo-Japanese War: A Photographic and Descriptive Review of the Great Conflict in the Far East, Gathered from the Reports, Records, Cable Despatches, Photographs, Etc., Etc., of Collier's War Correspondents.* New York: P. F. Collier, 1905.

Dell'Orto, Giovanna. *American Journalism and International Relations: Foreign Correspondence from the Early Days of the Republic to the Digital Age.* New York: Cambridge University Press, 2013.

Dennett, Tyler. *Roosevelt and the Russo-Japanese War: A Critical Study of American Policy in Eastern Asia in 1902–05, Based Primarily upon the Private Papers of Theodore Roosevelt.* Garden City, NY: Doubleday, Page & Company, 1925.
Desmond, Robert W. *Windows on the World: The Information Process in a Changing Society, 1900–1920.* Iowa City: University of Iowa Press, 1980.
De Tocqueville, Alexis. *Democracy in America*, vols. 1, 2. Translated by Henry Reeve. New York: The Colonial Press, 1899.
Dicken-Garcia, Hazel. *Journalistic Standards in Nineteenth-Century America.* Madison: University of Wisconsin Press, 1989.
Dunn, William J. *Pacific Microphone.* College Station: Texas A&M University Press, 2009.
Everett, Marshall. *Exciting Experiences in the Japanese-Russian War.* Chicago: The Educational Company, 1904.
Fox, John Jr. *Crittenden: A Kentucky Story of Love and War.* New York: Charles Scribner's Sons, 1900.
———. *Following the Sun Flag: A Vain Pursuit through Manchuria.* London: Constable, 1905.
Fraser, David. *A Modern Campaign: Or War and Wireless Telegraphy in the Far East.* London: Methuen & Co., 1905.
Griscom, Lloyd. *Diplomatically Speaking.* Boston: Little, Brown and Company, 1940.
Halstead, Murat. *The War between Russia and Japan: Containing Thrilling Accounts of Fierce Battles by Sea and Land.* S.l.: s.n., 1904.
Hare, James H., ed. *A Photographic Record of the Russo-Japanese War.* New York: P.F. Collier & Sons, 1905.
Haverstock, Nathan A. *Fifty Years at the Front: The Life of War Correspondent Frederick Palmer.* Washington, DC: Brassey's, 1996.
Hibberd, Matthew. *The Media in Italy: Press, Cinema and Broadcasting from Unification to Digital.* Maidenhead, England: Open University Press, 2008.
Howell, Thomas. *Soldiers of the Pen: The Writer's War Board of World War II.* Amherst: University of Massachusetts Press, 2019.
James, David H. *The Siege of Port Arthur: Records of an Eye-witness.* London: T. Fisher Unwin, 1905.
James, Lionel. *High Pressure: Being Some Record of Activities in the Service of The Times Newspaper.* London: John Murray, 1929.
Katovsky, Bill, and Timothy Carlson, eds. *Embedded: The Media at the War in Iraq.* Guilford, CT: Lyons Press, 2003.
Kendall, George Wilkins. *Dispatches from the Mexican War.* Norman: University of Oklahoma Press, 1999.
Kershaw, Alex. *Jack London: A Life.* New York, St. Martin's Press, 1999.
Knightley, Phillip. *The First Casualty: From Crimea to Vietnam; The War Correspondent as Hero, Propagandist, and Myth Maker.* New York: Harcourt Brace Jovanovich, 1975.
Kowner, Rotem, ed. *Rethinking the Russo-Japanese War, 1904–05*, vol. I: *Centennial Perspectives.* Leiden, Netherlands: Global Oriental/Brill, 2007.
Labor, Earle. *Jack London: An American Life.* New York: Farrar, Straus and Giroux, 2013.

Labor, Earle, Robert C. Leitz, and I. Milo Shepard, eds. *The Letters of Jack London*, vol. 1. Stanford, CA: Stanford University Press, 1993.

Larson, Magali Sarfatti. *The Rise of Professionalism: A Sociological Analysis*. Berkeley: University of California Press, 1977.

Lasswell, Harold D. *Propaganda Technique in the World War*. New York: Peter Smith, 1938.

Lippmann, Walter. *Public Opinion*. New York: Harcourt, Brace, 1922.

London, Jack. *The Letters of Jack London 1913–1916*, vol. 3. Edited by Earle Labor, Robert C. Leitz II, and I. Milo Shepard. Stanford, CA: Stanford University Press, 1988.

———. *Letters from Jack London: Including a Correspondence between London and Sinclair Lewis*. Edited by King Hendricks and Irving Shepard. Garden City, NY: Doubleday, 1970.

———. *The Star-Rover*. New York: Macmillan, 1915.

London, Jack, King Hendricks, and I. Milo Shepard, *Jack London Reports: War Correspondence, Sports Articles, and Miscellaneous Writings*. Garden City, NY: Doubleday, 1970.

London, Joan. *Jack London and His Times: An Unconventional Biography*. Seattle: University of Washington Press, 1939.

Lubow, Arthur. *The Reporter Who Would Be King: A Biography of Richard Harding Davis*. New York: Scribner Book Company, 1992.

Lynch, George, and Frederick Palmer, eds. *In Many Wars by Many War Correspondents*. With a foreword by John Maxwell Hamilton. Baton Rouge: Louisiana State University, 2010.

MacArthur, John R. *Second Front: Censorship and Propaganda in the Gulf War*. Berkeley: University of California Press, 1993.

Magri, Enzo. *Una vita da inviato*. Florence, Italy: Polistampa, 2008.

McCormick, Frederick. *The Menace of Japan*. Boston: Little, Brown and Company, 1917.

———. *The Tragedy of Russia in Pacific Asia*, vols. I–II. New York: The Outing Publishing Company, 1907.

McCullagh, Francis. *With the Cossacks: Being the Story of an Irishman Who Rode with the Cossacks throughout the Russo–Japanese War*. Uckfield, UK: The Naval and Military Press Ltd., 2004.

McKenzie, Frederick Arthur. *From Tokyo to Tiflis: Uncensored Letters from the War*. London: Hurst and Blackett, 1905.

McLaughlin, Greg. *The War Correspondent*. London: Pluto Press, 2002.

Millard, Thomas F. *The New Far East*. New York: Charles Scribner's Sons, 1906.

Milton, Joyce. *The Yellow Kids: Foreign Correspondence in the Heyday of Yellow Journalism*. New York: HarperCollins, 1989.

Mindich, David T.Z. *Just the Facts: How Objectivity Came to Define American Journalism*, New York: NYU Press, 2001.

Moorehead, Caroline, *Gellhorn: A Twentieth-Century Life*. New York: H. Holt, 2003.

Morris, Edmund. *The Rise of Theodore Roosevelt*. New York: Random House, 2010.

Mott, Frank Luther Mott. *American Journalism: A History of Newspapers in the United States Through 250 Years, 1690–1940*, New York: Macmillan, 1941.

Nojine, E.K. *The Truth about Port Arthur*. Edited by E.D. Swinton. Translated by A.B. Lindsay. London: John Murray, 1908.
O'Brien, Frank M. *The Story of the Sun, 1833–1918*. New York: G.H. Doran, 1918.
O'Connor, Richard. *Jack London: A Biography*. Boston: Little, Brown, 1964.
Osborn, Scott C., and Robert L. Phillips Jr. *Richard Harding Davis*. Boston: Twayne Publishers, 1978.
Palmer, Frederick. *With Kuroki in Manchuria*. New York: Charles Scribner's Sons, 1904.
———. *With My Own Eyes: A Personal Story of Battle Years*. Indianapolis: Bobbs–Merrill Company, 1933.
Persico, Joseph E. *Edward R. Murrow: An American Original*. New York: McGraw-Hill, 1988.
Prior, Melton. *Campaigns of a War Correspondent*. Edited by S.L. Bensusan. New York: Longman's Green & Co., 1912.
Ramsay, David. *The History of the American Revolution*, vol. 2. Philadelphia: R. Aitken & Son, 1789.
Read, James Morgan. *Atrocity Propaganda 1914–1919*. New Haven, CT: Yale University Press, 1941.
Redfern, Walter. *Writing on the Move: Albert Londres and Investigative Journalism*. Oxford, England: Peter Lang, 2004.
Reilly, Tom. *War with Mexico! America's Reporters Cover the Battlefront*. Edited by Manley Witten. Lawrence: University Press of Kansas, 2010.
Repington, Charles à Court. *The War in the Far East, 1904–1905: By the Military Correspondent of the Times*. London: John Murray, 1905.
R.H.D.: Appreciations of Richard Harding Davis. New York: Charles Scribner's Sons, 1917.
Ricalton, James. *China through the Stereoscope: A Journey through the Dragon Empire at the Time of the Boxer Uprising*. New York: Underwood & Underwood, 1901.
Rodgers, Marion Elizabeth. *Mencken: The American Iconoclast*. Oxford, UK: Oxford University Press, 2005.
Rosengarten, Frank. *The Italian Anti–Fascist Press: From the Legal Opposition Press to the Underground Newspapers of World War II*. Cleveland: Case Western Reserve Press, 1968.
Sakuyé Takahashi. *International Law Applied to the Russo–Japanese War with the Decisions of the Japanese Prize Courts*. New York: The Banks Law Publishing Company, 1908.
Schlesinger, Arthur M. *Prelude to Independence: The Newspaper War on Britain, 1764–1776*. Boston: Northeastern University Press, 1980.
Schudson, Michael. *Discovering the News: A Social History of American Newspapers*. New York: Basic Books, 1978.
Schuyler, W.S., J.F. Morrison, Carl Reichmann, and Peyton C. March. *Reports of the Military Observers Attached to the Armies in Manchuria during the Russo–Japanese War*, Part I. Washington, DC: Government Printing Office, 1906.
Selle, Earl Albert. *Donald of China*. New York: Harper, 1948.
Shumpei Okamoto. *The Japanese Oligarchy and the Russo–Japanese War*. New York: Columbia University Press, 1970.

Sinclair, Andrew. *Jack: A Biography of Jack London*. New York: Harper & Row, 1977.

Slattery, Peter. *Reporting the Russo–Japanese War 1904–05: Lionel James's First Wireless Transmissions to the Times*. Folkestone, UK: Global Oriental, 2004.

Smith, Jeffery A. *War and Press Freedom: The Problem of Prerogative Power*. New York: Oxford University Press, 1999.

Sperber, A.M. *Murrow: His Life and Times*. New York: Fordham University Press, 1999.

Stein, M.L. *Under Fire: The Story of American War Correspondents*. New York: Julian Messner, 1968.

Steinbeck, John. *Once There Was a War*. New York: Penguin, 1977.

Steinberg, John W., Bruce W. Menning, David Schimmelpenninck van der Oye, David Wolff, and Shinji Yokote, eds. *The Russo–Japanese War in Global Perspective: World War Zero*. Leiden, Netherlands: Brill, 2005.

Story, Douglas. *The Campaign with Kuropatkin*. London: T. Werner Laurie, 1904.

Sweeney, Michael S. *From the Front: The Story of War, Featuring Correspondents' Chronicles*. Washington, DC: National Geographic Press, 2002.

———. *The Military and the Press: An Uneasy Truce*. Evanston, IL: Northwestern University Press, 2006.

Taburno, Ieronim Pavlovich. *The Truth about the War*. Translated by Victoria von Kreuter. Kansas City, MO: Franklin Hudson Publishing, 1905.

Treat, Payson J. *Diplomatic Relations between the United States and Japan, 1895–1905*. Gloucester, MA: Peter Smith, 1963.

Uchimura Kanzō. *Uchimura Kanzō Zenshū*, vol. 14. Tokyo: Iwanami Shoten, Shōwa, 1932–33.

Villiers, Frederic. *Port Arthur: Three Months with the Besiegers: A Diurnal of Occurrences*. London: Longman's Green, and Co., 1905.

Voss, Frederick S. *The Journalistic Coverage of World War II*. Washington, DC: Smithsonian Institution Press, 1994.

Warner, Denis, and Peggy Warner. *The Tide at Sunrise: A History of the Russo–Japanese War, 1904–1905*. London: Frank Cass, 2002.

Washburn, Stanley. *The Cable Game: The Adventures of an American Press–Boat in Turkish Waters during the Russian Revolution*. Boston: Sherman, French & Company, 1912.

Westwood, J.N., *Russia against Japan, 1904–1905: A New Look at the Russo-Japanese War*. New York: SUNY Press, 1986.

York, Bill. *John Fox, Jr., Appalachian Author*. Jefferson, NC: McFarland & Company, 2003.

DOCUMENTARY

Fillion, Michèle Midori. *No Job for a Woman: The Women Who Fought to Report World War II*, DVD. Directed by Michèle Midori Fillion. New York: Hurry Up Sister Productions, 2011.

BOOK CHAPTERS

Beaumont, Jacqueline. "The Making of a War Correspondent: Lionel James of the *Times*." In *The Impact of the South African War*, edited by David Omissi and Andrew Thompson, 124–37. Houndmills, UK: Palgrave, 2002.

Bottomore, Steve. "Frederic Villiers: War Correspondent." In *Re-Viewing British Cinema, 1900–1992: Essays and Interviews*, edited by Wheeler W. Dixon, 11–24. Albany, SUNY Press: 1994.

Ramsey, Neil. "The Grievable Life of the War–Correspondent: The Experience of War in Henry Crabb Robinson's Letters to *The Times*, 1808–1809." In *Emotions and War: Palgrave Studies in the History of Emotions*, edited by Stephanie Downes, Andrew Lynch, and Katrina O'Loughlin, 235–50. London: Palgrave Macmillan, 2015.

GOVERNMENT DOCUMENTS

"Convention (II) with Respect to the Laws and Customs of War on Land and Its Annex: Regulations Concerning the Laws and Customs of War on Land," The Hague, Netherlands, July 1899.

Correspondence Relating to the War with Spain and Conditions Growing out of the Same: Including the Insurrection in the Philippine Islands and the China Relief Expedition, April 15, 1898, to July 30, 1902, vol. 2. Washington, DC: Government Printing Office, 1902.

March, Peyton C. "Report No. 6, War Department, Office of the Chief of Staff, Washington, January 3, 1905." *Reports of Military Observers Attached to the Armies in Manchuria During the Russo–Japanese War, Part I*. Washington, DC: Government Printing Office, 1906.

U.S. War Department. *Annual Report of the War Department for the Fiscal Year Ending June 30, 1898. Report of the Chiefs of Bureaus*. Washington, DC: Government Printing Office, 1898.

ACADEMIC JOURNALS

Bottomore, Steve. "Frederic Villiers—War Correspondent." *Sights and Sounds: International Film Quarterly* 49, no. 4 (1980): 250–55.

Davies, Alan. "Broadcasting in the Spanish Civil War of 1936–1939." *Historical Journal of Film, Radio and Television* 19, no. 4 (1999): 473–513.

Fahmy, Shahira, and Thomas J. Johnson. "Embedded versus Unilateral Perspectives on Iraq War." *Newspaper Research Journal* 28, no. 3 (Summer 2007): 98–114.

Gervais, Thierry. "Witness to War: The Uses of Photography in the Illustrated Press, 1855–1904." *Journal of Visual Culture* 9, no. 3 (December 2010): 370–84.

Greenwood, John T. "The U.S. Army Military Observers with the Japanese Army during the Russo-Japanese War (1904–1905)." *Army History* 36 (Winter 1996): 1–14.

Hallahan, Kirk. "Ivy Lee and the Rockefellers' Response to the 1913–1914 Colorado Coal Strike." *Journal of Public Relations Research* 14, no. 4 (2002): 265–315.

Harris, Christopher R. "The Illustrated American: 'A Revelation of the Heretofore Untried Possibilities of Pictorial Literature.'" *Visuals Communication Quarterly* 6, no. 4 (Fall 1999): 47.

Harvey, A.D. "The Russo-Japanese War 19045: Curtain Raiser for the Twentieth Century World Wars." *RUSI Journal: Royal United Services Institute for Defense Studies* 148, no. 6 (2003): 58–61.

Jansen, Sue Curry. "Semantic Tyranny: How Edward L. Bernays Stole Walter Lippmann's Mojo and Got Away with It and Why It Still Matters." *International Journal of Communication* 7 (2013): 1094–111.

Johnson, Dan. "Exporting Exoticism: Captain Brinkley's Japan Described and Illustrated." *Bridgewater Review* 34, no. 1 (May 2015): 26–29.

Martin, Edward A. "On Reading Mencken." *The Sewanee Review* 93, no. 2 (Spring 1985): 243–50.

McCrachen, Donal P. "The Relationship between British War Correspondents in the Field and British Military Intelligence during the Anglo–Boer War." *Scientia Militaria: South African Journal of Military Studies* 43, no. 1 (2015): 99–126.

Kowner, Rotem. "Becoming an Honorary Civilized Nation: Remaking Japan's Military Image during the Russo–Japanese War." *The Historian* 64, no. 1 (2001): 18–38.

Park Pae–Keun, "Discussions Concerning the Legality of the 1910 'Annexation' of Korea by Japan." *Korea Journal* 50, no. 4 (2010): 13–41.

Rabaut, Jean. "Albert Londres, grand reporter." *L'histoire* 70 (September 1984): 74–79.

———. "Le grand reportage n'est plus ce qu'il était." *L'histoire* 41 (January 1982): 92–93.

Reilly, Tom. "Jane McManus Storms: Letters from the Mexican War, 1846–1848." *The Southwestern Historical Quarterly* 85, no. 1 (July 1981): 21–44.

Risley, Ford. "Peter Alexander: Confederate Chronicler and Conscience." *American Journalism* 15, no. 1 (Winter 1998): 35–50.

Steele, W. William. "Edo in 1868: The View from Below." *Monumenta Nipponica* 45, no. 2 (Summer 1990): 127–55.

Steinberg, John W. "Was the Russo-Japanese War World War Zero?" *The Russian Review* 67, no. 1 (January 2008): 1–7.

Stolarski, Christopher. "Another Way of Telling the News: The Rise of Photojournalism in Russia, 1900–1914." *Kritika: Explorations in Russian and Eurasian History* 12, no. 3 (Summer 2011): 561–90.

Sweeney, Michael S., Paul Jacoway, and Young Joon Lim. "Weighing the Costs: The Scripps–McRae League Reports the War in Cuba." *American Journalism* 31, no. 2 (Spring 2014): 213–35.

Valliant, Robert B. "The Selling of Japan: Japanese Manipulation of Western Opinion, 1900–1905." *Monumenta Nipponica* 29, no. 4 (Winter 1974): 415–38.

Waller, Gregory A. "Narrating the New Japan: Biograph's *The Hero of Liao-Yang* (1904)." *Oxford University Press* 47, no. 1 (Spring 2006): 43–65.

Zollman, Florian. "Is it Either Or? Professional Ideology vs. Corporate-media Constraints." *Westminster Papers in Communication and Culture* 6, no 2 (2009): 97118. DOI: http://doi.org/10.16997/wpcc.126.

MASTER'S THESES AND DISSERTATION

Aswell, Paul L. "Wartime Press Censorship by the U.S. Armed Forces: A Historical Perspective." Master's thesis, Louisiana State University, 1978.
MacDermid, Susan Cheryl. "Print Capitalism and the Russo–Japanese War." Master's thesis, University of British Columbia, 1981.
Morton, Jerry Lee. "The History of the Journalism Program at Michigan State University." PhD dissertation, Michigan State University, 1991.
Ornatowsi, Gregory Kent. "Press, Politics, and Profits: The *Asahi Shimbun* and the Prewar Japanese Newspaper." Master's thesis, Harvard University, 1985.

REFERENCE WORKS

"Fuller, Hector." *Who's Who in America.* Chicago: A.N. Marquis & Co., 1908.
Kowner, Rotem. *Historical Dictionary of the Russo–Japanese War.* Lanham, MD: Scarecrow Press, 2006.
Vaughn, Stephen L. *Encyclopedia of American Journalism.* Abington, U.K.: Routledge, 2007.

MAGAZINES

"A 'Cash' Transaction in Korea." *Collier's Weekly*, June 4, 1904, 8.
Archibald, James F.J. "Russia Makes Rules to Govern War Correspondents." *Collier's Weekly*, April 20, 1904, 13.
Bigelow, Poultney. "In Camp at Tampa." *Harper's Weekly*, June 4, 1898, 550.
"Collier's Easter Number." *Collier's Weekly*, April 2, 1904, n.p.
Davis, Richard Harding. "Marking Time in Tokio: The Forty–Eighth Ronin." *Collier's Weekly*, May 21, 1904, 8–9.
———. "Marking Time in Tokio: The Tea House of the Hundred and One Steps." *Collier's Weekly*, May 28, 1904, 10–11.
———. "Marking Time in Tokio: The War Dogs Dine Out." *Collier's Weekly*, May 7, 1904, 9.
———. "Marking Time in Tokio: A War Drama." *Collier's Weekly*, May 14, 1904, 11–12.
———. "On the Track of the Army." *Collier's Weekly*, November 5, 1904, 22–30.
Dunn, Robert L. "In Korea with the Kodak." *Collier's Weekly*, August 13, 1904, 20–23.

———. "Ways That Are Dark, and Tricks That Are Vain." *Collier's Weekly*, July 23, 1904, 9–10.
Fox, John Jr. "The Backward Trail of the Saxon." *Scribner's Magazine* 37, no. 3 (March 1905): 274–80.
———. "Hardships of the Campaign." *Scribner's Magazine* 36, no. 1 (July 1904): 38–45.
———. "Making for Manchuria." *Scribner's Magazine* 36, no. 6 (December 1904): 691–95.
———. "On the War–Dragon's Tail." *Scribner's Magazine* 37, no. 1 (January 1905): 54–59.
———. "The Trail of the Saxon." *Scribner's Magazine* 35, no. 6 (June 1904): 658–61.
———. "The White Slaves of Haicheng." *Scribner's Magazine* 37, no. 2 (February 1905): 196–203.
Fuller, Hector. "Getting into Port Arthur—I." *The Reader Magazine*, November 1904, 607–15.
———. "Getting into Port Arthur—II." *The Reader Magazine*, December 1904–January 1905, 38–47, 143–56.
"Good Things to Come in *Collier's*." *Collier's Weekly*, April 16, 1904, n.p.
"The Greatest War Photographs Ever Taken." *Collier's Weekly*, November 5, 1904, 6.
Harper's Weekly, [no title], August 13, 1898, 786–87.
"Has the War Correspondent Seen His Last Fight?" *The American Review of Reviews*, April 1913, 487.
Hearn, Lafcadio. "A Letter from Japan." *The Atlantic* 94 (November 1904): 625–44.
Kentarō Kaneko. "The Secret of Japan's Success." *Collier's Weekly*, June 4, 1904, 7–8.
Millard, Thomas F. "The Fruits of Japan's Victory." *Scribner's Magazine* 38, no. 2 (August 1905): 240–51.
———. "The War Correspondent and His Future." *Scribner's Magazine* 37, no. 2 (February 1905): 242–48.
Mirriam, Edmund F., ed. *The Watchman* 86, no. 86 (September 8, 1904): 5.
"Outdoor Men and Women: Heroes of the Camera." *Outing Magazine*, April–September 1905, 729–33.
Palmer, Frederick. "About 'Jimmy' Hare: A Personal Sketch of the Collier's War Photographer with the Japanese First Army." *Collier's Weekly*, February 25, 1905, 18.
———. "The Greatest Battle since Gettysburg." *Collier's Weekly*, November 5, 1904, 11–14, 26–30.
———. "Japan Is Prepared for a Long War." *Collier's Weekly*, April 9, 1904, 6–7.
———. "Off for the Front!" *Collier's Weekly*, May 14, 1904, 10–11.
———. "War Correspondence from the Two Capitals." *Collier's Weekly*, April 23, 1904, 20–24.
———. "With the First Japanese Army in Manchuria." *Collier's Weekly*, May 28, 1904, 11.
Partridge, Bernard. "Wisdom of the East." *Punch, or the London Charivari*, March 16, 1904, 183.

"A Remarkable Photograph in Harper's Weekly." *Collier's Weekly,* May 21, 1904, 11.
Roosevelt, Theodore. "Davis and the Rough Riders." *Scribner's Magazine* 60, no. 1 (July 1916): 89.
"A Russian Trench Captured by the Japanese in a Night Attack." *Collier's Weekly,* November 5, 1904, 10.
"Russo-Japanese War Extra." *Collier's Weekly,* March 26, 1904, 1–3.
Washburn, Stanley. "Floating Mines in Naval War: Evils Which the Hague Conference Should Attack." *Outlook,* June 8, 1907, 281–86.
Whigham, H.J. "Kuropatkin's 'Old Man of the Sea.'" *Collier's Weekly,* August 6, 1904, 8.
"The Woes of the Poor War Correspondents: They Are All Longing for the Good Old Days of Shafter and Otis." *The Fourth Estate: A Weekly Newspaper for Publishers, Advertisers, Advertising Agents and Allied Interests* 544 (July 30, 1904): 12.

ORAL HISTORY

The Reminiscences of Stanley Washburn, 1950, in the Oral History Collection of Columbia University, New York.

NEWSPAPERS

Albuquerque (NM) *Journal*
Arkansas Democrat (Little Rock)
Arkansas Gazette (Little Rock)
Baltimore Evening Herald
Baltimore Sun
Boston Globe
Brooklyn (NY) *Daily Eagle*
Chicago Daily News
Corriere della Sera (Milan, Italy)
Daily New Era (Lancaster, PA)
Daily News (New York)
Danville (KY) *News*
Dayton (OH) *Daily News*
Evening Item (Richmond, IN)
Fort Wayne (IN) *Daily News*
The Gazette (Montreal, QC)
Glasgow (Scotland) *Herald*
Hamilton County Ledger (Noblesville, IN)
Hawaii Herald (Hilo)
Hawaiian Star (Honolulu)

Houston Chronicle
Houston Post
Hong Kong Times
Illustrated London News
Indianapolis News
Indianapolis Star
Korea Joongang Daily
L'Illustration (Paris)
Los Angeles Times
Marion (OH) *Star*
Minneapolis Journal
News Herald (Port Clinton, OH)
New York Herald
New York Journal
New York Times
New York Tribune
Pacific Commercial Advertiser (Honolulu)
Philadelphia Inquirer
Pittsburgh Post-Gazette
Pittsburgh Press
The Province (Vancouver, BC)
The Richmond (IN) *Item*
Reno (NV) *Gazette-Journal*
Saint Louis Globe Democrat
Saint Louis Post-Dispatch
Saint Louis Republic
Saint Paul (MN) *Globe*
San Francisco Call
San Francisco Chronicle
San Francisco Examiner
Sioux City (IA) *Journal*
Spokane (WA) *Chronicle*
Star-Tribune (Minneapolis)
The Sun (Chanute, KS)
Sydney (Australia) *Morning Herald*
Syracuse (NY) *Journal*
The Times (London)
Times-Standard (Eureka, CA)
Vicksburg (MS) *Evening Post*
Victoria (BC) *Daily Times*
Washington Evening Star
Washington Post
Wet Mountain Tribune (Westcliffe, CO)
Wilkes–Barre (PA) *Leader*
Winnipeg (MB) *Tribune*

WEB PAGES

"American Society of Newspaper Editors Code of Ethics." PBS. https://www.pbs.org/newshour/extra/app/uploads/2014/03/mediaethics_handout6.pdf.

Au, Pak Hung, and Keiichi Kawai. "Media Capture and Information Monopolization in Japan." Munich Personal RePEc Archive, 2010. https://core.ac.uk/download/pdf/12027645.pdf.

"Biographical Note." Stanley Washburn. Minnesota Historical Society Manuscripts Collection, Minnesota Historical Society. http://www2.mnhs.org/library/findaids/01250.xml.

Chomsky, Noam. "What Makes Mainstream Media Mainstream." Lecture at Z Media Institute, June 1997. Information Clearing House. https://web.archive.org/web/20190119121556/http://www.informationclearinghouse.info/article26193.htm.

Cimino, Marcello. Presentazione di Adolfo Rossi. "L'agitazione in Sicilia: Inchiesta sui Fasci dei lavatory." http://www.spazioamico.it/Adolfo%20Rossi.htm.

"Expecting an Attack from Russian Cavalry—Alert Japanese Near Tehling, Manchuria." New York: Underwood & Underwood, 1906, Library of Congress. https://www.loc.gov/resource/cph.3b26198/.

"The Eye of the Storm—How Alfred Waud's Sketches Captured the Carnage of the U.S. Civil War." *Military History Now*, April 21, 2017. https://militaryhistorynow.com/2017/04/21/the-eye-of-the-storm-how-alfred-wauds-sketches-captured-the-carnage-of-the-u-s-civil-war/.

"The German Army Marches through Brussels." Eyewitness to History. http://www.eyewitnesstohistory.com/brussels.htm.

Gervais, Thierry. "'Le plus grand des photographes de guerre': Jimmy Hare, photoreporter au tournant du XIXe et du XXe siècle." *Études photographiques* 26 (2010). https://proxy.library.ohio.edu/login?url=https://search-proquest-com.proxy.library.ohio.edu/docview/864672684?accountid=12954.

Han Wan–Sang. "Preparing for the Next Hundred Years under the Mindset of the March First Independence Movement." Korea.Net, February 25, 2019. http://korea.net/NewsFocus/Column/view?articleId=168221.

"He Wielded Pen and Sword." Northwood Village. July 25, 2011. http://www.northwoodvillage.org.uk/tchudsonarticles/he-wielded-pen-and-sword-by-t-c-hudson/.

"The Henry Crabb Robinson Project." University of London. http://www.crabbrobinson.co.uk/the-project/.

"John Fox, Jr., 1862–1919." http://carnegiecenterlex.org/wp-content/uploads/2018/01/John-Fox-Jr.-Biography.pdf.

Kerschbaumer, Ken. "Bloomobile: Iraq's Coolest Truck." *Broadcasting and Cable*. http://www.broadcastingcable.com/article/148693-Bloomobile_Iraq_s_Coolest_Truck.php.

Kim, Christine. "A Chaotic Prelude to Korean Subjugation." *Korea Joongang Daily*, August 26, 2010. http://koreajoongangdaily.joins.com/news/article/article.aspx?aid=2925134.

Kranzler, Bryna. "The Accidental Anarchist: Eyewitness Account of the Russo-Japanese War." https://www.theaccidentalanarchist.com/eyewitness-account/.

Kull, Steven. "Misperceptions, the Media and the Iraq War." The PIPA/Knowledge Networks Poll. Program on International Policy Attitudes and Knowledge

Networks, October 2, 2003, https://web.archive.org/web/20031202082736/http://www.pipa.org/OnlineReports/Iraq/Media_10_02_03_Report.pdf, 1–21.

Lee, Bartholomew. "Wireless—Its Evolution from Mysterious Wonder to Weapon of War, 190–205." *AWA Review*, California Historical Radio Society. http://www.californiahistoricalradio.com/wp-content/uploads/2013/01/BartWirelessWar190205Lee.pdf.

"Maj Walter Kirton." Find a Grave. https://www.findagrave.com/memorial/117027507/walter-kirton.

Mexican News. "The News Media and the Making of America, 1730–1865." http://americanantiquarian.org/earlyamericannewsmedia/exhibits/show/news-in-antebellum-america/item/22.

"Military Censorship in Imperial Russia, 1904–1917." The Rossica Society. http://www.rossica.org/RVG/_pdf/Imperial_Military_Censorship/Military%20Censorship%20in%20Imperial%20Russia%201904%20-%201917.pdf.

"On This Day: Who Is the Criminal." *The New York Times*. http://movies2.nytimes.com/learning/general/onthisday/harp/0813.html.

"Photo of the Week: Mexican-American War." Amon Carter Museum of American Art, Fort Worth, TX. https://www.cartermuseum.org/interact/notes-from-underground/photo-of-the-week-mexican-american-war.

"Professor Ricalton, with Japanese Officers of 11th Division, at Foot of Takushan, Port Arthur." New York: Underwood & Underwood, 1905. Library of Congress. https://www.loc.gov/item/2004665580/.

"Reporting America at War: Martha Gellhorn; High Explosives for Everyone." Public Broadcasting Service. https://www.pbs.org/weta/reportingamericaatwar/reporters/gellhorn/madrid.html.

"Ricalton, James A." Historical Photographs of China. University of Bristol. https://www.hpcbristol.net/photographer/james-ricalton.

"Robert Lee Dunn." Find a Grave. https://www.findagrave.com/memorial/103238587/robert-lee-dunn.

"The Rough Riders Storm San Juan Hill." Eyewitness to History. http://www.eyewitnesstohistory.com/pfroughriders.htm.

"Rough Riders: The World of 1898; The Spanish-American War." Library of Congress. https://www.loc.gov/rr/hispanic/1898/roughriders.html.

"Russian-Japanese War 1904–1905 Photo Gallery Part I." All World Wars: Photographs by Viktor K. Bulla. https://www.allworldwars.com/Russian-Japanese-War-1904-1905-Photo-Gallery-by-Victor-Bulla-Part-I.html.

Spark, Nick T. et al. "Suddenly and Deliberately Attacked: The Story of the Panay Incident." http://www.usspanay.org/attacked.shtml.

Thompson, Clive. "Stereographs Were the Original Virtual Reality." *Smithsonian Magazine*, October 2017. https://www.smithsonianmag.com/innovation/sterographs-original-virtual-reality-180964771/.

"Victor Bulla." Nailya Alexander Gallery, New York. http://www.nailyaalexandergallery.com/russian-photography/victor-bulla.

"War Correspondent Ellis Ashmead-Bartlett." The Anzac Centenary Nation Program. https://anzacportal.dva.gov.au/history/conflicts/gallipoli-and-anzacs/events/battle-landing/war-correspondent-ellis-ashmead.

Index

ABC News, 211
Abe, Lieutenant Y., 76
accreditation: Boer War, 20–21; defined by Hague Convention, 19–20; Japanese correspondents, 13; Spanish-American War, 17–18; Western correspondents with Japan, xv, 22, 31–32, 101, 105, 171, 172, 178, 192, 202; Western correspondents with Russia, 30, 32–33, 183–85, 186, 187, 189–90; World War I, 206–8; World War II, 62
Afghanistan, war in (2001), 182n46, 212n15
Albertini, Luigi, 133–34, 136, 143
Aleksandr II, 3
Alekseev, Evgenii Ivanovich, 51, 185, 186
Alger, Russell A., 17–18
al Qaeda, 211
American Revolution, 6–7, 116
American Society of Newspaper Editors, 8
Amur River, 3
Anglo-Japanese Alliance, 4, 49, 104
Anshantien, 103, 124, 141
Antung. *See* Dandong
Archibald, James F. J., 32, 188, 191

Artimeev, Colonel, 185, 187
Asada Nobuoki, 142
Asahi Shimbun, 11
Ashmead-Bartlett, Ellis, 149, 195
Associated Press, 8, 12, 16, 21, 22, 34, 78, 100, 141, 178, 183–84, 185, 191, 194, 207
Athearn, Pop, 49, 55
attachés, military, xvi, 205–6. *See also* MacArthur, Arthur; March, Peyton C.; Pershing, John J. "Black Jack"
atrocity stories, 19, 99, 207, 209

Babin, Gustave, 151
Baker, Newton, 203
Baltic Fleet, Russian, 35, 65, 202
Baltimore Evening Herald, 35
Barry, Richard, 201–2
Barzini, Ettore, 134
Barzini, Luigi Jr., 143
Barzini, Luigi Sr., 21, 27, 93, 100, 131–44, *139*, 201, 205; "feminine" style of war correspondence, 19, 204–5; Mukden, battle of, witness, 131–32, 138
Bass, John, 33, 56
Bayan, 50, 51
Bell, Charles Moberly, 47
Bernays, Edward, 209

Beveridge, Albert, 30, 174, 175
Bigelow, Poultney, 18
Blaine, James G., 56
Bloom, David, 182n46
Boer War, 4, 20–21, 27, 32, 46, 78, 114, 135
Borghese, Scipione, 132
Boxer Rebellion, 33, 134–35, 164
Brill, William H., 22, 23, 25, 78, 99, 100, 102, 103–4, 140, 141
Brindle, Ernest, 190
Brinkley, Frank, 106
Brooklyn Daily Eagle, 199
Brown, Harry, 49, 51, 52, 55
Bulla, Aleksandr, 157
Bulla, Karl, 156
Bulla, Victor K., 156–58, 191
Burleigh, Bennet, 11, 13, 21, 45, 54, 100, 132, 207, 210
Busan, 73
bushidō, 83

Cable News Network (CNN), 211
The Call of the Wild, 70
Cameron, Simon, 16
El Caney, battle of, 95
CBS News, 211
censorship: banning of press from combat zone, xiv, 23–24, 26, 54, 56, 69, 92, 98, 173, 190; justification by Japan, 28–30; Meiji era, prewar, 9, 10–12; photography, of, 24, 69, 72–73; protested by war correspondents, 28, 30, 78, 99; regulations, Japanese, 31–32, 79; regulations, Russian, 32, 187; relaxation by Japan, 30–31, 60, 76, 93, 107, 136; Russo-Japanese War, examples and strength, xiv–xvi, 12, 56, 69–70, 84, 103, 107–8, 135, 136, 138, 183, 193, 201; self-, 12, 16, 62, 64, 189. *See also* individual wars, telegraph
Central News Agency, 33, 78
Century Magazine, 71, 94
Chapelle, Dickey, 212n17

Chefoo. *See* Yantai
Chefoo, SS, 50, 55
Chefoo Daily News, 50, 176
Chemulpo. *See* Incheon
Chemulpo, battle of, 50, 157, 162
Chicago Daily News, 33, 56, 57, 58, 60, 61, 64, 191
Chicago Evening Post, 184
China. *See* individual locations
China, SS, 97
Chinampo. *See* Nampo
Chinese Eastern Railway, 3
Chinese Telegraph Company, 192
Chomsky, Noam, 209–10
Christie, Dugald, 192
Cincinnati Post, 17
Civil War, American, 8, 14–16, 148, 204
Cleveland Press, 17
Collier, Peter F., 113, 148
Collier's Weekly, 6, 21, 22, 26, 28, 32, 33, 34, 64, 71, 74, 81, 97, 113, 119, 120, 122, 132, 147, 148, 157, 160, 162, 188, 191, 192, 205
Collins, Robert Moore, 33
collodion wet-plate process, 149–50
Columbia, SS, 2, 186, 191
Committee on Public Information (CPI), 208, 209
Corriere d'America, 143
Corriere della Sera, 19, 27, 131, 132–35, 136, 137, 138, 141, 143
Cowan, Ruth, 212n17
Coxey's Army, 70
Crane, Stephen, 16, 18
Creel, George, 208, 209
Creel Commission. *See* Committee on Public Information (CPI)
Creelman, James, 18, 19
Crimean War, xiv, 19, 172, 186, 204; impact on style of war correspondence, 19, 140; photography (collodion wet-plate process), 149–50
Crittenden, 96

Crystallizing Public Opinion, 209
Cuba: revolt against Spain, 114, 115, 212n17. *See also* Spanish-American War

Daguerre, Louis-Jacques-Mandé, 149
daguerreotype, 149–50
Daily Chronicle (London), 33
Daily Express (London), 71
Daily Mail (London), 12, 33, 50, 74, 190, 191
Daily Telegraph (London), 13, 21, 33, 54, 74, 109, 131, 190, 195, 207
Dalian. *See* Dalny
Dalny, xi, 3, 50, 53, 60, 101, 135, 136, 137, 171
Dana, Charles, 94
Dandong, 81, 82
Davis, Cecil, 97, 113, 119, 120
Davis, Oscar King, 33, 71, 80
Davis, Richard Harding, 16, 18, 25, 29, 72, 91, 92, 93, 95, 96, 97, 108, 118, 136, 140, 141, 212n17; Cuban war of independence, 115–17; early life and education, 114–15; "feminine" style of war correspondence, 204–5; Japanese people, writing on, 120–21, 126; playwright, 115; protests censorship, 98–99, 109, 122; quits war zone, xvi, 36, 103–4, 105, 107; San Juan Hill, battle of, 117–19; Second Army, travels with, 100–4; World War I, 126–27
de Forest, Lee, 47–49, 55
de Mille, Cecil B., 109
Denny, George 191
Department of Defense, U.S. *See* Pentagon
de Plançon de Rigny, Georges A., 185
Desert Storm. *See* Iraq, war in (1991)
de Tocqueville, Alexis, 7–8, 9
Dinwiddie, William, 33, 80
Donohoe, M.H, 33
Dunn, Robert L., 20–21, 71, 74–75, 148, 149, 160–61
Dunn, William J., 45

Eastern Telegraph Company, 48, 55
embedded correspondents, embedding, 62, 63, 65n75, 144, 210, 212n15
Emerson, Edwin Jr., 171, 191–92
Empress of China, RMS, 100, 172
Empress of Japan, RMS, 56
espionage, 24–25, 46, 48, 51, 53, 54, 58, 59, 69–70, 72, 136, 174, 175, 176, 185, 186, 192–93, 204, 210
Espionage Act (1917), 208
ethics, journalism: codes, 8, 213n36; fabricated news, 27, 199, 201
Etzel, Lewis Leonard, 190, 191
Eulsa Coerced Government Treaty, 26

Fairbanks, Charles W., 174
Falklands War, 203
Fawan, SS, 57–61, 173–74; seized by Russian navy, 58–69
"feminine" style of war correspondence, 16, 19, 85, 204–5. *See also* Godkin, E. L.; individual correspondents
Fengcheng, 83
Feng Hwang Cheng. *See* Fengcheng
Fenton, Roger, 149, 150
Figaro, 24
Fillmore, Millard, 199
First Amendment, 7–8, 208
First Army, Japanese, 21–22, 33, 34, 62, 74–76, 78–80, 83, 173; correspondents accredited to, 33–34, 78
Following the Sun Flag, 109
Forbes-Robertson, Johnston, 154
Fourth Army, Japanese, 34, 62
Fourth Estate, 80
Fox, John Jr., 25, 36, 91–109, 105, 125, 126136, 140, 141, 171; "feminine" style of war correspondence, 204–5; protests censorship, 99, 105, 109; quits war zone, xvi, 36, 103–4, 106, 107; Second Army, travels with, 100–104; Spanish-American War, correspondence in, 16, 95–96
Fox, John Sr., 93
Fox, Minerva Worth Carr, 93

Fox Broadcasting Company, 211
Franco-Prussian War, 154
Franklin, Benjamin, 6
Fraser, David, 33, 46, 48
Freud, Sigmund, 209
Fukushima Yasumasa, 22
Fuller, Hector, 30, 54, 63, 100, 171–80, 193; accreditation revoked, 179; arrest at Port Arthur, 174
Fuller, Rose, 177, 179

Gallipoli, battle of, 195
Garfield, James, 56
The Gazette (Montreal), 78
Gellhorn, Martha, 205, 212n17
Geneva Conventions, 20
Godkin, E. L., 19, 140, 141, 202. *See also* "feminine" style of war correspondence
Goebbels, Joseph, 209
Gordon, Charles George "Chinese," 55, 70
grand reportage, 133
"Great System." *See* press pools
Grenada, war in, 203
Griscom, Lloyd, 23, 25, 28, 30, 31, 72–73, 98–99, 171, 174, 178, 192
Guards, military, 76, 83, 91–92, 102, 103, 108. *See also* liaisons
Las Guásimas, 95
Gussie, SS, 17

Hague Convention, 19–20, 51
Haicheng, 91–92, 101, 102, 103, 136
Haimun, SS, 46, 48, 50–55
Hanjapu, 131, 145n3
Hare, James L. "Jimmy," 34, 71, 81, 147, 149, 158–60
Harper's Weekly, 18, 33, 71, 95, 148
Harrison, Benjamin, 56
Hatsuse, 28, 60
Hay, John, 58, 98, 174
Hayashi Todasu, 28–30, 107, 108
Hayes, Rutherford B., 59
Hayes, Webb C., 59
Hearn, Lafcadio, 121

Hearst, William Randolph, xiv, 18, 34, 69, 71, 74, 76, 77, 82, 97, 115, 116, 148
Heijo Maru, SS, 100, 101
Heimin Shimbun, 10–11, 28
Hip Sang, SS, 59
Hirose Takeo, 121–22
Hochi Shimbun, 11, 99
Hooker, Joseph, 16
Hosoya Sukeuji, 53

Ichinohe Hyōe, 63
Ijuin Gorō, 49
Illustrated American, 158
Illustrated London News, 125, 148, 149, 151, 152, 155
L'Illustration, 151, 159
illustrations, history of, 150–51
Incheon, 28, 34, 48, 53, 57–58, 71, 74, 161, 173; Japanese invasion of, 2, 21–22, 48, 75
Indianapolis News, 30, 54, 63, 100, 171, 172, 173, 174, 178, 179
Indianapolis Star, 179–80
Industrie, SS, 50
Ingram, Herbert, 148
In Many Wars by Many War Correspondents, 25
International News Service, 207
Iraq, war in (1991), 203–4
Iraq, war in (2003), 65n75, 182n46, 210, 211, 212n15
Iroquois, SS, 95
Irsky, 157
Itō Hirobumi, 5
Itō Sukeyuki, 22

The Jacket. See The Star Rover
James, David H., 13
James, Lionel, 45–56, 71, 100
Japan Mail, 106
Jiji Shimpo, 99
Jiro Okabé, 108
Le Journal de Paris, 196
"journalism of action," 19

Kaneko Kentarō, 5–6, *15*, 105
Kaofengshik, 141
Kasuga, 28, 52
Katsura Tarō, 30
Kendall, George, xiii–xiv
The Kentuckians, 95
Kettle Hill, battle of, 118–19
Kidd, Benjamin, 83
Kipling, Rudyard, 154
Kirton, Walter, 33, 78
kisha clubs, 10
Kitchener, Herbert, 55, 206
Kittredge, Charmian, 70, 72, 74, 76, 77
Knight, Edward F., 27, 33
Kobe, 100
Kodama Gentarō, 22
Kokumin Shimbun, 12, 70
Komura Jutarō, 6, 22, 30, 50, 72–73, 98–99, 105, 107
Korea: Japan, opposition to, 4; Japanese invasion of, 21–22, 26; protectorate, 26. *See also* Eulsa Coerced Government Treaty; individual locations; Korean people; Korean War
Korea, SS, 85
Korean people, 75, 76–77, 163
Korean War, 212n15
Koreets, 21, 50, 58
Kosuga, 59–60
Kōtuko Shūsui, 10–11
Kulien Cheng, battle of, 82
Kuroki Tamemoto, 141, 159, 191
Kuropatkin, Aleksei, 58
Kwantung, 51

Lamscott, M., 184
Lamsdorf, Vladimir, 183, 184
liaisons, military, xv, 69, 79, 101, 190, 202, 204
Liaodong Peninsula, 1, 3, 32, 34, 35, 48, 53, 60, 99, 101, 103, 106, 135–36, 171, 172, 173, 187, 190, 192, 194, 207
Liaoyang, battle of, 34, 64–65, 93, 104, 123, 136–37, 140–41, 191

Lippmann, Walter, 200, 202, 209
Little, Richard Henry, 58, 191
Little Shepherd of Kingdom Come, 93, 95, 96, 109
London, Bess, 70, 85
London, Jack, 25, 34, 69–86, *73*, 97, 104, 109, 123, 126, 140, 141, 159, 202, 204, 205; arrested, 71–72, 76–77, 84; "feminine" style of war correspondence, 19, 85, 204–5; prisoner in Korea, 76–77; quits war zone, xvi; romantic notions of war, xiv, 70
London Daily News, 19
London Daily Chronicle, 53
Londres, Albert, 133
Louisa Bay, 174, 176
Lubavin, Baron, 53
Lushun. *See* Port Arthur
Lusitania, RMS, 207
Lynch, George, 25, 53, 100, 108, 125; quits war zone, 103–4, 108

MacArthur, Arthur, xvi, 203
MacArthur, Douglas, xvi, 203
MacDonald, Ramsay, 180
MacGahan, Januarius, 19
MacHugh, Robert Joseph, 33
MacPherson, Ian, 206
Maine, USS, 9, 16
Makarov, Stepan Osipovich, 52
Manchuria. *See* individual locations
March, Peyton C., xvi, 203, 206
Marroni, Ettore, 134
Martin Eden, 86
Maxwell, William, 33
McCormick, Frederick, 184, 186, 194, 196n8, 205
McCormick, Robert Sanderson, 183
McCullagh, Francis, 2, 186, 191
McKenzie, Frederick Arthur, 12, 23, 33, 71, 74–75, 191, 206
McKinley, William, 19, 56, 116, 119, 158, 160
Meiji, Emperor, 9, 152

Meiji government, 2–3
Mencken, H. L., 35, 199–200, 201
Metropolitan Magazine, 127
Mexican-American War, xiii–xiv, 14, 149
Michimasa Soyeshima, 106–8, 171
Middleton, Henry, 191
Millard, Thomas F., 1, 4, 5, 183, 191, 192, 193, 194, 201
Miller, Henry B., 58
Ministry of Foreign Affairs, Japanese, 6, 22, 25, 30, 31, 49, 72–73, 100, 108, 178; entertains journalists, 23, 27, 71
Ministry of War, Japanese, 22, 26, 28, 30, 31, 34, 71, 137, 203–4
Minneapolis Times, 56
Minotao Islands, 57, 63
Mitsuo Fuchida, 1
Moji, 33, 71–72, 100
Mokpo, 74
Montgomery, Cora. *See* Storms, Jane McManus
Morgan, Gerald, 127
Morning Chronicle (London), 125
Morning Post (London), 27, 33
Morrison, George, 54
Morse, Samuel F. B., xiii
Mott, Gordon L., 179
A Mountain Europa, 93, 94
Mukden, battle of, 34–35, 64–65, 131, 136, 137, 143, 191, 192, 194, 207
Murrow, Edward R., 45
Mussolini, Benito, 143

Nabeshima Keijirō, 5
Nampo, 33, 34, 48, 49, 50
Nanshan Hill, battle of, 34, 171
Nashimoto Morimasa, 92
National Cash Register Company (NCR), 180
National Public Radio, 211
Neaudeau, Ludovic, 196n8
Newchwang. *See* Yingkou
New Orleans *Picayune*, xiii
Newspaper Enterprise Association, 32, 171

newspapers, American: bylines, 16; colonial era, 6–7; economics, 7–9; growth in nineteenth century, 7–8, 14; press development, 6–9; professional standards, 6–9. *See also* ethics, journalism; individual papers; individual wars; Penny Press
newspapers, British. *See* individual papers
newspapers, Japanese: censorship of, 9, 10–12; economics, 10; feudal era, 9; Meiji era, 9–12; subsidies, 5; Tokugawa era, 9; war, support for, 11, 92, 99, 202. *See also* censorship; individual papers; *kisha* clubs; public opinion
New York Herald, 2, 19, 27, 33, 71, 96, 117, 124, 186
New York Journal, 18, 71, 115, 148
New York Sun, 7, 94, 115, 117
New York Times, 16, 33, 46, 48, 49, 55, 71, 94, 134, 178, 179
New York World, 16, 70, 80, 191
Nicholas II, Tsar, 3–4, 19, 183–84
Nietzsche, Friedrich, 83
Nightingale, Florence, xiv
Nisshin, 52
Niva, 157
Nodzu Michitsura, 131, 141
Nogi Maresuke, 61, 62
Nojine, E. K., 186
Novi Krai, 185–87
Novoe Vremia, 193

objectivity, 8, 160, 210–11
Okada, T., 79, 80
Oku Yasukata, 91–92, 99, 100, 101, 102, 103, 107–8, 123, 124, 135, 136, 137, 138, 141, 155
Opium War, 3
Oregonian (Portland), 56
Osaka Asahi Shimbun, 11
Ōyama Gentarō, 22, 93
Ōyama Iwao, 136, 138, 142–43

Pallada, 186, 201
Palmer, Frederick, 12, 13, 22–23, 25, 26, 33, 71, 79, 83, 93, 126, 132, *140*, 141, 159, 203, 204, 206, 207
Panay, USS, 143
Paoshankan, 141
Pavlov, Alexander, 54
Pearl Harbor, 1
Penny Press, 7
Pentagon, 210, 212n15
Perry, Matthew C., 2
Pershing, John J. "Black Jack," xvi, 203
Pescadores, 3
Pesteech, E. F., 32, 188, 189, 193
Petropavlovsk, 52, 63
Philadelphia Inquirer, 80
Phillips, Percival, 71
photography, history of, 147, 149; halftone printing, 149–50; Kodak, 162; technological advancements, 148. *See also* daguerreotype; collodion wet-plate process
Pitzuwo, 60
Plehve, Viacheslav Konstantinovich, 183, 184
Polk, James K., 14
Port Arthur, 1, 3, 45, 51, 55, 58, 59–60, 63, 64, 65, 100, 101, 183, 192–193, 195, 201; besieged on land, 12–13, 34, 48, 50, 54, 57, 61–62, 98, 136–37, 139, 165, 171–78, 195, 202; capitulation, 34, 137, 155, 178; defenses, 187; life within, 139, 178, 185–87; naval blockade of, 2, 34, 52, 53, 57, 61, 98, 121, 171, 174, 175, 178; surprise attack, 1–2, 21, 29, 48, 71, 74, 135, 148, 152, 172, 189, 191
Portsmouth, N.H., 35, 105
postmodernism, 201
Preece, William, 55
press pools, xv, 69, 79–80, 190, 202, 204
Prior, Melton, 13, 56, 100, 125, 149, 151, 154, 202; drawings of Japanese people, 152–53, 155; quits war zone, 103–4

prisoners of war, 176, 191, 193
Program on International Policy Attitudes, 211
propaganda, 28, 70, 85, 93, 201, 202, 207, 208, 209; British, xvi; French, xvi; Japanese, 5, 12–13, 26, 80; Russian, 37n13
Propaganda, 209
Public Broadcasting Service (PBS), 211
public opinion, 84–85, 108–9, 202, 204, 208, 211; American, 4, 5–6; British, 4, 5; Japanese, xvi, 4–6, 11, 12–13, 69–70, 97–99, 171, 201, 202; national unity, 10, 121. *See also* Russo-Japanese War
Public Opinion, 200, 209
public relations. *See* propaganda, public opinion
Pulitzer, Joseph, 16, 191
Punch, 153
Pyle, Ernie, 205
Pyongyang, 22, 34, 74, 75, 76, 81, 82

racism: American, 6, 12, 60, 78–79, 82–83, 84, 89n61, 203; Japanese, 82, 106
radio: commercial, 45; Russo-Japanese War, in, 45–55, 59; speed of correspondence, 55
radiotelegraphy, 47, 55
Reed, Thomas B., 56
Remington, Frederic, 95, 115, 116
Repington, Charles à Court, 2
Retvizan, 186, 201
Reuters, 12, 33, 47, 191
Review of Reviews, 19
Ricalton, James, 149, 156, 164–65, 201–2
Richmond (Indiana) *Item*, 172, 178
Riis, Jacob A., 117, 150
The Risen Sun, 6
Roberts, Frederick, 20
Robinson, Henry Crabb, 39n55
Rockefeller, John D., 209

Roosevelt, Theodore, xvi, 18, *29*, 33, 35, 61, 84, 95, 95, 98, 104, 105, 106, 117, 119, 161, 207
Rossi, Adolfo, 133
Rough Riders, 18, 83, 95
Rozhestvenskii, Zinovii Petrovich, 35
Russell, William Howard, xiv, 19, 140, 141; "father" of war correspondence, xiv; knighthood, xiv
Russian Revolution (1905), 205
Russian Revolution (1917), 205
Russo-Chinese Bank, 194
Russo-Japanese War: causes, 3–4; conclusion of, 35–36, 61, 105; impact on world events, xv, 201, 205–6, 210; Japanese mobilization, xv, 12, 21, 71, 172; Japanese strategy in, 2, 21, 34, 28–29; Japan's justification for, 6, 11, 106–8; Russian expansionism, 3–4; subsequent wars, impact on, xvi, 193, 203; weaponry, 1, 12–13, 132, 202. *See also* accreditation; censorship; individual battles; World War Zero
Russo-Turkish War, 154

Sakai Toshihiko, 10
Sakhalin Island, 3, 35
Samson, SS, 54–55
San Francisco Chronicle, 163
San Francisco Examiner, 71, 74, 78, 81, 82
San Juan Hill, battle of, 95, 117–19
Sataké, Viscount, 108
Scheff, Fritzi, 109
Scovel, Sylvester, 16–17
Scribner's Magazine, 93, 96, 97, 102, 104, 105, 109, 117, 125, 191
Scripps, E. W., 17, 32
The Sea Wolf, 71
Second Army, Japanese, 34, 53, 62, 91–92, 119, 135, 137; correspondents accredited to, 100

Sedition Act (1918), 208
Segawa Asanoshin, 106
Seoul, 2, 22, 48, 74, 75, 76, 77, 78, 81
Shafter, William R., 19, 80, 89n47, 118
Shaho, 137
Shandong Peninsula, 3, 48, 173
Shanghai, 28, 53, 54
Shanghai Mercury, 177
Shanghai News, 176
Shenyang, battle of. *See* Mukden, battle of
Sherman, William Tecumseh, 16
Shimonoseki, 71–72, 73
Siberia, SS, 48, 71
Sigsbee, Charles D., 16
Sino-Japanese War, 1, 3, 4, 29, 148, 166, 201
Sioux City (Iowa) *Journal*, 161
Smith, Al, 180
social media, 200, 210, 211
South Manchurian Railway, 4, 35
Spanish-American War, 16–19, 33, 70, 80, 95–96, 117–19, 158, 164, 204; censorship, 17, 18
Spanish Civil War, 45, 85, 205
The Sphere (London), 78
spies, spying. *See* espionage
Stampa, La, 133, 134
Standard (London), 33
Stanton, Edwin, 16
The Star Rover, 86
Stead, William T., 19
stereotypes, 200
Stevenson, Robert Louis, 114
St. Louis Post-Dispatch, 193
Stoessel, Anatolii Mikhailovich, 173, 176, 178, 187
Stone, Melville E., 183–84
Storms, Jane McManus, xiii–xiv
Story, Douglas, 11, 32, 171, 188, *189*, 190, 191, 193, 194, 210
Straight, Willard, 12, 23
Suematsu Kenshō, 5
Suminoye Maru, 33

Sunan-guyŏk, 75
Sungari, 58
Swinton, Earnest, 206–7

Taburno, Ieronim Pavlovich, 193–94
Taiwan, 3
Takahira Kogorō, 98–99
Takeuchi, 100
Taliban, 212n15
Tanaka Giichi, 22–23
Tang River, 141
telegraph: censorship, 28, 32, 69, 80, 81, 108, 136, 138, 173, 183–84; channel of news, xiii, 8, 27–28, 46, 138, 183–84, 192, 204; security threat, 16–17, 20, 27, 108, 136, 192
Telissu, battle of, 99, 102
Le Temps, 5, 34
Tennyson, Alfred, xiv
Teshima, Captain, 77
Third Army, Japanese, 34, 61, 62, 65, 131, 135, 156, 165; correspondents accredited to, 62, 195
Tianjin, 136, 137
Tiensuitien, 141
Tientsin. *See* Tianjin
Times (London), 2, 19, 33, 46, 47, 48, 49, 52, 53, 54, 55, 64, 71, 106, 109, 117, 133, 195
Times of India, 47
Tōgō Heichahirō, 1, 35
Tokutomi Sohō, 12, 70
Tonami Kurakichi, 49, 51, 52, 53, 64
The Trail of the Lonesome Pine, 109
Trans-Siberian Railway, 3
Tsessarevich, 186
Tsushima Strait, battle of, 35, 65, 199

Uchida Yasuya, 4
Uchimura Kanzō, 13
Underwood & Underwood, 164, 165
unilateral journalist, 63
United Press, 207

Variag, 21, 50, 58
Victor-Thomas, Charles, 34
Vietnam War, 116, 212n15
Villiers, Frederick, 149, 154–56
Vladivostok, 3, 4, 183, 186, 190
von Gottenburg, 34

Wafangdian, 101
Wa-fang-tien. *See* Wafangdian
Walker, Jimmy, 180
war correspondents: canteen, 34; "golden age," xiii–xiv, 14–19, 70; traveling kit, 25–26. *See also* individual correspondents; individual wars
War News from Mexico, 14, 24
Washburn, Stanley, 45, 56–65, 173–74, 176
Washburn, William Drew, 56
Washington Post, 68n75, 178, 179, 212n15
Waud, Alfred, 148
Weihai, 48, 55
Whigham, Henry J., 191, 194
White Fang, 86
Wiju, 76, 81; battle of, 81–82
Wilhelm II, Kaiser, 6, 184
Williams, J. Sheldon, 78
Wilson, Woodrow, 203, 208
Woodville, Richard Caton, 14, 24
Worcester, HMS, 172
World War I, xvi, 33, 55–56, 64, 143, 147, 158, 188, 195, 203, 206, 207, 209; adopts Russo-Japanese War censorship, xvi, 203, 205–7
World War II, 3, 45, 85, 203, 205, 212n15
"World War Zero," xv, xviiin5

Yalu, battle of the, 22, 57, 81–82, 98, 148, 155, 159
Yalu River, 58, 59, 60, 75, 76, 79, 83, 135, 159, 162

Yamamoto Gonnohyōe, 22
Yantai, 48, 53, 54, 57, 59, 60, 104, 105, 125, 162, 173, 174, 175, 176, 178, 185, 186, 191
Yashima, 28, 60, 202
"yellow peril," 6, 153

Yihetuan Movement. *See* Boxer Rebellion
Yingkou, 32, 58, 64, 106, 192
Yorozu Chōhō, 11
Yoshino, 28

Zulu War, 151

About the Authors

Dr. Michael S. Sweeney is a professor in the E.W. Scripps School of Journalism at Ohio University, where he teaches reporting, writing, editing, ethics, and journalism history. He is the author of more than twenty books and monographs, including *Secrets of Victory: The Office and Censorship and the American Press and Radio in World War II*, which was named Book of the Year by the American Journalism Historians Association. Recognized as an expert on the history of wartime censorship, he has also published *The Military and the Media: An Uneasy Truce* and *From the Front: The Story of War Featuring Correspondents' Chronicles*. He received awards from the American Journalism Historians Association for lifetime achievement in both research and teaching. From 2012 to 2018, he edited *Journalism History*, the oldest academic publication in the United States devoted to the history of the mass media. He lives in Athens, Ohio, with his wife, Carolyn, and Yorkie-beagle, Fiddich.

Natascha Toft Roelsgaard is a doctoral student in the E.W. Scripps School of Journalism at Ohio University, where she teaches reporting, writing, public relations, civil rights history, and journalism history. Her scholarship centers on the historical significance of the underappreciated journalistic work of immigrants and minorities in the United States, particularly the work of progressive women journalists within black press history. Her work has been published in *Journalism History* and she has received awards from the American Journalism Historians Association, including the Maurine Beasley Award for Outstanding Paper on Women's History. She currently resides in Athens, Ohio, but spends most summers on the eastern coast of her native Denmark.